W0010101

mediterranean kitchen

mediterranean kitchen

MURDOCH
B O O K S

contents

mediterranean kitchen

The Mediterranean Sea includes within its shores countries as distinct as France and Lebanon or Greece and Tunisia, and numerous races, languages, religions and cultures all call the Mediterranean home. Yet when we imagine the food of this region, local differences seem to hold little sway before the seductive allure of sun and sea, before the intoxicating sounds and smells of outdoor markets, or when faced with the promise of lazy lunches at roadside cafes.

And these images are not entirely misleading. Mediterranean cooking is distinguished by its close connection to the land and climate, its preference for fresh, locally produced ingredients, and its ancient tradition of hospitality and pleasure in communal eating. Centuries of trade and the movement of people have also meant that many of the same ingredients, techniques and ideas appear—in local guises—from one end of the Mediterranean to the other.

land and climate

The variety of ingredients one associates with the Mediterranean seems to suggest a land of plenty. Historically however, and even today in areas, it has been a place of struggle for many. Hemmed in by desert to the south and mountains to the north, much of the Mediterranean is hilly, barren terrain, with a dry, hot climate. The result is traditional cooking that has been greatly shaped by the need to be frugal. Thus, fruit and vegetables are dried or preserved in vinegar or alcohol; fish is salted; milk curdled into butter or cheese; and every part of an animal is used, from the tongue to the tail. But what may be lacking in abundance is more than compensated for with variety. Situated at the crossroads between Europe, Africa and Asia, the Mediterranean has always been subject to the ebb and flow of people, ideas and trade, and this has had as much of an influence on the formation of classic Mediterranean cuisine as has the physical environment.

a very brief history

The ancient Romans (building on the work of the ancient Greeks and others) are credited with firmly establishing the three cornerstones of Mediterranean cuisine—wheat, olive oil and vine—and many elements typical of modern Mediterranean life date to the ancient era, or earlier. Orchards, cereal crops, lagoon fishing, the irrigation of land and the distillation of alcohol are just a few examples. After the fall of Rome, however, usually given as AD476, much of Western Europe lost the skills and knowledge of the Classical age. This was not the case in the East, where great civilizations were flourishing. The Byzantine Empire, with Constantinople as its capital, developed into an economic and artistic centre and, further east, Islam was emerging as the dominant force. At its height, the Islamic Empire stretched from Asia to North Africa, across to Spain and into Sicily. From around the eighth to the twelfth centuries, there was a great flourishing of the arts, mathematics, sciences and culinary skills, and Islam formed a crucial link between the East—countries such as Persia, India and China—and Europe.

The second millennium brought many great changes. In 1096, the First Crusade began. This period also saw the emergence of powerful tribes including the Seljuk Turks, and the Mongols who toppled the Abassid Caliphate in Baghdad, Islam's capital, in 1258. They in turn fell to the Mamluks, a soldier-slave caste of the Turks. In the fourteenth century, the Black Death decimated the populations of Europe and the Mediterranean; Spain became a powerful force under the House of Aragon; and the defeat of the Hispano-Muslims at Granada in 1492 marked the beginning of the end of Islam's dominance in Spain. The following year, Constantinople fell to Mehmet II, the leader of the Ottoman Turks: these warrior people would eventually come to control over half the Mediterranean. In the Western part of the Mediterranean in the sixteenth century, the expelled Muslims from Spain moved to North Africa and Morocco, and Italian city-states became the centre of the Renaissance. The Age of Exploration got under way, bringing unimagined riches to Europe and opening it up to the rest of the world.

The effect of these forces on Mediterranean food and cooking has been great and varied, but a few defining elements do exist, which link all the many cultures, countries and histories. Of great importance is the role of the Islamic civilization on the area. Though the essentials of Mediterranean food and agricultural techniques were established in the Classical age, these were revived and perfected by the Arabs, who introduced farming practices that were crucial in stabilizing the unreliable soils. The spice trade, though existing long before the Arabs arrived, also thrived during the Middle Ages, forever changing the Mediterranean diet. As well, wherever they went, the Arabs took their own culinary traditions and ingredients and also those of the conquered peoples, in particular those of the Persians. Techniques and combinations seen today, such as the flavouring of meat with fruit or the popularity of intensely sweet, syrupy desserts, hark back to Persian influences. The Arabs also adopted the Persian notion that food, cooking and dining could be things of great beauty and worthy of lavish care—expressed, for example, in the Persian idea that paradise could be found in an orchard. At the great feasts of the Abassid Caliphs of Baghdad, guests ate extraordinary meals to the sound of music floating in the background, accompanied by singing and poetry recitals. These sumptuous feasts were later matched by those of the Ottoman Palace of Topkapi in Istanbul, Turkey, during the rule of Mehmet the Conqueror and Suleyman the Magnificent, and contemporary Turkish cuisine reflects this history. The Turkish armies also contributed, by bringing kebabs, pilafs, meatballs and stuffed vegetables to the conquered lands in the Eastern Mediterranean.

During the European Renaissance, the rise of haute cuisine saw the development of, among many things, table manners and the use of the fork. As well, the discovery of the Americas brought strange new foods to the Mediterranean, including tomatoes, pumpkins, potatoes, vanilla and chocolate. These newcomers were to dramatically alter the region's cuisines, and many classic dishes of the Mediterranean date to this time.

traditions and techniques

One of the most enjoyable expressions of the Mediterranean attitude to food preparation and eating is the tradition of small appetizers. Known variously as antipasto in Italy, mezze or meze in the Middle East, Turkey and Greece, and tapas in Spain, this practice of serving small dishes to whet the appetite or to accompany alcohol has been a feature of Mediterranean eating since ancient times. Dishes are usually strongly flavoured and can range from the simple to the elaborate: marinated olives, cubes of feta cheese, strips of prosciutto wrapped around fresh figs, creamy eggplant (aubergine) dips or platters of deep-fried assorted seafood. These appetizers are a particular feature of Turkish, Spanish and Lebanese eating, and are often what first entices people to learn more about Mediterranean food.

Mediterranean cooking, on the whole, does not involve complicated techniques or unusual cooking equipment. Most of the more laborious tasks, such as rolling couscous grains by hand, have been replaced by largely acceptable commercially produced alternatives, and many dishes involve only quick grilling (broiling), barbecuing or frying. There are, of course, a number of dishes that demand the exact opposite— long, slow roasting over coals (or in the oven) or patient simmering in aromatic stock. The tradition of outdoor cooking is alive and well, and the smells, sights and sounds of marketplaces from Provence to Algiers are the sorts of things that travellers dream about.

regional cuisine

Though the cuisines of the Mediterranean share many things—ingredients, cooking techniques, flavour combinations—it is not always possible to speak of one cuisine, or even to speak of a country's cuisine. Rather, it is more accurate to speak of a regional cuisine, such as that of Provence, or of Catalonia, or of Sicily. Today, despite—or perhaps because of—the movement towards large-scale production and specialization that has occurred across the Mediterranean, there is still great respect for and reliance on regionally produced goods and dishes. Local foods such as cheeses, hams, oils, breads and wine are all fiercely championed and protected, as is seasonal eating.

the mediterranean kitchen

Looking at the ingredients of the Mediterranean is a fascinating way of learning about the dishes of the region. On the backs of camel trains, packed in Phoenician sailing ships, or marched with victorious armies, ingredients have crisscrossed the Mediterranean for thousands of years. The dishes of the region reflect this, with saffron appearing in Spanish paella, and Tunisian merguez sausage popular in southern French cooking. By looking at the ingredients of the Mediterranean, it is possible to learn not only about the region's recipes but also a little bit about its history and customs. As well, focusing on ingredients encourages us to remember that good food does not just appear—it grows, swims or walks, is discovered or nurtured and perfected—but is inextricably linked with the land, sea and people that produced it. There is something very exciting about knowing where an ingredient comes from and that care has been taken in its production. Fresh produce markets are springing up everywhere and, while they may not have the exotic headiness of a market in Cairo, they are normally excellent places to buy fresh produce. Use the index at the back of this book if looking for a particular ingredient or recipe. Most ingredients are readily available, but hunt out specialist stores for greater variety.

mediterranean pantry

breads

Few meals in the Mediterranean are not accompanied by bread of one sort or another. For many, bread is of religious significance, a gift from God. Bread is usually bought fresh as needed, from specialist bakeries or hot out of communal ovens in marketplaces. France and Italy are famous for their baguettes, pizzas and rustic hearty loaves; Turkey for its long flat pide; Egypt for its bread rings; and the Middle East and North African countries are specialists in all sorts of flatbreads. Bread can be flavoured with olives, herbs, sesame seeds and nuts. Uses, too, are as varied as the breads themselves: bread is added to stews and soups, used to scoop up juices, made into simple but delicious rolls, and sliced, toasted and topped with fresh ingredients for serving with other appetizers.

bread flours

Flours used for bread-making vary throughout the region, though most bread recipes can be made with strong bread flour, as well as plain (all-purpose) flour. The increased gluten content of strong flour will make the bread rise more, giving it a lighter texture. Plain (all-purpose) flour makes a denser loaf, typical of the rustic bread from Italy and France, though it is also used in the flatbreads of the Eastern Mediterranean.

yeast

This microscopic, living, single-celled organism causes food to ferment, converting it into alcohol and carbon dioxide. It is crucial for making leavened bread as it is the interaction of carbon dioxide, moisture, warmth and sugar that allows yeast to grow, enabling dough to rise. Yeast is readily available in supermarkets and is sold as either compressed fresh yeast or as active dry yeast. Fresh yeast is alive and moist and must be stored in the refrigerator. Dry yeast is also alive but the dehydrated yeast cells are dormant until they are mixed with warm liquid. Dry yeast should be stored in a cool, dry place and can be frozen or refrigerated. It must be returned to room temperature before dissolving so that it will become active.

baguettes

The baguette was invented in the nineteenth century and today is virtually synonymous with France. The first baguette was based on Viennese bread, and was made from white flour and a sourdough starter, then rolled up into a slim, light, crusty loaf. Today, a 'true' baguette must be approximately 70 cm (28 inches) in length and 250 g (9 oz) in weight. In France, people buy their baguettes direct from specialist *boulangeries*, which, by law, must exist in every village. Baguettes become stale very quickly and so batches are baked up to three times a day to be absolutely fresh for each meal.

pan bagnat

slice the bread rolls in half and remove some of the soft centre from the tops. Cut the garlic clove in half and rub the insides of the rolls with the cut sides. Sprinkle both sides of the bread with olive oil, vinegar, salt and freshly ground black pepper.

put all the salad ingredients on the base of the rolls, cover with the other half and wrap each sandwich in foil. Press firmly with a light weight and stand in a cool place for 1 hour before serving. Serves 4.

1 French baguette sliced into 4 chunks, or 4 crusty bread rolls
1 garlic clove
60 ml (¼ cup) olive oil
1 tablespoon red wine vinegar
3 tablespoons basil leaves, torn
2 tomatoes, sliced
2 hard-boiled eggs, sliced
70 g (2½ oz) tin tuna
8 anchovy fillets
1 small cucumber, sliced
½ green pepper (capsicum), thinly sliced
1 French shallot, thinly sliced

ciabatta

The name of this classic country Italian bread means 'slipper', in reference to its shape. Recipes vary across Italy but, generally, the bread is formed from a wet dough made with flour, water, milk, yeast, olive oil and *biga*, a starter dough made using a small amount of flour, water and yeast. The wet dough allows large bubbles to form and also gives a thin crust. The starter *biga* gives the bread a rich, fresh taste. Ciabatta, and other country-style loaves such as pugliese, are best eaten on the day they are made or bought. Stale ciabatta can be used for bruschetta and crostini.

simple country-style bread

starter
185 ml (³/₄ cup) milk, warmed
2 teaspoons honey
1 teaspoon dried yeast or 7 g (¹/₄ oz) fresh yeast
125 g (1 cup) plain (all-purpose) flour

dough
1 teaspoon dried yeast or 7 g (¹/₄ oz) fresh yeast
2¹/₂ teaspoons salt
500 g (4 cups) plain (all-purpose) flour

to make the starter, mix the milk and honey in a large bowl with 3 tablespoons warm water. Sprinkle the yeast over the top and stir to dissolve. Leave in a draught-free spot to activate. If the yeast does not bubble and foam in 5 minutes, it is dead, so throw it away and start again. Add the flour and whisk to form a thick paste. Cover loosely with plastic wrap and leave at room temperature overnight.

to make the dough, sprinkle the yeast over the starter. Break up the starter by squeezing it between your fingers. Gradually add 250 ml (1 cup) water, combining it with the starter. Mix in the salt and flour with your fingers until the mixture comes together to form a soft dough.

turn the dough out onto a lightly floured work surface and knead for 10 minutes, or until smooth and elastic. Put the dough in a lightly oiled bowl and cover with a damp tea towel. Leave to rise in a draught-free place for 1–1¹/₂ hours, or until doubled in size. Knock back, turn out onto a lightly floured surface and knead for 1–2 minutes until smooth.

divide the dough in half and shape into round loaves, then flatten them slightly. Lightly grease a large baking tray with oil and dust with flour. Put the loaves on the tray and score a crisscross pattern 5 mm (¹/₄ inch) deep across the top of each loaf. Dust lightly with more flour.

cover with a damp tea towel and leave to rise in a draught-free place for about 40 minutes, or until doubled in size. Preheat the oven to 200°C (400°F/Gas 6). Bake for 30–35 minutes or until the bread sounds hollow when tapped underneath. Transfer to a wire rack to cool. Makes 2 loaves.

bruschetta

4 Roma (plum) tomatoes, chopped
80 ml (¹/₃ cup) olive oil
1 tablespoon balsamic vinegar
2 tablespoons chopped basil
8 slices day-old crusty Italian bread
1 garlic clove, peeled
chopped basil, extra, to garnish

combine the tomatoes, olive oil, balsamic vinegar and chopped basil. Season well.

toast the bread on one side. Rub the toasted side lightly with a peeled clove of garlic. Top with the tomato mixture and garnish with the extra chopped basil. Serve immediately. Makes 8.

note: Bruschetta should be made only when needed but crostini can be made in advance. Crostini are smaller than bruschetta and are made by drizzling olive oil over both sides of the bread slices, then toasting in the oven. Traditionally, they are served as an antipasto, topped with various flavourings such as tapenade. Do not keep crostini for too long as the oil will become stale. Store in an airtight container for 2 or 3 days and crisp them up in an oven heated to 180°C (350°F/Gas 4) for about 10 minutes before you use them.

flatbreads

The most basic of all breads, flatbreads are the ancestors of the modern loaf. They are the staples of the poorest people in the Mediterranean, and include lavash, pitta and Sardinian *carta de musica*. Flatbreads are cooked on hearths, chargrill pans (griddles), on the sides of ovens and over open fires, and can be made from low-gluten grains like barley, buckwheat and corn. Flatbreads not only add carbohydrate to a meal but also often act as the dish or cutlery, as a scoop or wrap for the food.

Middle Eastern lavash (left) and pitta bread pockets (right).

flatbread with za'atar

1 tablespoon dried yeast or 30 g (1 oz) fresh yeast
1 teaspoon sugar
405 g (3¼ cups) plain (all-purpose) flour
125 ml (½ cup) olive oil
4 tablespoons za'atar (see page 207)
1 tablespoon sea salt flakes

put the yeast and sugar in a small bowl with 60 ml (¼ cup) warm water and stir until dissolved. Leave in a draught-free place for about 10 minutes, or until bubbles appear on the surface. The mixture should be frothy and slightly increased in volume. If the yeast doesn't bubble and foam, it is dead, so throw it away and start again.

sift the flour and ½ teaspoon salt into a large bowl. Make a well and pour in the yeast mixture and 315 ml (1¼ cups) warm water. Gradually combine to form a dough, then knead on a floured work surface for 10–15 minutes until smooth and elastic, gradually adding 1 tablespoon olive oil as you knead. Cover and set aside in a warm place for 1 hour, or until risen.

punch down the dough with your fist and then knead again. Set aside and leave to rise for about 30 minutes. Knead briefly and divide into 10 portions. Roll each portion until smooth and round. Roll each into a circle about 5 mm (¼ inch) thick. Set aside covered with a tea towel for another 20 minutes.

preheat the oven to 220°C (425°F/Gas 7). Lightly grease 2 baking trays. Place the rolls on the trays and gently press the surface with your fingers to create a dimpled effect. Brush with the remaining oil and sprinkle with za'atar and salt. Bake for 12–15 minutes. Serve warm. Makes 10.

pitta, pide and lavash

Pitta is the staple bread of the Middle East. It is known as *khubz* in Arabic but is more commonly known in the west by its Greek name, pitta. Turkish pide is a slightly thicker version of pitta. Both, however, are a flatbread with a chewy crust and a hollow pouch that makes them extremely versatile. Typically, the bread is split open and filled with a variety of meats, salads and dips, such as hummus or baba ghannouj. It can also be used as a scoop for dips and to wrap foods such as kebabs.

Lavash probably originated in Armenia though it is eaten in Syria, Turkey and Lebanon. It is rolled paper-thin and cooked in a special oven called a *tannur*.

Keep pitta and pide bread sealed in a plastic bag in the refrigerator. To refresh it, sprinkle it lightly with water and reheat it in a warm oven.

focaccia

Eaten since Roman times, this yeasted bread dough is an Italian flatbread. The dough is rolled flat, dimpled with fingermarks and then drizzled with lots of olive oil and salt. Originally it was cooked over an open fire, which provided the inspiration for its name, from the Latin *focus*, meaning 'fireplace'. There are many regional variations that use a range of toppings such as olives, onions, herbs or tomatoes.

There are many kinds of focaccia in Italy and each is named according to the region it is eaten in. In Naples it is known as pizza, in Tuscany it is called stiacciata, and in Venice fugassa.

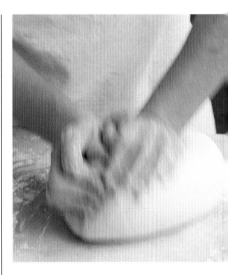

kneading

Don't be tempted to cut short the kneading time as it affects the texture of the finished bread. Kneading firstly distributes the yeast evenly throughout the dough and, secondly, allows the flour's protein to develop into gluten, which gives the dough elasticity and strength.

Make the dough in a large bowl so you have enough room to bring it together. Knead on a well-floured surface until the dough is really elastic, then use the heel of your hand to stretch it into a rectangle. Transfer the dough to a baking tray, lightly dusted with cornmeal.

basic focaccia

put the yeast in a large bowl with the sugar and add 250 ml (1 cup) lukewarm water. Stir together well. Leave in a draught-free spot to activate. If the yeast does not bubble and foam in 5 minutes it is dead, so throw it away and start again.

put the flour, half the olive oil and a large pinch of salt in a large bowl or in a food processor with a dough hook attachment and pour the yeast mixture into the middle. Knead the dough for about 5 minutes, either using the dough hook or with your hands on the work surface, until it forms a soft and slightly sticky ball.

transfer the dough to a lightly greased bowl and smear with a film of oil to prevent it drying out. Cover with a tea towel and leave to rise in a warm place for about 2 hours, or until doubled in size.

punch down the dough to its original size. Roll the dough out to a 10 x 20 cm (4 x 8 inch) rectangle, then use the heels of your hands, working from the centre of the dough outwards, to make a 20 x 30 cm (8 x 12 inch) rectangle. Lightly grease a baking tray and dust with cornmeal. Transfer the dough to the tray, cover with a damp cloth and leave to rise for 30 minutes.

preheat the oven to 220°C (425°F/Gas 7). Scatter the olives over the surface and press them firmly into the dough. Sprinkle with salt and rosemary. Bake for 20 minutes, or until golden brown. As soon as the focaccia comes out of the oven, drizzle it with the remaining oil and sprinkle with coarse salt. Serve warm. Makes 1 focaccia.

2 teaspoons dried yeast or 15 g (½ oz) fresh yeast
1 teaspoon sugar
405 g (3¼ cups) strong white flour
100 ml (3½ fl oz) extra virgin olive oil
cornmeal
175 g (6 oz) green olives
coarse sea salt
20–24 small rosemary sprigs

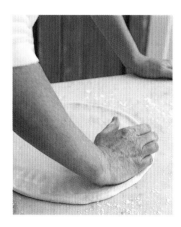

pizza

The most famous of all the flatbreads, Italian pizza is loved the world over and has probably been around since ancient Greek and Roman times. There are countless variations but it is the pizza of Naples in southern Italy that is considered to be the true pizza. The first Neapolitan pizzas were pale affairs, topped with garlic, lard, anchovies and salt. It was the tomato that was to transform pizza into the dish we know today. The Neapolitans were the first Europeans to embrace this strange new fruit, successfully growing it from seeds brought from the New World in the sixteenth century. The original tomato pizza was most probably pizza marinara, though the classic Neapolitan creation is the supremely simple yet irresistible pizza margherita.

basic pizza dough

1 tablespoon caster (superfine) sugar
2 teaspoons dried yeast or 15 g (½ oz) fresh yeast
460 g (3⅔ cups) plain (all-purpose) flour
½ teaspoon salt
3 tablespoons olive oil
cornmeal

put the sugar and yeast in a bowl and stir in 80 ml (2½ fl oz) of lukewarm water. Leave in a draught-free spot to activate. If the yeast does not bubble and foam in 5 minutes, it is dead, so throw it away and start again.

mix the flour and salt in a bowl or in a food processor fitted with a plastic blade. Add the olive oil, 135 ml (5 fl oz) lukewarm water and the yeast mixture. Mix until the dough loosely clumps together. Transfer to a lightly floured work surface and knead for 8 minutes, or until you have a soft dough that is not sticky but is dry to the touch.

rub the inside of a large bowl with olive oil. Roll the ball of dough around in the bowl to coat it with oil, then cut a shallow cross on the top of the ball. Leave the dough in the bowl, cover with a tea towel or put in a plastic bag and leave in a warm spot for 1–1½ hours until doubled in size (or leave in the refrigerator for 8 hours to rise slowly).

punch down the dough to its original size, then divide into 2 portions. (At this stage the dough can be stored in the refrigerator for up to 4 hours, or frozen. Bring back to room temperature before continuing.)

Add the olive oil to the flour and salt in a large bowl and mix until the dough loosely comes together.
Transfer to the work surface and knead, adding a little flour or a few drops of warm water if necessary.
After leaving the dough to rise, punch it down to its original size, then divide into 2 portions.

working with one portion at a time, push the dough out to make a thick circle. Use the heels of your hands and work from the centre of the circle outwards, to flatten the dough into a 30 cm (12 inch) circle with a slightly raised rim. (Use a rolling pin if necessary.) The pizza dough is now ready to use, as instructed in the recipe. Cook on a lightly oiled baking tray, dusted with cornmeal, and get it into the oven as quickly as possible. Makes 2 x 30 cm (12 inch) pizza bases.

pizza marinara

preheat the oven to 240°C (475°F/Gas 9). Put the pizza base on a baking tray dusted with cornmeal and spoon the tomato sauce onto the base, spreading it up to the rim. Sprinkle over the dried oregano and garlic cloves and drizzle with the olive oil. Bake for 12 minutes, or until the crust is browned and the centre is bubbling. Drizzle with a little more oil and serve. Makes 1 x 30 cm (12 inch) pizza.

1 x 30 cm (12 inch) pizza base
1 quantity tomato sauce
  (see page 106)
pinch of dried oregano
3 garlic cloves, chopped
olive oil

pizza margherita

preheat the oven to 240°C (475°F/Gas 9). Put the pizza base on a baking tray dusted with cornmeal and spoon the tomato sauce onto the base, spreading it up to the rim. Scatter with the mozzarella and basil and drizzle with the oil.

bake for 12–15 minutes, or until golden and puffed. Remove from the oven and brush the rim with a little extra olive oil before serving. Makes 1 x 30 cm (12 inch) pizza.

1 x 30 cm (12 inch) pizza base
1 quantity tomato sauce
  (see page 106)
150 g (5½ oz) mozzarella
  cheese, chopped
9 small basil leaves
1 tablespoon olive oil

pizza dough

10 g (¼ oz) dried yeast
1 teaspoon caster (superfine)
 sugar
500 g (4 cups) plain
 (all-purpose) flour
2 tablespoons olive oil

1 tablespoon olive oil,
 plus extra for brushing
375 g (13 oz) minced
 (ground) lamb
1 onion, finely chopped
40 g (¼ cup) pine nuts
1 tomato, peeled, seeded
 and chopped
¼ teaspoon ground
 cinnamon
pinch allspice
2 teaspoons chopped
 coriander (cilantro), plus
 extra for serving
2 teaspoons lemon juice
60 g (¼ cup) Greek-style
 natural yoghurt

turkish pizza

combine the yeast, sugar and 185 ml (¾ cup) warm water. Cover and leave in a draught-free place for 10 minutes, or until bubbles appear on the surface. If it hasn't foamed after this time, it is dead, so throw it away and start again.

sift the flour and ½ teaspoon salt and make a well. Add the yeast mixture and oil. Mix with a flat-bladed knife, using a cutting action, until a dough forms. Knead for 10 minutes, or until smooth. Put in a large oiled bowl, cover with plastic wrap and leave for 45 minutes, or until doubled in size.

heat the oil in a frying pan over medium heat and cook the lamb for 3 minutes, or until browned. Add the onion and cook, stirring, over low heat for 8 minutes, or until soft. Add the pine nuts, tomato, cinnamon and allspice, ¼ teaspoon cracked pepper and some salt. Cook for 8 minutes, or until dry. Stir in the coriander and lemon juice.

preheat the oven to 230°C (450°F/Gas 8). Punch down the dough, then knead for 8 minutes, or until elastic. Roll out into 24 ovals. Spoon some filling onto each base. Pinch together the two short sides to form a boat shape. Lightly brush with oil, and place the pizzas on a greased baking tray. Bake for 10 minutes. Serve with a dab of yoghurt and some coriander. Makes 24.

Cooks in the Eastern Mediterranean have their own forms of pizza that make wonderful use of the local ingredients. The Turkish boat-shaped pizza usually features minced (ground) lamb flavoured with pine nuts, spices and coriander (cilantro), while in Lebanon, pizza is often given a burst of tartness with a dash of pomegranate juice, followed by a sprinkling of dried chilli flakes.

1 Spread the softened onion over the bread base.

2 Arrange the anchovies in the traditional lattice pattern.

pissaladière

put the yeast in a bowl with 2 tablespoons lukewarm water. Leave in a warm, draught-free place for 10 minutes, or until foamy. If it hasn't foamed after this time, it is dead, so throw it away and start again.

sift the flour and ¼ teaspoon salt into a large bowl, make a well in the middle and add the yeast mixture, egg, oil and 2 tablespoons warm water. Bring the ingredients together with a wooden spoon and when clumped together, transfer to a lightly floured work surface. Knead to a soft, pliable dough, adding a little more water or flour as needed. Continue kneading for 6–8 minutes, or until smooth and elastic. Lightly oil a clean large bowl and put the dough in it. Roll the dough around to coat with oil, cover the bowl with a dry tea towel and put in a warm place for 1 hour, or until doubled in size.

to make the filling, heat the oil in a large, heavy-based frying pan, add the garlic, thyme and onion and cook, stirring occasionally, over very low heat for 1 hour, or until the onion is soft and buttery but not brown. Discard the garlic and thyme, add the nutmeg and season well.

brush a 30 cm (12 inch) pizza tray with oil. Punch down the dough and lightly knead into a ball. Roll out to a 30 cm (12 inch) circle and put on the oiled tray. Spread the onion over the surface leaving a 1 cm (½ inch) border. Make a diamond cross-hatch pattern on top with the anchovies. Intersperse with the olives. Slide the tray into a large plastic bag and leave to rise again for 30 minutes. Preheat the oven to 200°C (400°F/Gas 6).

bake for 20–25 minutes, or until the dough is cooked and golden. Reduce the heat slightly to 190°C (375°F/Gas 5) if the crust starts to overbrown towards the end of baking. Cut into wedges for serving. Serves 4–6.

2 teaspoons dried yeast or 15 g (½ oz) fresh yeast
185 g (1½ cups) plain (all-purpose) flour
1 egg, beaten
1 tablespoon olive oil

filling

60 ml (¼ cup) olive oil
2 garlic cloves
1 thyme sprig
4 large onions, thinly sliced
pinch ground nutmeg
30 g (1 oz) drained anchovy fillets, halved lengthways
16 pitted black olives

This French take on the traditional Italian pizza takes its name from *pissalat*, meaning puréed anchovies. It can vary in its topping from onions and anchovies to onions and anchovies flavoured with tomatoes or simply anchovies puréed with garlic. Traditional to Nice, it can be made with a bread or pastry base.

grains and flours

People have been pounding and grinding away at plant grains for thousands of years, perfecting the process whereby the fruit and seeds of wild grasses are transformed into edible foods. Such grass plants, which include wheat, barley, corn, millet and rice, are known as cereals, named after Ceres, a pre-Roman goddess of agriculture. Records show that the cultivation of barley and wheat date to 6000BCE and the ancient civilizations of Asia Minor, Mesopotamia, Palestine and Syria all relied on barley as their staple food.

Today, wheat is the most widely used grain—to the degree that 'flour' is almost taken as meaning wheat flour—and is used in making countless different breads and pastas. However, all cereal grains as well as vegetables such as dried potatoes, chickpeas or nuts (chestnuts), can be ground into flour. In the Mediterranean, as well as wheat flours, processed cereals such as couscous, semolina and polenta are important basic ingredients.

besan flour

Made from finely ground chickpeas, besan is a nutritious high-protein flour. It is not extensively used in the Mediterranean, appearing mainly in the regional cooking of Nice in southern France and Sicily in Italy. Uses include as a thickener for stews and soups and as a batter for fish. It can be bought ready-ground from specialist supermarkets.

deep-fried squid

145 g (1⅓ cups) besan flour
½ teaspoon paprika
1½ teaspoons ground cumin
½ teaspoon baking powder
250 ml (1 cup) soda water
oil, for deep-frying

6 squid, cleaned and thinly
**   sliced into rings**
flat-leaf (Italian) parsely and
**   preserved lemon, to serve**
lemon juice, olive oil, and
**   garlic, to garnish**

to make the batter, sift the flour, paprika, cumin and baking powder into a bowl, add ¼ teaspoon black pepper, mix together and make a well in the centre. Gradually add the soda water, whisking until smooth. Season with salt. Cover and leave for 30 minutes.

fill a large heavy-based saucepan or wok one-third full of oil and heat until a cube of bread dropped into the oil browns in 15 seconds.

dip the squid into the batter, allowing any excess to drip away. Cook in batches for 30–60 seconds, or until pale gold and crisp all over. Drain well on crumpled paper towels and keep warm.

serve with a salad of flat-leaf parsley and some finely sliced preserved lemon rind. Drizzle over the salad some lemon juice and olive oil, scatter over a finely chopped garlic clove, and toss well. Top with the squid rings and serve immediately. Serves 4 as a starter.

Also known as – gram
flour or chickpea flour

burghul

Burghul is a processed food made by par-boiling or steaming wheat kernels until soft then drying and grinding them. This ancient technique is possibly mankind's first attempt at processing food. Burghul has a slightly nutty flavour and is used extensively in Greek, Turkish and Middle Eastern cuisines. Unlike cracked wheat, which has not been pre-cooked, burghul needs only minimal cooking to be made edible. Among burghul's uses is tabbouleh, famed as an excellent mezze dish or accompaniment to grilled (broiled) meat. Burghul also features in *kibbeh*, the national dish of Lebanon and Syria. These thick pastes of minced (ground) meat and burghul are pounded together, shaped and cooked.

Also known as – bulgar

tabbouleh

130 g (³/₄ cup) burghul
3 ripe tomatoes
1 Lebanese (short) cucumber
4 spring onions (scallions), sliced
120 g (4 cups) chopped flat-leaf (Italian) parsley
25 g (¹/₂ cup) chopped mint

dressing
80 ml (¹/₃ cup) lemon juice
60 ml (¹/₄ cup) olive oil
1 tablespoon extra virgin olive oil

put the burghul in a bowl, cover with 500 ml (2 cups) water and leave for 1¹/₂ hours.

cut the tomatoes in half, squeeze gently to remove any excess seeds and roughly chop into 1 cm (¹/₂ inch) cubes. Cut the cucumber in half lengthways, remove the seeds with a teaspoon and cut the flesh into 1 cm (¹/₂ inch) cubes.

to make the dressing, put the lemon juice and 1¹/₂ teaspoons salt in a bowl and whisk until thoroughly combined. Season well with freshly ground black pepper and slowly whisk in the olive oil and extra virgin olive oil.

drain the burghul and squeeze out any excess water. Spread the burghul out on a clean tea towel or paper towels and leave to dry for about 30 minutes. Put the burghul in a large salad bowl, add the tomato, cucumber, spring onion, parsley and mint, and toss well to combine. Pour the dressing over the salad and toss until evenly coated. Serves 6.

COUSCOUS

Celebrated throughout Morocco, Algeria and Tunisia, this cereal is processed from hard wheat semolina flour. Traditionally, the semolina flour is laid out on a large round mesh frame, sprinkled with salted water, and laboriously rolled into tiny balls of grain. The balls are then passed through three progressively finer sieves, sorting the grains into a uniform size before drying in the sun. Today, machines do this work and couscous is mostly sold pre-prepared and par-steamed using a Tunisian process. Couscous is a valued high-carbohydrate dish, often served with meat and vegetable dishes. It is Morocco's national dish and is served every day, though rarely as part of the evening meal. At feasts it is the final dish, served to ensure no guest leaves hungry. In Sicily, couscous is the traditional accompaniment to fish stews, and in Egypt it may be served as a dessert with honey, nuts and dried fruits.

vegetable couscous with chicken

heat the grill (broiler). Bring 250 ml (1 cup) water to the boil in a saucepan, add the couscous, then take the pan off the heat and leave it to stand for 10 minutes.

heat the oil in a frying pan and fry the onion and zucchini until lightly browned. Add the pepper and semi-dried tomatoes, then stir in the couscous. Stir in the orange zest, 2 tablespoons of the orange juice and the mint.

put the chicken in a small shallow baking dish and dot it with butter. Sprinkle with the remaining orange juice and season well. Grill (broil) the chicken for 8–10 minutes, turning it over halfway through. The skin should be browned and crisp when done. Serve the chicken on the vegetable couscous with any juices poured over it. Serves 2.

95 g (½ cup) instant couscous
1 tablespoon olive oil
½ onion, finely chopped
1 zucchini (courgette), sliced
½ red pepper (capsicum), chopped
6 semi-dried (sun-blushed) tomatoes, chopped
½ teaspoon grated orange zest
125 ml (½ cup) orange juice
25 g (½ cup) mint, chopped
4 chicken thighs or 2 chicken breasts, skin on
1 tablespoon butter, softened

cooking couscous

Traditionally, couscous is cooked in a *couscoussier*, which is similar to a steamer. It is placed over an accompanying stew or boiling water containing aromatics such as cinnamon and the couscous cooks by steaming. The result is separate, perfumed grains. The method used here is quicker but does not achieve the same light result. A second stage helps: add some butter to the cooked, fluffed up couscous, cover with foil and steam in the oven for 15 minutes.

sweet couscous

**80 g (½ cup) combined pistachio nuts, pine nuts
  and blanched almonds**
45 g (¼ cup) dried apricots
90 g (½ cup) pitted dried dates
250 g (1⅓ cups) instant couscous
55 g (¼ cup) caster (superfine) sugar
90 g (3¼ oz) unsalted butter, softened

to serve

2 tablespoons caster (superfine) sugar
½ teaspoon ground cinnamon
375 ml (1½ cups) hot milk

preheat the oven to 160°C (315°F/Gas 2–3). Spread the nuts on a baking tray and bake for 5 minutes, or until light golden. Allow to cool, then coarsely chop and put in a bowl. Slice the dried apricots into matchstick-sized pieces and quarter the dates lengthways. Add both to the bowl and toss to combine.

put the couscous and sugar in a large bowl and cover with 250 ml (1 cup) boiling water. Stir, then add the butter and a pinch of salt. Stir to melt the butter. Cover with a tea towel and set aside for 10 minutes. When the couscous has absorbed all the water, fluff with a fork, then toss half the fruit and nut mixture through.

to serve, pile the warm couscous in the centre of a platter. Arrange the remaining nut mixture around the base. Combine the sugar and cinnamon in a small bowl and serve separately for sprinkling. Pass around the hot milk in a jug for guests to help themselves. Serves 4–6.

freekeh

Eaten over much of the Middle East and North Africa, this is a roasted green wheat—green because the whole wheat grains are harvested while still young. Freekeh is very nutritious, containing high levels of protein, fibre, vitamins and minerals, as well as being low in starch. It has a rich, smoky flavour, and is used in broths of meat or chicken and is also a traditional dish of Ramadan, the Muslim month of fasting. The Bedouins make it into a rice-like dish. To use, the grains are boiled then allowed to stand for 15 minutes so that the grains can swell and soften further. Freekeh is available in a cracked and wholegrain form.

Also known as – freek

polenta

Also known as cornmeal, these ground, dried corn kernels are traditionally made and eaten in the mountainous areas of northern Italy. As well as the grains, the name also refers to its most common use: a type of porridge, often flavoured with butter and Parmesan cheese, which is lightly cooked. It is then poured into a tray in the middle of the table and eaten as an accompaniment to the main meal. Like many processed grains, cooking polenta initially involved significant amounts of tireless stirring over a hot fire. This is less the case today, with commercial preparations of polenta greatly reducing the cooking time.

Polenta comes in different grades, which are matched to the dish they are being served with: coarser versions go with richer, heartier accompaniments, while the finer grade suits delicate sauces. Cooked polenta is often cooled, then cut into squares and baked or fried. A white version, *polenta bianca*, is eaten in the Veneto area of Italy. Depending on the coarseness of the grain, polenta may take 40 minutes to cook.

making polenta

1 Pour the polenta into the water in a steady, even stream.

2 Stir the polenta occasionally to prevent sticking.

put the specified amount of cold water and salt in a deep heavy-based saucepan and bring to the boil. Add the polenta in a steady stream, using a wooden spoon to stir the water vigorously in a whirlpool action as you pour the polenta in.

after adding all the polenta, reduce the heat so the water is just simmering and keep stirring for the first 30 seconds to prevent lumps.

the finished texture of the polenta will improve the more you stir it. Leave it to bubble away for about 40 minutes, stirring every few minutes to prevent it sticking. When cooked, it should be thick enough to fall from the spoon in lumps.

grilling polenta

1 Pour the cooked wet polenta into a flat dish and allow to cool.

2 Once cool, cut the polenta into squares, rectangles or triangles.

3 Brush with olive oil and grill (broil) for a crisp exterior.

pour the cooked polenta onto a flat plate or serving dish and leave to cool. Do not store the polenta in the refrigerator or condensation will form and make it stick when grilled (broiled). Cut the polenta into triangles or strips.

lightly brush the pieces of polenta with olive oil and grill (broil) or cook on a chargrill pan (griddle) for about 3 minutes on each side. You can use grilled polenta for canapé bases as well as an accompaniment to stews and sauces.

shaping polenta

1 To shape, pour the polenta into a dish, smooth and allow to cool.

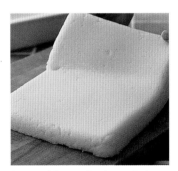

2 Carefully transfer the cooled polenta to a work surface.

3 Slice horizontally, then layer with sauce and re-form in the dish.

polenta can easily be moulded into shapes for layering with sauce. Pour the polenta into a deep serving dish, bearing in mind you want it to be no more than 2.5 cm (1 inch) thick or it will be too stodgy.

the polenta will mould itself to the shape of the dish. Allow to cool completely. Once cooled, the polenta will be very pliable and easy to handle. Carefully turn the polenta out of the dish and onto a board. Use a long sharp knife to slice it. The polenta slices can then be layered with sauce and re-formed in the dish.

semolina

This flour is obtained from the first milling of durum wheat, usually the very hard durum wheat. Semolina can be coarse, medium or fine. Fine semolina flour is known as *semola di grano* in Italy, and it is this grade that is used for making pasta and bread. In Greece, Turkey, Syria, Egypt and Lebanon, sweet semolina cakes, pastries and puddings are popular, often made rich through the addition of honey, or perfumed with the use of spices such as vanilla or cinnamon.

syrup
**575 g (2½ cups) caster
(superfine) sugar
2 tablespoons lemon juice**

**125 g (4½ oz) unsalted butter
170 g (¾ cup) caster
(superfine) sugar
2 teaspoons finely grated
lemon zest
3 eggs
185 g (1½ cups) semolina
125 g (1 cup) self-raising
flour
125 ml (½ cup) milk
80 g (½ cup) blanched
almonds, toasted and
finely chopped
blanched flaked almonds,
to decorate**

greek halvas fourno

preheat the oven to 170°C (325°F/Gas 3). Grease a 30 x 20 cm (12 x 8 inch) cake tin.

dissolve the sugar in a saucepan with 750 ml (3 cups) water over high heat. Add the lemon juice and bring to the boil. Reduce the heat to medium and simmer for 20 minutes. Remove from the heat and allow to cool.

while the syrup is cooking, cream the butter, sugar and lemon zest with electric beaters until light and fluffy. Add the eggs one at a time, beating well after each addition.

sift together the semolina and flour and fold into the butter mixture alternately with the milk. Mix in the chopped almonds, then spread the mixture into the tin and arrange rows of flaked almonds on top. Bake for 35–40 minutes, or until the cake is golden and shrinks slightly from the sides of the tin. Prick the surface with a fine skewer, then pour the cooled syrup over the hot cake. When the cake is cool, cut it into squares or diamonds. Serves 6–8.

semolina and nut diamonds

preheat the oven to 210°C (415°F/Gas 6–7). Lightly grease a 23 cm (9 inch) square baking tin and line the base with baking paper. Cream the butter and sugar in a bowl until light and fluffy. Stir in the semolina, ground hazelnuts and baking powder. Add the eggs, orange zest and juice and fold through until well combined. Spoon into the tin, smooth the surface and bake for 20 minutes, or until golden and just set. Leave in the tin.

meanwhile, make the syrup. Put the sugar, cinnamon sticks and about 830 ml (3⅓ cups) water in a saucepan over low heat and stir until the sugar has dissolved. Increase the heat and boil rapidly, without stirring, for 5 minutes. Pour into a heatproof measuring jug then return half to the saucepan. Boil for 15–20 minutes, or until thickened and reduced to about 170 ml (⅔ cup). Stir in the orange zest.

add the lemon juice and orange flower water to the syrup in the jug and pour it over the cake in the tin. When absorbed, turn the cake out onto a large flat plate. Slice into 4 equal strips, then slice each strip diagonally into 3 diamond-shaped pieces. Discard the end scraps but keep the pieces touching together.

to make the topping, combine the almonds and hazelnuts and scatter over the cake. Pour the thickened syrup and orange zest over the nuts and leave to stand for 30 minutes before serving. Using a cake slice, transfer the diamonds to individual plates and serve with whipped cream or honey-flavoured yoghurt. Makes 12.

115 g (4 oz) unsalted butter, softened
125 g (heaped ½ cup) caster (superfine) sugar
125 g (1 cup) semolina
110 g (1 cup) ground roasted hazelnuts
2 teaspoons baking powder
3 eggs, lightly beaten
1 tablespoon finely grated orange zest
2 tablespoons orange juice
whipped cream or honey-flavoured yoghurt, to serve

syrup
690 g (3 cups) caster (superfine) sugar
4 cinnamon sticks
1 tablespoon thinly sliced orange zest
80 ml (⅓ cup) lemon juice
125 ml (½ cup) orange flower water

topping
60 g (½ cup) slivered almonds
70 g (½ cup) roasted hazelnuts, coarsely chopped

pasta

There can be no ingredient more instantly connected with Italian cooking than pasta. Originally a southern Italian, and particularly Sicilian, creation, its popularity spread when Mussolini moved the cultivation of wheat, and therefore pasta, to other areas of Italy. From there, it has spread throughout the world with the migrations of Italians. Today, there are over 200 different types of pasta, and it seems as if every region in Italy prefers its own particular type. Generally, however, southern Italians favour dried pasta made without egg while northern Italians tend to eat fresh egg and filled pastas. Pasta is not confined to Italy; many other countries in the region use it. Dishes include Greek *pastitsio*, a dish of layered macaroni and meat, topped with a rich béchamel sauce, Spanish *fideos* and Turkish ravioli in yoghurt.

dried pasta

This is made with durum wheat (semolina) flour and water. It is a tough dough that can be easily forced through special machines known as dies. As it passes through the die, the pasta is shaped and cut to length, then slowly dried on trays in hot rooms. Dried pasta includes short pastas such as penne, macaroni and conchiglie and long shapes such as spaghetti, linguine and tagliatelle. Dried pasta can also be made with durum wheat (semolina) flour and eggs; this is usually shaped into filled pasta such as ravioli or cut as ribbons and dried as nests. Semolina pasta is sometimes eaten fresh in the south of Italy where it is formed into shapes such as orecchiette, meaning 'little ears'.

spaghetti alla puttanesca

1 small red chilli
1 tablespoon capers
4 tablespoons olive oil
1 small onion, finely chopped
2 garlic cloves, thinly sliced
6 anchovy fillets, finely chopped
400 g (14 oz) tin chopped tomatoes
1 tablespoon finely chopped oregano or ¼ teaspoon
  dried oregano
100 g (3½ oz) black olives, pitted and halved
400 g (14 oz) spaghetti
1 tablespoon finely chopped flat-leaf (Italian) parsley

cut the chilli in half, remove the seeds, then chop it finely. Rinse the capers, squeeze them dry and, if they are large, roughly chop them.

heat the olive oil in a large saucepan and add the onion, garlic and chilli. Gently fry for about 6 minutes, or until the onion is soft. Add the anchovies and cook, stirring and mashing, until they break down to a smooth paste.

add the tomato, oregano, olives and capers and bring to the boil. Reduce the heat, season and leave to simmer for about 10 minutes, or until the sauce has reduced and thickened.

meanwhile, cook the pasta in a large saucepan of boiling salted water until *al dente*. Drain briefly, leaving some of the water still clinging to the pasta, then add to the sauce with the parsley. Toss well before serving. Serves 4.

note: Cooking pasta until it is *al dente* means 'to the tooth'. That is, the pasta should retain a little bite. When you drain the pasta, leave a little water to stop the from pasta sticking together.

pasta alla norma

1 large eggplant (aubergine),
    cut into 2.5 cm (1 inch)
    thick slices
350 g (12 oz) fresh tomatoes
    or 400 g (14 oz) tin
    chopped tomatoes
170 ml (2/3 cup) olive oil
2 garlic cloves, thinly sliced
handful torn basil leaves
400 g (14 oz) conchiglie
160 g (2/3 cup) ricotta cheese

put the eggplant slices in a bowl of salted water for 10 minutes. Drain and dry on a tea towel. If using fresh tomatoes, remove the stems and score a cross in the base of each one. Put in boiling water for 20 seconds, then plunge into cold water. Drain and peel the skin away from the cross (it should slip off easily), then chop the tomatoes.

pour a generous amount of the olive oil into a frying pan and cook the eggplant in batches over medium-high heat until golden brown and soft inside, adding more of the oil as you need it. Drain the cooked eggplant in a colander or on paper towels. Carefully cut the eggplant into 2.5 cm (1 inch) thick sticks and set aside.

remove all but 2 tablespoons of the oil from the frying pan, add the garlic and cook until light golden brown. Add the tomato and season. Cook until the sauce has reduced and thickened. Add the eggplant and the basil leaves, mix well and set aside.

cook the pasta in a large saucepan of boiling salted water until *al dente*. Drain briefly, leaving some of the water clinging to the pasta, then return the pasta to the saucepan with the eggplant mixture and two-thirds of the ricotta.

mix briefly, check for seasoning and serve immediately with the remaining ricotta crumbled over the top. Serves 4.

1 Cook the eggplant slices until golden on both sides.

2 Add the pasta to the eggplant mixture and gently stir to mix.

pastitsio

preheat the oven to 180°C (350°F/Gas 4). Grease a 1.5 litre (6 cup) ovenproof dish. Cook the macaroni in a large saucepan of boiling salted water for 10 minutes, or until *al dente*. Drain and return to the pan. Melt the butter in a small saucepan until golden, then pour it over the macaroni. Stir in the nutmeg and half the cheese and season with salt and freshly ground black pepper. Leave until cool, then mix in the egg and set aside.

to make the meat sauce, heat the oil in a large frying pan, add the onion and garlic and cook over medium heat for 6 minutes, or until the onion is soft. Increase the heat slightly, add the beef and cook, stirring, for 5 minutes, or until the meat is browned. Add the wine and cook over high heat for 1 minute until evaporated. Add the stock, tomato paste, oregano, salt and pepper. Reduce the heat, cover and simmer for 20 minutes.

meanwhile, make the béchamel sauce. Melt the butter in a small saucepan over low heat. Stir in the flour and cook for 1 minute, or until pale and foaming. Remove from the heat and gradually stir in the milk. Return to the heat and stir constantly until the sauce boils and thickens. Reduce the heat and simmer for 2 minutes. Add the nutmeg and some salt and pepper. Allow to cool a little before stirring in the beaten egg. Stir 3 tablespoons of the béchamel into the meat sauce.

spread half the meat sauce in the dish, then layer half the pasta over it. Cover with the remaining meat sauce and then the remaining pasta. Press down firmly with the back of a spoon. Spread the béchamel sauce over the pasta and sprinkle the remaining cheese on top. Bake for 50 minutes, or until golden. Let the pastitsio stand for 15 minutes before serving. Serves 6.

**150 g (5½ oz) elbow
   macaroni**
40 g (1½ oz) butter
¼ teaspoon ground nutmeg
**60 g (2¼ oz) kefalotyri or
   Parmesan cheese, grated**
1 egg, lightly beaten

meat sauce
2 tablespoons oil
1 onion, finely chopped
2 garlic cloves, crushed
**500 g (1 lb 2 oz) minced
   (ground) beef**
125 ml (½ cup) red wine
250 ml (1 cup) beef stock
**3 tablespoons tomato paste
   (purée)**
1 teaspoon chopped oregano

béchamel sauce
40 g (1½ oz) butter
**1½ tablespoons plain
   (all-purpose) flour**
375 ml (1½ cups) milk
pinch nutmeg
1 egg, lightly beaten

fresh egg pasta

This is made from eggs and doppio zero (00) flour, a soft wheat flour, sometimes with a little semolina flour added. This mixture gives a soft pliable pasta that can be easily shaped by hand. Fresh egg pasta is used to make lasagne sheets, is folded into shapes like tortellini or is cut into ribbons. It is simple to make fresh pasta at home and it has a lighter and more slippery texture than dried semolina pasta.

home-made fresh pasta

500 g (4 cups) doppio zero (00) or plain (all-purpose) flour
4 eggs
chilled water

mound the flour on a work surface or in a large bowl. Make a well in the centre. Break the eggs into the well and whisk with a fork, incorporating the flour as you whisk. You may need to add a little chilled water (1/4 teaspoon at a time) to make a loosely massed dough. Turn the dough onto a lightly floured surface—it should be soft, pliable and dry to the touch. Knead for 6–8 minutes, or until smooth and elastic with a slightly glossy appearance. Cover with a tea towel and leave for 30 minutes. The dough is then ready to roll out.

to make the dough in a processor, mix the flour for 2–3 seconds, then add the eggs with the motor running. Mix again for 5 seconds, or until the mixture looks like coarse meal. Mix until a loose ball forms, then continue for 4–5 seconds until the machine slows and stops. If the dough seems too sticky to form a smooth ball, add 2 teaspoons flour, mix briefly and continue adding small amounts of flour until the ball forms. If the mixture is too dry, add chilled water, a teaspoon at a time. Transfer to a floured work surface and knead for 3 minutes, or until elastic. Cover with a tea towel and leave for 30 minutes. Makes 700 g (1 lb 9 oz).

1 Break the eggs into the flour, set directly on the work surface.

2 Whisk with a fork, incorporating the flour as you work.

3 Knead until the dough is smooth and elastic.

working with fresh pasta

rolling out the dough Divide the dough into 2 or 3 manageable portions. Work with 1 portion at a time, keeping the rest covered. Flatten the dough onto a lightly floured surface and roll out from the centre to the outer edge, rotating the dough often. When you have a 5 mm (¼ inch) thick circle of dough, fold it in half and roll it out again. Do this 4 times to give a smooth circle of pasta, then roll to a thickness of 2.5 mm (⅛ inch), mending any tears with a little pasta from the edge of the circle and a little water. Transfer to a lightly floured tea towel. If the pasta is to be filled, keep it covered so it doesn't dry out. If the sheets are to be cut into lengths or shapes, leave them uncovered while you roll out the other portions, so that the surface will dry out before cutting.

using a pasta machine Divide the dough into 6 to 8 flattened rectangular pieces and cover with plastic wrap. Dust the work surface with semolina (to make the pasta heavier). Flatten the first piece of pasta so that it is easier to roll through the machine. Feed the pasta through the rollers on the widest setting. Fold the flattened pasta in half or thirds, so that it fits across the rollers. Repeat this process 3 times, making the setting smaller each time until the dough is the correct thickness.

cutting by hand Roll out the pasta into long flat sheets of the width you want and dust them with semolina to help prevent the cut noodles sticking together. Roll up each sheet loosely and cut into slices of whatever width you want. Bear in mind that thicker widths are easier to handle when they are unrolled. Toss the strips in more semolina to keep them separate or hang them up to dry, as above.

cutting by machine Attach the cutting blades to your machine: the wide one for tagliatelle and the narrower one for linguine. Feed a sheet of pasta into the machine and carefully collect the cut pasta as it comes out at the other end. Either hang up the pasta to dry over a broomstick or on a pasta dryer or coil it into wide nests. To keep the nests from sticking, toss them in a little semolina.

filling Roll out a sheet of pasta, brush with egg wash (1 egg beaten with 2 teaspoons milk) and add the filling at short intervals. Put another sheet of pasta on top and press down. Cut around the mounds. Alternatively, roll out a sheet of pasta, cut out shapes with a knife or cutter and then put a mound of filling in the centre. Brush the edge with egg wash. Cover with another piece of pasta the same shape or fold the piece of pasta in half. A third method is to lay a sheet of pasta over a ravioli mould. Press the pasta into the indents, then add a spoonful of filling to each one. Brush the edges with egg wash, lay another sheet of pasta over the top and seal by rolling over with a rolling pin.

When cutting strips of pasta, always work with manageable lengths.

Use a wheel, knife or pasta cutter to cut neat filled pasta shapes.

4 Roll out the dough until very thin, rotating the dough often.

5 Alternatively, use a machine to achieve the desired thickness.

making fresh pasta

The most difficult part of making pasta at home is measuring the ingredients exactly. Variable egg sizes and the moisture content of the flour can affect how much of each you actually need. Just remember that the dough should be quite hard to knead and not too moist: simply add more flour or egg accordingly.

pulses

Pulses are an important source of protein and are a staple food throughout the Mediterranean, particularly in areas where little or no meat is eaten. The term technically refers to the edible seeds of any legume but, in practice, it usually signifies only the dried seeds, which includes beans, peas and lentils. Mediterranean marketplaces offer countless different pulses, varying in size, shape and colour, but the most commonly used ones are green and brown lentils and beans such as borlotti (cranberry), broad (fava), chickpeas and haricot beans.

borlotti beans

Especially popular in Italian cooking, borlotti beans are relatively large, slightly kidney-shaped and have a pale, pinkish brown colour, with darker specks. The beans have a distinctive nutty flavour and a creamy texture, and are ideal for soups, stews and salads. Dried borlotti beans need to be soaked overnight; they are also available canned.

Also known as – cranberry beans

braised borlotti beans

soak the beans in cold water overnight, then drain. Put in a large saucepan and add the red wine, onion, cloves, half the olive oil and 875 ml (3½ cups) water. Cover and bring to the boil. Reduce the heat, remove the lid and simmer for 1 hour.

heat the remaining oil in a small saucepan. Strip the leaves off the rosemary sprig and chop finely. Add to the oil with the garlic and red chilli flakes and cook for 1 minute. Add to the beans and simmer for ½–1 hour until the beans are tender.

drain the beans, reserving the cooking liquid. Return the liquid to the saucepan and simmer until it thickens. Season. Return the beans to the pan and simmer for another 5 minutes. Stir in the parsley and cool for 15 minutes. Serve either warm or cold. Serves 4–6.

350 g (1¾ cups) dried borlotti (cranberry) beans
435 ml (1¾ cups) dry red wine
1 small onion, finely chopped
3 cloves
125 ml (½ cup) olive oil
1 rosemary sprig
3 garlic cloves, crushed
pinch red chilli flakes
3 tablespoons chopped flat-leaf (Italian) parsley

broad beans

These beans are one of mankind's oldest foodstuffs and it is said they hark back to the time of the pharaohs. It is appropriate then, that in Egypt, *ful mudammas* (or *ful medames*), made with a type of broad bean, is the national breakfast dish. The dish was traditionally made by mixing the beans with lentils and cooking in water overnight in a special pot, ready for eating the next morning. Simple seasonings and toppings such as lemon wedges, olive oil and hard-boiled eggs were typical but today buffalo milk or tomato sauce may also be added.

Also known as – fava beans

broad bean and garlic dip

200 g (1 cup) dried broad (fava) beans
2 garlic cloves, crushed
¼ teaspoon ground cumin
1½ tablespoons lemon juice
up to 80 ml (⅓ cup) olive oil
2 tablespoons chopped flat-leaf (Italian) parsley
flatbread, for serving

rinse the beans well, then put in a large bowl, cover with 500 ml (2 cups) of water and leave to soak overnight.

if using peeled beans, transfer them and their soaking water to a large heavy-based saucepan. If using the unpeeled brown beans, drain, then add to the pan with 500 ml (2 cups) fresh water. In either case, bring to the boil, cover, and simmer over low heat for 5–6 hours. Check the water level from time to time and add a little boiling water, as necessary, to keep the beans moist. Do not stir, but shake the pan occasionally to prevent the beans sticking. Set aside to cool slightly.

purée the contents of the pan in a food processor, then transfer to a bowl and stir in the garlic, cumin and lemon juice. Gradually stir in enough olive oil to give a dipping consistency, beginning with 60 ml (¼ cup). As the mixture cools it may become thick, in which case stir through a little warm water to return the mixture to dipping consistency.

spread over a large dish and sprinkle with the parsley. Serve with the flatbread, cut into triangles. Serves 6.

buying

When buying the dried beans, you can choose between the ready-peeled white variety or the small, brown ones. Split broad (fava) beans, which are already skinned, are available from specialist and health food stores. If the whole beans are used in a recipe, they will need to be skinned after soaking. To do this, pierce each skin with your fingernail, then peel it off or squeeze each bean to allow the skin to pop off.

tuna with beans

**400 g (14 oz) dried cannellini
  beans**
1 bay leaf
1 garlic clove
150 ml (5 fl oz) olive oil

1 small red onion, finely sliced
**2 tablespoons finely chopped
  flat-leaf (Italian) parsley**
**400 g (14 oz) tin tuna in olive
  oil, drained**

soak the beans overnight in plenty of cold water.

rinse them and transfer to a very large saucepan. Cover with plenty of cold water and bring to the boil. Add the bay leaf, garlic clove and 1 tablespoon olive oil, cover and simmer for 1–1½ hours or until tender, depending on the age of the beans. Salt the water for the last 15–20 minutes of cooking. The beans should keep their shape and have a slight bite rather than being soft.

drain well, remove the bay leaf and garlic and transfer the beans to a shallow serving dish. Add the onion and remaining olive oil and season with salt and pepper. Toss well, then chill.

toss through two-thirds of the parsley and taste for seasoning. Break the tuna up into bite-sized pieces and toss through the beans. Sprinkle the remaining parsley over the top and serve. Serves 4.

cannellini beans

These are white, kidney-shaped beans, mildly flavoured and slightly fluffy in texture when cooked. They are good all-purpose beans, and are popular in Italy and France, used in soups, casseroles, stews and salads. Like haricot, cannellini beans are mostly used dried rather than fresh. The dried beans need to be soaked for a few hours to soften them before using. Tinned beans can also be used—add them at the end of the cooking time or they will quickly disintegrate.

Also known as – Italian haricot beans or white kidney beans

chickpeas

Grown in the Levant and Egypt since ancient times, it is not surprising that chickpeas contribute some of the most popular Middle Eastern dishes, including hummus and falafel. They have a meaty sweetness to them that makes them ideal for a range of dishes, from soups and stews to stuffings and salads.

Despite the name, chickpeas are beans not peas, and there are two main kinds: the large white garbanzo and the smaller brown dessi. Chickpeas are wonderfully versatile and nutritious: they contain dietary fibre, protein, iron, vitamin B1 and potassium, and they can be boiled, roasted, ground, mashed and milled. They are available dried or pre-prepared in tins. Dried chickpeas need to be soaked overnight.

hummus

220 g (1 cup) dried chickpeas
2 tablespoons tahini (see page 202)
4 garlic cloves, crushed
2 teaspoons ground cumin
80 ml (¹/₃ cup) lemon juice
3 tablespoons olive oil
large pinch cayenne pepper
extra lemon juice, optional
extra virgin olive oil, to garnish
paprika, to garnish
chopped flat-leaf (Italian) parsley, to garnish

put the chickpeas in a bowl, add 1 litre (4 cups) water, then soak overnight. Drain and put in a large saucepan with 2 litres (8 cups) water, or enough to cover the chickpeas by 5 cm (2 inches). Bring to the boil, then reduce the heat and simmer for 1 hour 15 minutes, or until the chickpeas are very tender. Skim any scum from the surface. Drain well, reserving the cooking liquid and leave until cool enough to handle. Pick through for any loose skins and discard them.

put the chickpeas, tahini, garlic cloves, cumin, lemon juice, olive oil, cayenne pepper and 1¹/₂ teaspoons salt in a food processor and combine until thick and smooth. With the motor running, gradually add enough of the reserved cooking liquid, about 185 ml (³/₄ cup), to form a smooth creamy purée. Season with a little salt or some extra lemon juice.

spread onto flat bowls or plates, drizzle with the extra virgin olive oil, sprinkle with paprika and scatter parsley over the top. Serve with warm pitta bread. Makes 750 ml (3 cups).

falafel

put the broad beans in a large bowl, cover well with water and soak for 48 hours. Drain, then rinse several times in fresh water. Put the chickpeas in a large bowl, cover well with water and soak for 12 hours.

drain the broad beans and chickpeas well, then combine in a food processor with the onion and garlic until smooth.

add the ground coriander, cumin, parsley, chilli powder, bicarbonate of soda and coriander leaves. Season with salt and freshly ground black pepper, then mix until well combined. Transfer to a large bowl and set aside for 30 minutes.

shape tablespoons of mixture into small balls, flatten to 5 cm (2 inch) rounds, put on a tray and refrigerate for 20 minutes.

fill a deep, heavy-based saucepan one-third full of oil and heat to 180°C (350°F), or until a cube of bread dropped in the oil browns in 15 seconds. Cook in batches for 1–2 minutes, or until golden. Drain on paper towels. Serve hot or cold with hummus, baba ghannouj and pitta bread. Makes 30.

150 g (1 cup) dried split
  broad (fava) beans
220 g (1 cup) dried chickpeas
1 onion, roughly chopped
6 garlic cloves, roughly
  chopped
2 teaspoons ground
  coriander
1 tablespoon ground cumin
15 g (½ cup) chopped
  flat-leaf (Italian) parsley
¼ teaspoon chilli powder
½ teaspoon bicarbonate
  of soda
3 tablespoons chopped
  coriander (cilantro) leaves
light oil, for deep-frying

lentils

Tiny, flat, lens-shaped pulses, lentils have long played a daily part in Mediterranean cooking. Thought to be native to the Middle East, archaeological evidence suggests the plants may have existed in areas such as Greece, Palestine and Syria as long ago as 8000BCE. Their reputation is a mixed one. An excellent source of protein and readily available, lentils have been a vital food of the poor for centuries. This same reliability, however, combined with a mild flavour, has led many to disregard them over the years. Perhaps aware of this, cooks in the Mediterranean combine them with strongly flavoured ingredients such as English spinach and silverbeet (Swiss chard), lemon, meat and spices and use them in stews, soups and casseroles.

When buying lentils, look for bright, shiny pulses with no hint of dust, damp or mould. Do not buy in bulk as lentils become harder and drier with time. They then take longer to cook and are more likely to break up during cooking. Lentils don't need to be soaked before they are cooked. Pick over lentils before cooking as they can conceal small stones, then rinse and discard any lentils that float.

types of lentils

castelluccio Castelluccio in Umbria is home to Italy's most famous lentils, the *lenticchie di Castelluccio*. These small grey-brown lentils are organically grown on the plains that surround the hilltop town. Castelluccio lentils are used in the soups and braised dishes of the area or are simply cooked in water and then dressed with olive oil and lemon juice.

green and brown Also known as continental lentils, these are the largest of all lentils. They keep their shape when cooked, thus are a good way to add texture to casseroles and soups. Green and brown vary in size and colour and aren't always easy to differentiate from each other—treat in the same way.

puy Tiny, speckled grey-green lentils that are grown organically and contain more minerals than other varieties. *Lentilles vertes du Puy* from France are governed by the French *appellation d'origine contrôlée* (AOC) and must be from that area. The same type of lentils are grown elsewhere—these are sold simply as puy lentils.

red Also called Egyptian lentils, these break down when cooked and can be used for making soups and purées.

braised sausages with puy lentils

1 tablespoon olive oil
55 g (2 oz) pancetta, cubed
1 red onion, finely chopped
6 French Toulouse sausages or other meaty pork sausage
1 garlic clove, peeled and smashed
1 thyme sprig leaves
150 g (²/₃ cup) puy lentils
375 ml (1 ½ cups) tinned chicken consommé
150 g (5½ oz) baby English spinach leaves, finely chopped (about 4 handfuls)
2 tablespoons crème fraîche

heat the oil in a wide heavy-based frying pan (with a lid) and fry the pancetta until it is browned. Take it out, using a slotted spoon, and put it in a bowl. Put the onion in the pan and cook until it is soft and only lightly browned. Take the onion out, using a slotted spoon, and add it to the pancetta. Put the sausages in the same pan and fry them until they are brown all over. Return the pancetta and onion to the pan.

add the garlic, thyme leaves and lentils to the frying pan, and mix everything together. Add the consommé and bring to the boil. Cover, then slowly simmer for 25 minutes. Add the spinach and stir through.

season the lentils with salt and freshly ground black pepper and stir in the crème fraîche. Serve the sausage and lentils in shallow bowls, with crusty bread. Serves 2.

rice

Though rice is not as important as wheat in the Mediterranean diet, it is still eaten daily in many parts, particularly in the eastern areas. The ancient Persians first imported rice from China and India, and began cultivation of the crop about 2000 years ago. Later, the Arab conquest of the region brought rice to southern Italy and Spain in the eighth century. Today, far from being considered an accompaniment, rice forms an important base for many traditional dishes, many of which reflect the great age of Persian, Arab and Ottoman cooking, with dishes such as aromatic pilafs, perfumed saffron rice dishes, Spanish paellas and southern Italian risottos.

At Antica Riseria Ferron in the Veneto, Italy, (above right), rice is husked by hand then polished to produce perfect white grains.

white rice

White rice—in its numerous guises—is the most common choice of rice right throughout the Mediterranean, though there are locally grown exceptions. All white rice has had the husk removed and been milled, and has good storing qualities (which partly accounts for its popularity), but different varieties of white rice have different qualities, such as the absorbent qualities, grain shape, degree of stickiness and the hardness of the core. These determine which variety is used in a particular dish.

other rice types and forms

camargue red This is from the Camargue region of southern France and has a distinctive nutty flavour and chewy texture. It is served there with duck and game.

ground rice Though more typical of Asian rather than Mediterranean cooking, ground rice (rice flour) is also occasionally used, mostly as an ingredient in milk puddings. It is available in various varieties and brands including white and brown rice flour.

long-grain rice

This absorbent, fine-grained rice contains relatively high amounts of a starch called amylose, which does not dissolve easily. As a result, grains tend to stay separate and fluffy after cooking. This quality is essential to the famed pilafs of the Middle East. There are many variations—they can be steamed or baked, made with burghul as is done in Syria, or flavoured in different ways— but all rely on the correct texture of the rice for their success. The most celebrated pilafs are those that are inspired by the cooking of the Ottoman empire, using unusual ingredients such as cherries and pomegranates, spices and other aromatics.

lamb pilaf

1 large eggplant (aubergine), about 500 g (1 lb), cut into 1 cm (½ inch) cubes
125 ml (½ cup) olive oil
1 large onion, finely chopped
2 teaspoons ground cumin
1 teaspoon ground cinnamon
1 teaspoon ground coriander
300 g (1½ cups) long-grain white rice
500 ml (2 cups) chicken or vegetable stock

500 g (1 lb 2 oz) minced (ground) lamb
½ teaspoon allspice
2 tablespoons olive oil, extra
2 vine-ripened tomatoes, cut into wedges
3 tablespoons toasted pistachios
2 tablespoons currants
2 tablespoons chopped coriander (cilantro) leaves, to garnish

put the eggplant in a colander, sprinkle generously with salt and leave for 1 hour. Rinse well and squeeze dry in a clean tea towel. Heat 2 tablespoons oil in a large, deep frying pan with a lid, add the eggplant and cook over medium heat for 8–10 minutes, or until golden and cooked through. Drain on paper towels.

heat the remaining oil, add the onion and cook for 4–5 minutes, or until soft but not brown. Stir in half of each of the cumin, cinnamon and coriander. Add the rice and stir to coat, then add the stock, season and bring to the boil. Reduce the heat and simmer, covered, for 15 minutes, adding a little more water if the pilaf starts to dry out.

meanwhile, put the lamb in a bowl with the allspice and the remaining cumin, cinnamon and coriander. Season and mix well. Roll into balls the size of macadamia nuts. Heat the extra oil in the frying pan and cook the meatballs in batches over medium heat for 5 minutes each batch, or until lightly browned and cooked through. Drain on paper towels. Add the tomato to the pan and gently cook, turning, for 3–5 minutes, or until lightly golden. Remove from the pan.

stir the eggplant, pistachios, currants and meatballs through the rice (this should be quite dry by now). Serve surrounded by the cooked tomato and garnished with the coriander leaves. Serves 4.

short-grain rice

The key to culinary gems such as risotto and paella is short-grain rice. The reason for this is its sticky, soft texture when cooked, which in turn is due to its relatively high amounts of the starch amylopectin. This starch easily dissolves in water, thus producing the characteristic creamy result. As well as risotto and paella, short-grain is also used in moulds, puddings and stuffings.

types of short-grain rice

paella rice Spaniards may argue over the authenticity of ingredients such as rabbit, snails and various seafood in their national dish, but all agree that the key to success is getting the rice right. Correct texture is everything: paella should not be fluffy like pilaf or oozy like risotto but somewhere in between—slightly creamy, glistening with oil and flavour. Bomba rice, from the Spanish region of Calasparra, is the premium variety for cooking paella and was the first Spanish rice to be awarded demonination of origin status. Valencia is another prized Spanish grain.

risotto rice Risotto is another superb example of the culinary potential of short-grain rice. Risotto rice is divided into three grades: *superfino*, *fino* and *semifino*. Arborio rice, in the first, highest grade, is a large plump grain, rich in amylopectin, the starch that dissolves in cooking to produce a sticky risotto. The *semifino* Vialone Nano is a stubby small grain, containing more of another starch, amylose, which does not soften easily in cooking, so giving the cooked grain more of a bite in the middle. It is ideal for looser Veneto-style risottos, soups or *arancini* (rice croquettes). A new variety developed in 1945 by a Milanese rice grower is Carnaroli, a cross between Vialone and a Japanese strain. Small production makes this *superfino* grain relatively expensive. The outer skin has enough of the soft starch to dissolve and make the risotto creamy but it also contains more of the tough starch than any of the other risotto rices and so keeps a good, firm consistency. A good *fino* rice is Europa.

chicken paella

60 ml (¼ cup) olive oil

1 large red pepper (capsicum), seeded and cut into 5 mm (¼ in) strips

600 g (1 lb 5 oz) chicken thigh fillets, cut into 3 cm (1¼ in) cubes

200 g (7 oz) chorizo, cut into 2.5 cm (1 inch) slices

200 g (7 oz) mushrooms, thinly sliced

3 garlic cloves, crushed

1 tablespoon grated lemon zest

700 g (1 lb 9 oz) ripe tomatoes, roughly chopped

200 g (7 oz) green beans, cut into 3 cm (1¼ inch) lengths

1 tablespoon chopped rosemary

2 tablespoons chopped flat-leaf (Italian) parsley

¼ teaspoon saffron threads dissolved in 60 ml (¼ cup) hot water

440 g (2 cups) paella rice such as Bomba or Valencia

750 ml (3 cups) hot chicken stock

6 lemon wedges, to serve

heat the olive oil in a paella pan, or in a heavy-based deep frying pan over medium heat. Add the red pepper and cook, stirring, for 6 minutes. Remove from the pan. Add the chicken, toss through and cook for 10 minutes, or until brown on all sides. Remove from the pan. Add the chorizo to the pan and cook for 5 minutes. Set aside with the chicken. Add the mushrooms, garlic and lemon zest to the pan, and cook over medium heat for about 5 minutes.

stir in the tomato and red pepper, and cook for another 5 minutes, or until the tomato is soft. Add the beans, rosemary, parsley, saffron mixture, rice, chicken and chorizo. Stir briefly and add the stock. Do not stir at this point. Reduce the heat and simmer for 30 minutes. Remove from the heat, cover and leave to stand for 10 minutes. Serve with lemon wedges. Serves 6.

seafood risotto

12 baby clams or pipis
375 ml (1½ cups) white wine
**875 ml (3½ cups) vegetable
stock**
2 bay leaves
1 celery stalk, chopped
6 French shallots, chopped
60 ml (¼ cup) lemon juice
**12 raw king prawns
(shrimps), peeled and
deveined**
**12 scallops, cleaned and
roes removed**
**1 squid tube, cut into
12 slices**
1 tablespoon olive oil
2 tablespoons butter
**80 g (²⁄₃ cup) finely chopped
spring onions (scallions)**
4–6 garlic cloves, crushed
**1½ tablespoons finely
chopped thyme**
330 g (1½ cups) arborio rice
90 g (⅓ cup) sour cream
**35 g (⅓ cup) grated
Parmesan cheese**
**2 tablespoons chopped
flat-leaf (Italian) parsley**
**shaved Parmesan cheese,
to serve**

scrub and rinse the clams to remove any grit, discarding any that are opened or damaged. Put the wine, stock, bay leaves, celery, shallots, lemon juice and 625 ml (2½ cups) of water in a saucepan and bring to the boil for 5 minutes. Reduce the heat to a simmer, then add the clams and cook for 3 minutes, or until they open. Using a slotted spoon, transfer the clams to a bowl, discarding any that did not open. Add the prawns to the stock and cook for 2 minutes, or until pink and curled, then transfer to the bowl with the clams. Add the scallops and squid and cook for 1 minute, then transfer to the bowl. Strain the stock, then return to the pan and keep at a low simmer.

heat the oil and half the butter in a large heavy-based saucepan over medium heat. Add the spring onion, garlic and chopped thyme and cook, stirring constantly, for 1 minute. Stir in the rice and cook for 1 minute, or until well coated.

add 125 ml (½ cup) of the hot stock. Stir constantly over medium heat until all the stock is completely absorbed. Continue adding more stock, 125 ml (½ cup) at a time, stirring constantly for 25 minutes, or until the stock is absorbed. Add the seafood with the final addition of stock. The rice should be tender and creamy.

remove from the heat and stir in the sour cream, Parmesan cheese and parsley. Season. Serve with shaved Parmesan cheese. Serves 4 (or 6 as a starter).

1 Add the stock to the rice mixture, stirring constantly.

2 Deep-fry the arancini in batches, to a golden crispness.

arancini

leave the saffron to soak in the wine while you prepare the risotto. Melt the butter in a saucepan. Add the onion and garlic, and cook over low heat for 4 minutes, or until softened but not browned. Heat the stock to simmering point in another saucepan.

add the thyme and rice to the onion. Cook, stirring, for 1 minute. Add the wine and saffron, and stir until all the wine is absorbed. Add several ladles of the hot stock, stirring continuously so that the rice cooks evenly. Keep adding enough stock to just cover the rice, stirring frequently. Repeat this process for about 20 minutes, or until the rice is thick and creamy.

add more water or chicken stock if the rice is not fully cooked. Make sure all the liquid is absorbed. Remove from the heat and stir in the Parmesan cheese, then spread out onto a tray covered with plastic wrap. Leave to cool and, if possible, leave in the refrigerator overnight.

to make the arancini, roll a small amount of risotto into a walnut-sized ball. Press a hole in the middle with your thumb, put a cheese cube inside and press the risotto around it to enclose it in a ball. Repeat with the rest of the risotto. Roll each ball in the breadcrumbs, pressing down to coat well.

heat enough oil in a deep saucepan to fully cover the arancini. Heat the oil to 180°C (350°F), or until a cube of bread dropped into the oil browns in 15 seconds. Deep-fry the arancini in batches, without crowding the pan, for 3–4 minutes. Drain on paper towels and leave for a couple of minutes before eating. Serve hot or at room temperature. Makes 20.

pinch saffron threads
250 ml (1 cup) white wine
100 g (3½ oz) butter
1 onion, finely chopped
1 large garlic clove, crushed
750 ml (3 cups) chicken stock
2 tablespoons thyme
220 g (1 cup) risotto rice such as Vialone Nano
50 g (½ cup) grated Parmesan cheese
100 g (3½ oz) mozzarella or fontina cheese, cubed
75 g (3/4 cup) dried breadcrumbs
oil, for deep-frying

market garden

artichokes

The globe artichoke is a member of the thistle family—in fact, it is the unopened bud of the plant's brilliant blue flower. It was most probably introduced to the region by the Arabs, finding its way to Spain and Sicily around the mid-fifteenth century. It is particularly popular in Italian, Spanish and French cooking, and is also a feature of Mediterranean Jewish cooking. When very young, artichokes are eaten whole, even raw in salads; the more mature buds are stuffed, boiled, fried or quartered; and large ones are boiled and eaten one leaf at a time, dipped into a vinaigrette or hollandaise sauce. Artichokes are also sold in jars or tins, whole or quartered, in olive oil or brine.

artichokes in aromatic vinaigrette

2 tablespoons lemon juice
4 large globe artichokes
2 garlic cloves, crushed
1 teaspoon finely chopped oregano

½ teaspoon ground cumin
½ teaspoon ground coriander
pinch dried chilli flakes
3 teaspoons sherry vinegar
60 ml (¼ cup) olive oil

add the lemon juice to a large bowl of cold water. Trim the artichokes, cutting off the stalks to within 5 cm (2 inches) of the base of each artichoke and removing the tough outer leaves. Cut off the top quarter of the leaves from each. Slice each artichoke in half from top to base, or into quarters if large. Remove each small, furry choke with a teaspoon, then put each artichoke in the bowl of acidulated water to prevent it from discolouring while you prepare the rest.

bring a large non-aluminium saucepan of water to the boil, add the artichokes and a teaspoon of salt and simmer for 20 minutes, or until tender. The cooking time will depend on the artichoke size. To test, press a skewer into the base. If the artichoke is soft and offers little resistance, it is ready. Strain, then put the artichokes on their cut side to drain.

combine the garlic, oregano, cumin, coriander and chilli flakes in a small bowl. Season with salt and pepper and blend in the vinegar. Beating constantly, slowly pour in the olive oil to form an emulsion. This step can be done in a small food processor.

arrange the artichokes in rows on a serving plate. Pour the vinaigrette over the top and leave to cool completely before serving. Serves 4.

note: Choose heavy globe artichokes with firm heads and stems, and leaves that are tightly overlapping. Artichokes are best used on the day of purchase but can be stored in a plastic bag in the refrigerator for up to 3 days if necessary.

Asparagus is native to Europe and Asia and has been cultivated in the Mediterranean since ancient Greek times, often combined with spices and strong flavourings. Today, asparagus tends to be matched with ingredients such as eggs, cheese, ham and lemon. It is available in green, white and purple varieties, green being the most abundant and affordable of the three. White asparagus is achieved by growing the vegetable without sunlight, either in special black tents or, traditionally, by covering the shoots with soil. It is highly prized in France, and also in Bassano, Italy, which, according to legend, discovered the variety after a hailstorm in the 1550s left only the underground white parts undamaged. Sweet-flavoured purple asparagus gets its colour from a pigment, which is destroyed by heat.

asparagus

asparagus and mint frittata

6 eggs
35 g (1¼ oz) Pecorino or Parmesan cheese, grated
5 g (¼ cup) mint leaves, finely shredded

200 g (7 oz) baby asparagus spears
2 tablespoons extra virgin olive oil

break the eggs into a large bowl, beat well, then stir in the cheese and mint and set aside.

trim the woody part of the asparagus, then cut the asparagus on the diagonal into 5 cm (2 inch) pieces. Heat the oil in a 20 cm (8 inch) frying pan that has a heatproof handle. Add the asparagus and cook for 5 minutes, or until tender. Season, then reduce the heat to low.

pour the egg mixture over the asparagus and cook for 8–10 minutes. Use a spatula to pull the side of the frittata away from the side of the pan and tip the pan slightly so the uncooked egg runs underneath the frittata.

when the mixture is nearly set but still slightly runny on top, place the pan under a low grill (broiler) for 1–2 minutes, until the top is set and just browned. Serve warm or at room temperature. Serves 4.

using asparagus

When buying fresh asparagus make sure that the tips of the spears are tightly closed and the stalk is firm and green with no tinges of yellow. It is generally prepared with the minimum of fuss—steamed or gently grilled (broiled), or used in primavera sauces for pasta and risottos. The white asparagus needs a longer cooking time, and is served with hollandaise sauce. Cook purple asparagus only briefly to retain its colour.

basil

For an ingredient that seems Mediterranean down to its roots, basil was only introduced from India in the fifteenth century. Today it is essential in Italian and southern French cooking, where its fresh spiciness and aroma enhance countless cooked dishes and salads. Pesto, that most famous use of basil, is traditionally associated with Genoa in Italy, though it probably originated with the Persians, and is served with minestrone, pasta and bread. The French version of pesto is pistou, which originated in Provence.

pesto

30 g (²/3 cup) basil leaves   **100 ml (3¹/2 fl oz) olive oil**
1¹/2 tablespoons pine nuts   **4 tablespoons grated**
2 garlic cloves   **Parmesan cheese**

combine the basil, pine nuts and garlic with a pinch of salt in a mortar or food processor and pound or process to a paste. Slowly add the oil until thick. Stir in the Parmesan cheese and some pepper. Add salt if necessary. Refrigerate in a sterilized jar, covered with a layer of olive oil, for up to 3 weeks. Makes approximately 200 ml (7 fl oz).

using basil

Basil loses its flavour easily, so is usually added to dishes at the end of cooking time. Sometimes, however, basil might be cooked in a soup or stew in order that its flavour marries with the other ingredients. If possible, use only the freshest basil, never drooping or blackened leaves. Unless the recipe calls for julienned basil, it is best to tear the basil leaves with your hands rather than cut them with a knife, as this tends to bruise the basil and cause it to go brown.

note: To prepare a sterilized storage jar, preheat the oven to 120°C (250°F/Gas¹/2). Wash the jar and lid in hot soapy water and rinse with hot water. Put the jar in the oven for 20 minutes, or until fully dry. Do not dry with a tea towel.

minestrone alla genovese

put the dried beans in a large bowl, cover with cold water and leave to soak overnight. Drain and rinse under cold water.

to make the soup base, melt the butter in a large saucepan and add the onion, garlic, parsley, sage and pancetta. Cook over low heat, stirring once or twice, for about 10 minutes, or until the onion is soft and golden.

add the celery, carrot and potatoes and cook for 5 minutes. Stir in the tomato paste, tomato, basil and borlotti beans. Season with plenty of freshly ground black pepper. Add the stock and bring slowly to the boil. Cover and leave to simmer for 2 hours, stirring once or twice.

check to see that the potatoes have broken up: if they haven't, roughly break them up with a fork against the side of the pan. Taste for seasoning, then add the zucchini, peas, runner beans, cabbage and pasta. Simmer until the pasta is *al dente*. Serve with a dollop of pesto and some grated Parmesan. Serves 6.

225 g (8 oz) dried borlotti
   beans
50 g (1³/₄ oz) butter
1 large onion, finely chopped
1 garlic clove, finely chopped
15 g (¹/₂ cup) finely chopped
   flat-leaf (Italian) parsley
2 sage leaves
100 g (3¹/₂ oz) pancetta,
   cubed
2 celery stalks, halved
   and sliced
2 carrots, sliced
3 potatoes, peeled
1 teaspoon tomato paste
   (purée)
400 g (14 oz) tin chopped
   tomatoes
8 basil leaves
3 litres (12 cups) chicken or
   vegetable stock
2 zucchini (courgettes), sliced
205 g (1¹/₃ cups) shelled peas
125 g (4¹/₂ oz) runner beans,
   cut into 5 cm (2 inch) lengths
¹/₄ cabbage, shredded
150 g (5¹/₂ oz) small pasta
200 ml (7 fl oz) pesto
grated Parmesan cheese

Nearly every region in Italy has its own style of minestrone. This version from Genoa, in Liguria, is always served with a spoonful of pesto, which is stirred through at the end, though in some areas rice is added. Minestrone should always be accompanied by plenty of freshly grated Parmesan.

bay leaves

making a bouquet garni

Wrap the green part of a leek around a bay leaf, a sprig of thyme, a sprig of parsley and celery leaves. Tie the bundle with string, leaving it long at one end for easy removal. Vary the herbs to suit the dish.

The ancient Romans and Greeks both held these glossy green leaves in high esteem, using them to make laurel wreaths to crown their poets, athletes and military victors. In cooking, they are used fresh and dried to add a strong, slightly peppery flavour to many dishes: stuffings and stews, milk infusions for baked custards or béchamel sauce, and whole baked fish dishes in the Eastern Mediterranean. The leaves also flavour rice while it is cooking, and are a key element in bouquet garni. Wash fresh leaves well and store them in the refrigerator for up to three days. Dried bay leaves will keep in an airtight container for up to six months.

beans and peas

Fresh beans and peas are one of the delights of the Mediterranean market over spring and summer. Native to the Americas, beans of all sizes, shapes and colours are grown today around the world. In the Mediterranean, there are numerous varieties of green beans—such as runner, broad (fava) and French beans—and also yellow and white varieties. As well, there are pretty borlotti beans, with their creamy red pods, and French beans also appear in purple or cream shades.

Originally from Asia, peas have been a part of the Mediterranean culinary scene since classical times; ancient Athenians enjoyed hot pea soup and Romans snacked on fried peas. Today, they come in three main varieties, the garden pea, the field or grey pea, and the increasingly elusive wild Mediterranean pea. The French snowpeas (mangetout) and sugar snap peas are both varieties of the garden pea. So, too, are the wonderfully sweet petits pois, which are garden peas that have been harvested when young.

using beans and peas

Green beans are largely interchangeable in recipes, and are used in soups and braised dishes and as accompaniments. Peas are most often used as a vegetable side dish, but are also very good in risottos, soups and pasta dishes. When buying, make sure beans are crisp and bright: they should literally snap when bent. When young, broad (fava) beans can be eaten in their pods like snowpeas (mangetout), but as they age, the pods toughen and the beans inside develop a grey, leathery skin. Double-pod before using, or use frozen ones. Runner beans need to be stringed down each side unless they are very young. Petits pois should be shelled before cooking.

turkish green beans with tomato and olive oil

80 ml (1/3 cup) olive oil
1 large onion, chopped
3 garlic cloves, finely chopped
400 g (14 oz) tin chopped tomatoes
1/2 teaspoon sugar
750 g (1 lb 10 oz) green beans, trimmed
3 tablespoons chopped flat-leaf (Italian) parsley

heat the olive oil in a large frying pan, add the onion and cook over medium heat for 4–5 minutes, or until softened. Add the garlic and cook for another 30 seconds.

add the tomato, sugar and 125 ml (1/2 cup) water, then season with salt and freshly ground black pepper. Bring to the boil, then reduce the heat and simmer for 10 minutes, or until reduced slightly.

add the beans and gently simmer for another 10 minutes, or until the beans are tender and the tomato mixture is pulpy. Stir in the parsley. Check the seasoning, and adjust if necessary. Serve immediately, as a side dish. Serves 4.

beans and peas with braised artichokes

cut each artichoke heart into 12 segments. Pod the beans and peas and blanch them for 1 minute in boiling water, then refresh in iced water. If the broad beans are very large and old you may also want to remove the pale green outer skin.

heat the olive oil in a large saucepan or deep frying pan and add the artichoke segments, onion and pancetta. Cook gently for 15 minutes, stirring frequently. Season with salt and pepper. Add the beans and peas and cook for 5 minutes. (If the broad beans are large, add them before the peas as they will need 1–2 minutes longer.) Stir in the garlic, add the white wine and cook for 10 minutes more, or until all the liquid has evaporated.

pierce the artichokes with a knife to see if they are tender. If they need more cooking, add a dash of water and cover. When cooked, add the mint, taste for seasoning and leave to stand for a few minutes to allow the flavours to develop. Serves 6.

750 g (1 lb 10 oz) cleaned artichoke hearts

1 kg (2 lb 4 oz) fresh broad (fava) beans in pods (300 g/ 10½ oz podded weight)

400 g (14 oz) fresh peas in pods (150 g/5½ oz podded weight)

3 tablespoons extra virgin olive oil

1 red onion, quartered and thinly sliced

185 g (6¼ oz) smoked pancetta

2 garlic cloves, chopped

125 ml (½ cup) white wine

2 tablespoons chopped mint

beetroot

Native to the Mediterranean, this root vegetable was first grown for its young leaves, but is now cultivated for its sweet, purple-red root. Not all beetroot are deep red; golden and white varieties also exist, and chioggia is an Italian variety with alternating red and white rings. When cooking beetroot, take care to prevent it from bleeding. Don't cut or peel before it is cooked, and wash it carefully to prevent the skin breaking. Store beetroot in the crisper drawer of the refrigerator for up to two weeks, and one or two days for the leaves. Beetroot is also sold in tins.

french fresh beetroot and goat's cheese salad

1 kg (2 lb 4 oz) fresh beetroot (4 bulbs with leaves)
200 g (7 oz) green beans
1 tablespoon red wine vinegar
2 tablespoons extra virgin olive oil
1 garlic clove, crushed
1 tablespoon drained capers, coarsely chopped
100 g (3½ oz) goat's cheese

trim the leaves from the beetroot and set aside. Scrub the bulbs and wash the leaves well. Add the whole bulbs to a large saucepan of salted water, bring to the boil, then reduce the heat and simmer, covered, for 30 minutes, or until tender when pierced with the point of a knife.

meanwhile, bring another saucepan of water to the boil, add the beans and cook for 3 minutes, or until just tender. Remove with a slotted spoon and plunge briefly into a bowl of cold water. Drain well. Add the beetroot leaves to the same saucepan of water and cook for about 5 minutes, or until tender. Drain, plunge into a bowl of cold water, then drain again. Finally, drain and cool the beetroot, then peel the skins off and cut the bulbs into thin wedges.

put the red wine vinegar, oil, garlic, capers and ½ teaspoon each of salt and pepper in a screw-top jar and shake.

divide the beans, beetroot leaves and bulbs among 4 serving plates. Crumble goat's cheese over the top of each and drizzle with dressing. Serve with fresh crusty bread. Serves 4.

broccoli

broccoli and chilli sauce with orecchiette

250 g (9 oz) broccoli
400 g (14 oz) orecchiette
80 ml (⅓ cup) extra virgin
  olive oil
2 garlic cloves, finely chopped
½ large red chilli, finely
  chopped

1 tablespoon chopped
  rosemary
25 g (¼ cup) grated
  Parmesan cheese, plus
  extra to serve
extra virgin olive oil, to serve

bring a large saucepan of salted water to the boil. Cut the broccoli into small florets and add them to the water with the pasta. Cook until the pasta is *al dente* (the broccoli will be very tender and may have broken up) then drain, reserving a small cup of the water.

heat the olive oil in the saucepan and add the garlic, chilli and rosemary. Gently cook for 1–2 minutes until the garlic is light golden brown. Remove from the heat, add the broccoli and pasta and mix well—the broccoli should break up and create the sauce.

add a little of the cooking water to loosen the pasta if necessary, then season well and stir in the Parmesan. Serve immediately with a drizzle of olive oil and the extra Parmesan. Serves 4.

Meaning 'little arms' in Italian, broccoli is related to kohlrabi, cauliflower and cabbage. There are many varieties of broccoli in the Mediterranean, but one of the most common is the calabrese (first grown in Calabria, Italy), which has green, densely packed heads. There are also purple, lime-green and white varieties, as well as the hybrid broccolini. Broccoli rabe, once a cheap staple over much of the Southern Mediterranean, is less common nowadays. It is a non-heading, slightly bitter variety of broccoli that is also eaten in Asia (and known as Chinese flowering cabbage). Broccoli is eaten raw, steamed or boiled, added to crepes or tossed with pasta, or served with hollandaise sauce. When buying, look for firm, tightly closed green heads, with no tinges of yellow.

cabbages

Though cabbage is not one of the high-flyers of the vegetable world, it has provided sustenance to Mediterranean people for centuries. Originally, a wild native variety would have been used, a far cry from the robust examples now available. There are two main types: loose-leaved and firm-hearted. Loose-leaved cabbages tend to be green or tinged with red, and include the darker green Savoy cabbage among their numbers, while firm-hearted cabbages are red, white or green. A third type is cavolo nero, meaning 'black cabbage'. This dark green cabbage turns almost black when cooked and has a unique flavour, nuttier than regular cabbage.

Firm-hearted cabbages are mostly eaten raw in salads, while wrinkly Savoy cabbages are served steamed or boiled as a vegetable. The whole cabbage leaves are popular in Greek cooking for wrapping fillings. Cavolo nero, with its long curled leaves, is a classic ingredient in the Italian soup *la ribollita*, but it is also braised, steamed or baked and served as a vegetable accompaniment. Its strong flavour means that it can hold its own with bold ingredients such as bacon, chilli and cheese. If it's not available use dark green Savoy cabbage instead.

From left to right: Loose-leaved cabbage, firm-hearted red cabbage and cavolo nero.

Used both as a salad leaf and vegetable, chicory has a refreshing bitterness. It is popular in Italian and French cooking, where the crunchy leaves are often used for scooping up dips. As well, the whole chicory is halved or quartered, then grilled (broiled) or braised, and served with rich meats that will benefit from chicory's robust flavour. Radicchio, which means 'red chicory' in Italian, has a dark red bitter leaf that is either curled into a ball like a cabbage or has a longer looser structure. Radicchio is not as bitter as white chicory, and it adds wonderful colour to grilled (broiled) dishes and fresh salads. Other types of chicory include frisée and escarole; both have the distinctive bitter taste, though escarole is the mildest type of all.

chicory

chicory and pancetta al forno

450 g (1 lb) white chicory
1 large radicchio
150 g (5½ oz) pancetta or smoked bacon, thinly sliced
55 g (⅔ cup) fresh breadcrumbs

50 g (½ cup) grated Parmesan cheese
1½ tablespoons finely chopped thyme
1 garlic clove, finely chopped
560 ml (2¼ cups) thick (double/heavy) cream

preheat the oven to 180°C (350°F/Gas 4). Slice the white chicory in half lengthways (or if they are quite large, into quarters). Divide the radicchio into 6 or 8 wedges, depending on its size.

lightly butter a shallow 2.5 litre (10 cup) gratin dish. Put the chicory and radicchio in the dish in one layer, alternating the colours. Mix together the pancetta, breadcrumbs, Parmesan, thyme and garlic and season well. Sprinkle over the chicory and radicchio.

pour the cream over, cover with foil and bake for 50–60 minutes. Take the foil off the dish for the last 20 minutes so the pancetta and breadcrumbs become crisp. Rest for 10 minutes before serving. Serves 4.

chillies

These members of the capsicum family are native to Central and South America, and only reached the Mediterranean via India and Asia once Spanish and Portuguese traders established that link in the sixteenth century. They are not used extensively in Mediterranean cooking, with the exceptions being the cooking of Tunisia, Algeria and southern Italy. Chillies are known as *peperoncini* in Italy and those from Calabria in the south are especially valued. They feature in many local dishes and can be seen draped over balconies, drying in the sun, throughout much of the year. Chillies are generally served as a condiment, for example in Tunisian *harissa*, used in sauces such as the Catalan *salsa romesco* or added whole to dishes for flavour. They are used fresh or dried.

salsa romesco

4 garlic cloves, unpeeled
1 Roma (plum) tomato, halved and seeded
2 long fresh red chillies
40 g (¼ cup) blanched almonds

60 g (2¼ oz) sun-dried peppers (capsicums) in oil
1 tablespoon olive oil
1 tablespoon red wine vinegar

preheat the oven to 200°C (400°F/Gas 6). Wrap the garlic in foil, put on a baking tray with the tomato and chillies and bake for 12 minutes. Add the almonds and bake for 3–5 minutes more. Allow to cool.

transfer the almonds to a small food processor and process until finely ground. Squeeze the garlic and scrape the tomato flesh into the processor, discarding the skins. Split the chillies and remove the seeds. Scrape the flesh into the processor, discarding the skins. Pat the peppers dry, then chop them and add to the processor with the oil, vinegar, salt and 2 tablespoons water. Blend until smooth, adding more water if necessary, to form a dipping consistency. Makes 185 ml (¾ cup).

This classic sauce hails from Tarragona in Catalonia, northeast Spain, and is an essential accompaniment to seafood. Fishermen and cooks alike fiercely guard their own recipe, which may also contain fried bread and hazelnuts.

1 Squeeze the garlic out of its skin, adding just the soft flesh.

2 Blend the sauce ingredients until smooth and creamy.

coriander

Thought to be the world's most commonly used herb, every part of this Mediterranean native is used: roots, stems, leaves and seeds. The seeds, which are the plant's ripe, dried fruit, have been found in Egyptian tombs dating as far back as 960BCE and are also mentioned in the Bible.

Coriander is used daily by cooks throughout the Eastern Mediterranean, appearing in stews, sauces, soups and salads. In Morocco, generous quantities of the fresh leaves are added to soups including their national dish, *harira*. This soup has its origins in peasant Berber cooking and each town has its own local version. An important dish, it is often served at evening meals during Ramadan, the Muslim month of fasting. The leaves are also included in plates of fresh herbs that are placed on the table for people to pick at during the meal. The seeds, used whole or ground, are a distinct feature of Cypriot cooking and are an important component of *dukkah*, the Egyptian spice mix.

Also known as – cilantro

harira

2 tablespoons olive oil
2 small onions, chopped
2 large garlic cloves, crushed
500 g (1 lb 2 oz) lamb
  shoulder steaks, trimmed
  of excess fat and sinew,
  cut into small chunks
1 ½ teaspoons ground
  cumin
2 teaspoons paprika
½ teaspoon ground cloves
1 bay leaf

2 tablespoons tomato paste
  (purée)
1 litre (4 cups) beef stock
3 x 300 g (10½ oz) tins
  chickpeas, rinsed and
  drained
800 g (1 lb 12 oz) tin
  diced tomatoes
30 g (⅔ cup) finely chopped
  coriander (cilantro) leaves,
  plus extra, to garnish
small black olives, to serve

heat the oil in a large heavy-based saucepan or stockpot, add the onion and garlic and cook for 5 minutes until softened but not browned. Add the meat, in batches, and cook over high heat until the meat is browned on all sides. Return all the meat to the pan.

add the spices and bay leaf to the pan and cook until fragrant. Add the tomato paste and cook for 2 minutes, stirring constantly. Add the stock to the pan, stir well and bring to the boil.

add the chickpeas, tomato and chopped coriander to the pan. Stir, then bring to the boil. Reduce the heat and simmer for 2 hours, or until the meat is tender. Stir occasionally. Season, to taste.

garnish with coriander leaves and small black olives and serve with toasted pitta bread drizzled with a little extra virgin olive oil. Serves 4.

note: When using coriander in cooking, remember that the fresh leaves and small dried seeds taste completely different from each other and can't be used interchangeably.

cucumbers

greek tzatziki

2 Lebanese (short) cucumbers (about 300 g/10½ oz)
400 g (14 oz) Greek-style natural yoghurt
4 garlic cloves, crushed
3 tablespoons finely chopped mint, plus extra, to garnish
1 tablespoon lemon juice

cut the cucumbers in half lengthways, scoop out the seeds with a teaspoon and discard. Leave the skin on and coarsely grate the cucumber into a small colander. Sprinkle with a little salt and leave to stand over a large bowl for 15 minutes to drain off any bitter juices.

meanwhile, put the yoghurt, garlic, mint and lemon juice in a bowl and stir together.

rinse the cucumber under cold water then, taking small handfuls, squeeze out any excess moisture. Combine with the yoghurt mixture and season with salt and freshly ground black pepper. Serve immediately or refrigerate until ready to serve. Garnish with mint and serve as a dip with flatbread or as a sauce for seafood and meat. Makes 500 ml (2 cups).

This superbly refreshing summer treat is one of the oldest cultivated vegetables. Many varieties exist, Mediterranean cooks choosing from three sorts: the familiar long, smooth variety, also known as Lebanese (short) cucumbers; small ones for pickling, known by the French as cornichons (gherkins); and a local variety, long and thin and often hooked at the end, called continental or telegraph cucumbers. Cucumbers are eaten raw, used in salads, cooked in a soup or mixed with yoghurt and garlic to make world-famous Greek tzatziki. The Turks have their own version, called *cacik*, which contains chopped dill instead of mint. Cornichons are served as appetizers, with pâté.

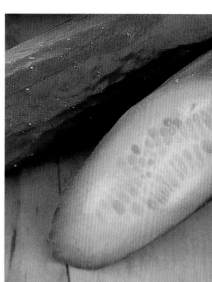

eggplants

These kings of the vegetable world were first introduced to the Mediterranean in the eighth century by the Arabs who themselves had only recently discovered them in Persia. Eggplants have a natural affinity with the robust flavours of Mediterranean cuisine and have become key ingredients in the region's cooking. Renowned for their great versatility in preparation, eggplants are stuffed, puréed, cubed, sliced and fried, and used in pickles. Famous dishes abound and include moussaka, baba ghannouj, ratatouille, numerous stuffed eggplant dishes and 'aubergine caviar'. In the Arab parts of the region, recipe names conjure up fabulous worlds: Turkish *hünkâr begendi*, a rich smoked eggplant and cheese sauce served as a bed for meatballs, is known as 'sultan's delight' and the stuffed eggplant dish *imam bayildi*, also from Turkey, means 'the priest fainted', though why exactly is open to conjecture.

Also known as – aubergines

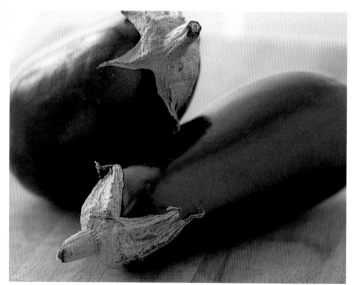

choosing eggplants

Eggplants vary in size and shape: from small, round pea shapes to large, fat pumpkin-shaped ones. Their colour too can vary, ranging from green, cream or yellow to pale or dark purple. When buying, choose eggplants that are heavy, shiny and firm. The best eggplants have dense, firm and sweet flesh, with small seeds. Eggplants that are old, or simply overmature, will be full of bitter seeds, and will need to be salted for up to an hour before they are used, to remove the unpleasant flavours.

baba ghannouj

2 large eggplants (aubergines)
3 garlic cloves, crushed
½ teaspoon ground cumin
80 ml (⅓ cup) lemon juice
2 tablespoons tahini

pinch cayenne pepper
1½ tablespoons olive oil
1 tablespoon chopped flat-leaf
 (Italian) parsley
black olives, to garnish

preheat the oven to 200°C (400°F/Gas 6). Prick the eggplants several times with a fork, then cook over an open flame for 5 minutes, until the skin is black and blistered. Transfer to a baking dish and bake for 40–45 minutes, or until the eggplants are very soft and wrinkled. Put in a colander over a bowl to drain off any bitter juices, leaving them for 30 minutes, or until cool.

carefully peel the skin from the eggplants, chop the flesh and put it in a food processor with the garlic, cumin, lemon juice, tahini, cayenne pepper and olive oil. Process until smooth and creamy. Alternatively, use a potato masher or fork. Season with salt and stir in the parsley. Spread in a flat bowl or on a plate and garnish with the olives. Serve with flatbread or pitta bread for dipping. Makes 435 ml (1¾ cups).

imam bayildi

1 kg (2 lb 4 oz) elongated
   eggplants (aubergine)
185 ml (³/₄ cup) olive oil
3 onions, finely chopped
3 garlic cloves, finely
   chopped
400g (14 oz) tin chopped
   Roma (plum) tomatoes
2 teaspoons dried organo
4 tablespoons chopped
   flat-leaf (Italian) parsley
¹/₄ teaspoon ground
   cinnamon
2 tablespoons lemon juice
pinch of sugar
125 ml (¹/₂ cup) tomato juice

preheat the oven to 180°C (350°F/Gas 4). Cut the eggplant in half lengthways. Heat half the olive oil in a large heavy-based frying pan and cook the eggplants on all sides for about 8–10 minutes, or until the cut sides are golden. Remove from the pan and scoop out some of the flesh, leaving the skins intact and some flesh lining the skins. Finely chop the scooped-out flesh and set aside.

heat the remaining oil in the same frying pan and cook the onion over medium heat for 8–10 minutes, or until soft. Add the garlic and cook for 1 more minute. Add the tomato, dried oregano, parsley, currants, cinnamon, reserved eggplant flesh and salt and pepper, to taste.

put the eggplant shells in a large baking dish and fill each with tomato mixture. Mix the lemon juice, sugar, tomato juice and some salt and pour over the eggplant shells.

cover and bake the eggplant shells for 30 minutes, then uncover and cook for another 10 minutes. To serve, transfer to serving plates and drizzle over any remaining juice. Serves 4.

Imam bayildi, a stuffed eggplant dish, is eaten all over the Arab world. Its name literally means 'the priest fainted', which is a bit of a mystery. It is not known if the priest fainted from overindulging in his sumptuous lunch or from the shock of the quantities of expensive olive oil used in the preparation.

moussaka

lay the eggplant on a tray, sprinkle well with salt and leave to stand for 30 minutes. Rinse under water and pat dry. Preheat the oven to 180°C (350°F/Gas 4).

heat 2 tablespoons olive oil in a frying pan, add the eggplant in batches and cook for 1–2 minutes each side, or until golden and soft. Add a little more oil when needed.

heat 1 tablespoon olive oil in a large saucepan, add the onion and cook over medium heat for about 5 minutes. Add the garlic, allspice and cinnamon and cook for 30 seconds. Add the lamb and cook for 5 minutes, or until browned, breaking up any lumps with the back of a spoon. Add the tomato, tomato paste and wine, and simmer over low heat for 30 minutes, or until the liquid has evaporated. Stir in the chopped parsley and season, to taste.

to make the cheese sauce, melt the butter in a saucepan over low heat. Stir in the flour and cook for 1 minute, or until pale and foaming. Remove the saucepan from the heat and gradually stir in the milk and nutmeg. Return the saucepan to the heat and stir constantly until the sauce boils and thickens. Reduce the heat and simmer for 2 minutes. Stir in 1 tablespoon of the cheese until well combined. Stir in the egg just before using.

line the base of a 3 litre (12 cup) ovenproof dish measuring 25 x 30 cm (10 x 12 inches) with a third of the eggplant. Spoon half the meat sauce over it and cover with another layer of eggplant. Spoon the remaining meat sauce over the top and cover with the remaining eggplant. Spread the cheese sauce over the top and sprinkle with the remaining cheese. Bake for 1 hour. Leave to stand for 10 minutes before cutting. Serves 6.

1.5 kg (3 lb 5 oz) eggplants (aubergines), cut into 5 mm (¼ inch) slices
125 ml (½ cup) olive oil
2 onions, finely chopped
2 large garlic cloves, crushed
½ teaspoon ground allspice
1 teaspoon ground cinnamon
750 g (1 lb 10 oz) minced (ground) lamb
2 large ripe tomatoes, peeled and chopped
2 tablespoons tomato paste (purée)
125 ml (½ cup) white wine
3 tablespoons chopped flat-leaf (Italian) parsley

cheese sauce
60 g (2¼ oz) butter
60 g (½ cup) plain (all-purpose) flour
625 ml (2½ cups) milk
pinch ground nutmeg
35 g (1¼ oz) kefalotyri or Parmesan cheese, finely grated
2 eggs, lightly beaten

fennel

In medieval Europe in the sixteenth century, an obscure fertility cult of peasants, known in Italian as the *benandanti* or 'good walkers', held nocturnal battles with witches, their sworn enemies. Fennel, noted for its healing properties, was wielded by the *benandanti*; the opposing forces had stalks of sorghum. Sadly for the peasants, the Inquisition eventually came to find them witches. As for fennel, the Italians are still fond of it and cultivate finnochio, also known as Florence fennel, for its thick stems and bulbous base, both of which may be eaten raw like celery. The distinctive aniseed flavour of fennel makes it a welcome ingredient in salads or it can be cooked as a vegetable. It goes particularly well with seafood. Tender baby fennel bulbs can be quartered and used like crudités for dipping in sauces.

roasted fennel and orange salad

8 baby fennel bulbs
100 ml (3½ fl oz) olive oil
2 oranges
1 tablespoon lemon juice
1 red onion, halved and thinly sliced
100 g (3½ oz) Kalamata olives
2 tablespoons roughly chopped mint
1 tablespoon roughly chopped flat-leaf (Italian) parsley

preheat the oven to 200°C (400°F/Gas 6). Trim and reserve the fronds from the fennel. Remove the stalks and cut a slice off the base of each fennel 5 mm (¼ inch) thick. Slice each fennel into 6 wedges, put in a baking dish and drizzle with 3 tablespoons olive oil. Season well. Bake for 40–45 minutes, or until the fennel is tender and slightly caramelized. Turn once or twice during cooking. Allow to cool.

cut a thin slice off the top and bottom of each orange. Using a small sharp knife, slice the skin and pith off the oranges. Remove as much pith as possible. Slice down the side of a segment between the flesh and the membrane. Repeat with the other side and lift the segment out. Do this over a bowl to catch the juices. Repeat with all the segments on both oranges. Squeeze out any juice remaining in the membranes.

whisk the remaining oil into the orange juice and the lemon juice until emulsified. Season well. Combine the orange segments, onion and olives in a bowl, pour on half the dressing and add half the mint. Mix well. Transfer to a serving dish. Top with the roasted fennel, drizzle with the remaining dressing, and scatter the parsley and remaining mint over the top. Chop the reserved fronds and sprinkle over the salad. Serves 4.

garlic

One of the smallest members of the onion family, garlic is also the most pungent and it's fair to say kitchens would be sadder places without it. In Mediterranean cooking, it imparts a crucial depth of flavour to many dishes. One crucial role, however, is its partnership with olive oil and egg yolk, that magic emulsion best known through French aïoli, and an essential part of the Provençal stew bourride. In Catalonia, the northeast region of Spain that includes Valencia and Barcelona, allioli is one of the classics of its cuisine. A pounded sauce of garlic, olive oil and salt, without egg yolk, it is notoriously difficult to perfect. In Greece, cooks blend garlic and olive oil with potatoes or bread to make skordalia; the Turks pound walnuts with garlic and oil to make tarator; the Spanish make ajo blanco, garlic and almond soup … and the list goes on.

bourride

preheat the oven to 160°C (315°F/Gas 2–3). Lightly brush the bread with oil and bake for about 10 minutes, or until crisp. Rub one side of each slice with garlic.

to make the aïoli, put the egg yolks, garlic and 3 teaspoons of the lemon juice in a mortar or food processor and pound with a pestle or mix until light and creamy. Add the oil, drop by drop from the tip of a teaspoon, whisking constantly until it begins to thicken, then add the oil in a very thin stream. (If you're using a processor, pour in the oil in a thin stream with the motor running.) Season, add the remaining lemon juice and, if necessary, thin with a little warm water. Cover and refrigerate.

to make the stock, soak the saffron in a tablespoon of hot water for 15 minutes. Put the saffron, wine, leek, carrot, onion, orange zest, fennel seeds, thyme and fish trimmings in a large saucepan with 1 litre (4 cups) water. Cover and bring to the boil, then simmer for 20 minutes,

garlic croutons
½ **stale baguette, sliced**
60 ml (¼ **cup) olive oil**
1 **garlic clove, halved**

aïoli
2 **egg yolks**
4 **garlic cloves, crushed**
5 **teaspoons lemon juice**
250 ml (1 **cup) olive oil**

stock
¼ **teaspoon saffron threads**
1 **litre (4 cups) dry white wine**
1 **leek, white part only, chopped**
2 **carrots, chopped**
2 **onions, chopped**
2 **long pieces orange zest**
2 **teaspoons fennel seeds**
3 **thyme sprigs**
2.5 **kg (5 lb 8 oz) whole firm white fish such as monkfish, sea bass, cod, perch, sole or bream, filleted, skinned and cut into 5 cm (2 inch) pieces (reserve the trimmings)**
3 **egg yolks**

1 Rub the toasted bread with the cut side of a garlic clove.

2 Use a selection of the freshest white fish possible.

skimming occasionally. Strain into a clean saucepan, pressing the solids with a wooden spoon to extract all the liquid. Bring the stock to a gentle simmer, add half the fish and poach for 5 minutes. Remove and keep warm while you cook the rest of the fish, then remove the fish from the pan and bring the stock back to the boil. Boil for 5 minutes, or until slightly reduced, and remove from the heat.

put half the aïoli and the egg yolks in a bowl and mix until smooth. Whisk in a ladleful of hot stock, then gradually add 5 ladlefuls, stirring constantly. Add to the rest of the hot stock and whisk over low heat for 3–5 minutes, or until the soup is hot and slightly thicker (don't let it boil or it will curdle). Season with salt and freshly ground black pepper.

to serve, put 2 garlic croutons in each bowl, top with a few pieces of fish and ladle over the soup. Serve immediately, with the remaining aïoli served separately. Serves 4.

using garlic

Garlic is at its pungent best when it is young and very fresh. As it ages, it becomes stale and starts to sprout. Garlic does not store well, contrary to popular belief, and should be bought as needed. Most commercially grown garlic has been dried to give it a longer shelf life, which also makes it stronger in flavour. The strength of the flavour you extract from garlic bears a direct relation to how finely it is chopped—sliced garlic will be less robust and crushed garlic very strongly flavoured, as more of its pungent oil is released. When choosing garlic look for hard, large, round bulbs and always check underneath for any signs of unwanted mould.

3 Add the stock ingredients to the pan, stirring to mix, then cover.

4 Add ladlefuls of stock to the aïoli and yolks, whisking constantly.

melokhia

The deep green leaves of this plant are used as a vegetable in the Eastern Mediterranean. In Egypt, it is used to make one of their national dishes, a peasant soup of the same name. The leaves give the soup a gelatinous texture, which can be a little unnerving for first-time tasters, though in Egypt, this filling and easily prepared soup is eaten daily in many parts. Like a number of Egypt's national dishes, its origins date back to the time of the pharaohs, and it is thought the word melokhia is a derivation of the Arab word *molook*, meaning monarch. Melokhia is normally bought fresh from markets in Egypt and other parts of the Eastern Mediterranean, but outside of the region, it is mostly available dried (occasionally frozen) from speciality food stores.

mint

This refreshing herb comes in several varieties, including peppermint and spearmint. It is popular in all sorts of salads (fruit, vegetable, and grain ones such as tabbouleh), numerous dips such as Turkish *cacik*, cold and cooked dishes, and in stuffings for pasta, meat and poultry. In the Eastern Mediterranean, it is often served in plates of fresh herbs as a palate cleanser, and added to tisanes and teas.

moroccan mint tea

This light sweet tea is often served before, and always after, a meal. It is prepared at any hour of the day when friends or guests arrive at a Moroccan home and is sipped constantly in cafes. Traditionally it is served from a silver teapot into ornately painted glasses. To make the tea in the traditional manner, heat the teapot and add 1 tablespoon green tea leaves, 30 g (1 oz) sugar and a large handful of fresh spearmint leaves and stalks. Fill with boiling water and brew for at least 5 minutes. Adjust the sweetness if necessary.

Mint tea is the national drink of Morocco. For a decorative touch, serve in ornate glasses, garnished with some fresh mint leaves.

mushrooms

Given that mushrooms are fungi that grow above the ground in dark, damp habitats and live off live, decaying and dead organic matter, they are pretty irresistible. Though not all mushrooms are edible, there are countless varieties of cultivated ones, and others gathered from the wild. The wild mushrooms are generally in season throughout autumn, with the exception of morels, which are picked in spring. Cultivated mushrooms such as button mushrooms are available all year round. Mushrooms are used in a range of Mediterranean dishes that take advantage of the different sizes and flavours available: flat mushrooms are stuffed, button mushrooms are more often used raw in salads or in sauces and the highly prized porcini mushrooms feature in risottos, on bread or with polenta.

mushrooms à la grecque

2 tomatoes
80 ml (⅓ cup) extra virgin
  olive oil
60 ml (¼ cup) white wine
2 spring onions (scallions),
  finely chopped
1 garlic clove, crushed
6 coriander seeds, lightly
  crushed

1 bay leaf
1 thyme sprig
500 g (1 lb 2 oz) button
  mushrooms
2 teaspoons lemon juice
pinch sugar
1 tablespoon chopped parsley

score a cross in the base of each tomato. Put them into a bowl of boiling water for 20 seconds, then plunge into cold water. Drain and peel the skin away from the cross. Finely chop the tomatoes, discarding the cores.

put the oil, wine, tomato, spring onion, garlic, coriander seeds, bay leaf, thyme and 250 ml (1 cup) water in a non-aluminium saucepan. Bring to the boil, cover and simmer for 10 minutes. Uncover the pan, add the mushrooms and simmer for a further 10 minutes, stirring occasionally. Lift out the mushrooms with a slotted spoon and put them in a serving dish.

boil the cooking liquid rapidly until about 250 ml (1 cup) remains. Remove the bay leaf and thyme. Add the lemon juice and season with salt, pepper and the sugar. Pour the liquid over the mushrooms and leave to cool. Serve the mushrooms cold, sprinkled with the chopped parsley. Serves 4.

Button mushrooms (top) and wild mushrooms (centre). Picking wild mushrooms is a national pastime in areas of France and Italy, where varieties such as porcini, chanterelles and morels can all be found.

cultivated mushrooms

These are available in varying stages of development and include the familiar button, open cup and flat (open or field). Button mushrooms, the smallest, have a mild flavour and keep their pale colour when cooked. They are most often used raw in salads or cooked in white sauces. The larger, open cup mushrooms are more flavoursome and so are ideal for stews and casseroles. Flat mushrooms have a good earthy flavour and a meaty texture; they are mostly grilled (broiled) or stuffed. To prepare, simply wipe cultivated mushrooms with a paper towel.

stuffed mushrooms

preheat the oven to 150°C (300°F/Gas 2). Gently wipe the large mushrooms with a damp cloth, remove and discard the stalks and rub the caps with a little lemon juice to keep them white. Wipe the button mushrooms clean and chop them finely, then add to a bowl with the remaining lemon juice and toss to mix.

heat the butter in a small frying pan, add the spring onion and garlic and cook, stirring, for 4 minutes. Add the chopped mushrooms and the wine and cook, stirring, for another 4 minutes. Remove from the heat and stir in the Parmesan, breadcrumbs, egg, cream and tarragon. Season with salt and freshly ground black pepper.

put the mushroom caps on a lightly oiled baking tray and stuff with the filling. Bake for 12 minutes. Sprinkle with the Parmesan and parsley and serve either warm or cold. Serves 4.

8 large flat mushrooms
1½ tablespoons lemon juice
12 button mushrooms
15 g (½ oz) butter
1 spring onion (scallion),
    finely chopped
1 garlic clove, crushed
2 tablespoons white wine
100 g (3½ oz) Parmesan
    cheese, grated, plus
    1 tablespoon, to serve
55 g (⅔ cup) breadcrumbs
1 egg, lightly beaten
3 tablespoons thick
    (double/heavy) cream
1 tablespoon chopped
    tarragon
1 tablespoon chopped parsley

using dried mushrooms

Soak dried mushrooms in warm water, then rinse thoroughly. The soaking water will be flavourful, so don't discard it; strain it and add to stock or a sauce. Dried mushrooms reconstitute up to 8 times their original weight. As well, the flavour of mushrooms is intensified when dried, so they should be used sparingly.

dried mushrooms

The most important dried mushroom in the Mediterranean is the porcini (cep) mushroom, which is considered the king of mushrooms. When in season, porcini mushrooms can be picked wild or bought from markets and vegetable shops. However, the season is only short and the mushrooms often prohibitively expensive, so dried porcini are often substituted. These are sold in small packets and are widely available. Other mushrooms that are more commonly found dried than fresh include morels and chanterelles (girolles). Morels are short, stubby mushrooms that resemble a domed sponge while chanterelles are golden yellow with a concave cap, with blunt, gill-like waves and folds on the underside.

culinary uses

Porcini mushrooms grow in the mountain forests around Genoa in northern Italy, and Genoese cuisine makes good use of them, featuring them in pasta dishes, risottos and with semolina or polenta. Morels are served with chicken or veal and are also used to make an excellent creamy mushroom sauce for pasta or toasted bread. Chanterelles are good multi-purpose mushrooms.

mushroom ragù with polenta squares

grease a 20 cm (8 inch) shallow square cake tin. Put the stock and a pinch of salt in a large saucepan and bring to the boil. Add the polenta in a steady stream, stirring constantly. Reduce the heat and simmer, stirring frequently, for 15–20 minutes. Remove from the heat and stir in the butter and Parmesan. Spread the mixture into the tin and refrigerate for 20 minutes.

soak the porcini mushrooms in 125 ml (½ cup) boiling water for 10 minutes, or until softened, then drain, reserving 80 ml (⅓ cup) liquid.

wipe the other mushrooms with a damp cloth. Thickly slice the Swiss brown mushrooms, and coarsely chop the field mushrooms. Heat 80 ml (⅓ cup) oil in a large frying pan, add the mushrooms, including the porcini mushrooms, cook for 4–5 minutes, then remove from the pan. Heat the remaining oil in the pan and cook the onion and garlic over medium heat for 2–3 minutes, or until translucent.

add the reserved soaking liquid, bay leaf, thyme and oregano to the pan, season and cook for 2 minutes. Return the mushrooms to the pan, add the parsley and vinegar and cook over medium heat for 1 minute, or until nearly dry. Remove the bay leaf and check the seasoning.

sprinkle the extra Parmesan over the polenta and heat under a medium grill (broiler) for 10 minutes, or until lightly browned and the cheese has melted. Cut into four 10 cm (4 inch) squares.

put a polenta square in the centre of each serving plate and top with the mushroom mixture. Garnish with some freshly ground black pepper. Serves 4.

500 ml (2 cups) vegetable stock or water
150 g (1 cup) polenta
20 g (¾ oz) butter
75 g (¾ cup) grated Parmesan cheese
5 g (⅛ oz) dried porcini mushrooms
200 g (7 oz) Swiss brown mushrooms
300 g (10½ oz) field mushrooms
125 ml (½ cup) olive oil
1 onion, finely chopped
3 garlic cloves, finely chopped
1 fresh bay leaf
2 teaspoons finely chopped thyme
2 teaspoons finely chopped oregano
15 g (½ cup) finely chopped flat-leaf (Italian) parsley
1 tablespoon balsamic vinegar
25 g (¼ cup) grated Parmesan cheese, extra

okra

This green, slender, slightly curved, ridged pod is popular in Egyptian cooking. It has a lot of small seeds and, if cut, a very glutinous texture. It is most often used in stews, combined with tomatoes, onions, other vegetables, herbs such as coriander (cilantro), and flavourings such as pomegranates and garlic. Whole okra is briefly fried with sugar and lemon juice to make an easy mezze dish, and its natural thickening properties are used to advantage in casseroles. In cooking, the glutinous texture of okra can be lessened considerably by soaking in a mixture of lemon juice and salt water before cooking. It is available fresh or canned. Baby okra, popular in Lebanese and Palestinian cooking, can also be bought occasionally; use in a similar fashion.

Also known as – ladies' fingers

okra with coriander and tomato sauce

60 ml (¼ cup) olive oil
1 onion, chopped
2 garlic cloves, crushed
500 g (1 lb 2 oz) fresh okra, or 800 g (1 lb 12 oz) tin okra

400 g (14 oz) tin chopped tomatoes
2 teaspoons sugar
60 ml (¼ cup) lemon juice
65 g (1¼ cups) coriander (cilantro), finely chopped

heat the oil in a large frying pan, add the onion and cook over medium heat for 5 minutes, or until translucent and golden. Add the garlic and cook for another minute.

add the okra to the pan and cook, stirring, for 4–5 minutes, then add the tomato, sugar and lemon juice, and simmer, stirring occasionally, for 3–4 minutes, or until softened. Stir in the coriander, remove from the heat and serve. Serves 4–6.

using okra

When buying, choose pods that are tender and healthy green in colour. They should snap rather than bend and should be no more than 10 cm (4 inches) long. If too ripe, the okra pod will feel very sticky. To prepare, gently scrub with a paper towel or a vegetable brush. Rinse and drain, then slice off the top and tail. If using okra as a thickener, blanch whole first, then slice and add to the dish 10 minutes before the end of cooking. In some recipes, the pod is used whole; this prevents the release of the sticky substances within.

onions

Onions have been a part of the Mediterranean since ancient Egyptian times, and possibly earlier. Their raw pungency has excited varying reactions: the Egyptians put them in mummies' bandages in the hope of reviving the dead while the nobility and priests of various cultures have at times shunned them. In cooking, however, onions add a depth of flavour to countless dishes, and are a delicious vegetable in their own right. They are added raw to salads, are baked, fried and grilled (broiled), used in stews, tagines and casseroles, and are stuffed, skewered and pickled. Onions are sold dry or fresh (green), as flakes, in a powder-like onion salt or as fried flakes. Store in a cool, dark place.

types of onions

The most common sort is the yellow onion (top left), which is available all year. Varieties include the sweet onion vidalia, Spanish red onions (bottom left), pickling onions and cipolline, small flat onions (bottom right). White onions are generally mild and slightly sweet. They can be used for cooking or in salads. Red onions, including torpedo onions (top right) have less flavour than other varieties, although they can be slightly sweeter. They are roasted, grilled (broiled) and used in salads.

cipolline agrodolce

1 kg (2 lb 4 oz) small onions (cipolline or pickling onions)	2 tablespoons white wine vinegar
2 tablespoons brown sugar	60 g (2¼ oz) butter

peel the onions, cut off the roots and remove the first layer of skin. Heat the sugar in a large heavy-based saucepan until it melts and starts to caramelize. Remove from the heat, add the vinegar and butter and stir well. Return to the heat, bring to the boil and add the onions. Add enough water to just cover the onions and simmer for 10 minutes. Cover the saucepan and simmer for another 20 minutes, or until the onions are tender. Serve hot or at room temperature. Serves 8.

oregano

This strongly flavoured herb is especially popular in Italian and Greek cooking. It is used both fresh and dried, but is much more commonly seen dried. Oregano is traditionally used to flavour tomato sauces, added to pizza toppings and combined with other robust ingredients such as meat that is being roasted. Oregano also goes well with some fish—the Sicilians, for example, use it in a marinade for swordfish, tuna or bonito, a relation of tuna. Oregano's flavour can dominate so should only be used sparingly.

parsley

There is something very wonderful about buying a bunch of fresh herbs that is big enough to be carried home in one's arms. It's this sort of image that makes everyone want to pack up sticks and move to the Mediterranean. Flat-leaf parsley is the region's most common variety, and is used in the same generous spirit with which it is sold. Examples include tabbouleh and the Middle Eastern bread salad *fattoush*, refreshing salads of four or five fresh herbs, in marinades for grilled (broiled) meat and fish, in bouquet garni and *herbes de Provence*, and in Italian sauces for pasta or seafood such as salsa verde.

salsa verde

4 anchovy fillets, drained
1 tablespoon capers
1 garlic clove, crushed
7 g (¼ cup) chopped flat-leaf (Italian) parsley
7 g (¼ cup) basil leaves
7 g (¼ cup) mint leaves
2 teaspoons red wine vinegar
3 tablespoons extra virgin olive oil
1 teaspoon Dijon mustard

Also known as – Italian parsley

put the anchovies, capers, garlic, parsley, basil and mint in a food processor and chop in short bursts until roughly blended. Transfer to a bowl and stir in the vinegar. Slowly mix in the oil, then the mustard. Season to taste. Makes 200 ml (7 fl oz).

peppers

Although sweet peppers are a tropical fruit, Mediterranean cooks treat them more as a vegetable salad ingredient. Highly versatile, they are grilled (broiled) or roasted and peeled for antipasto, stuffed whole with an assortment of fillings, used in soups and ragùs, pickled or dried, cut into chunks and skewered with lamb kebabs, and eaten raw in salads. Most sweet peppers are green at first, then turning red, yellow or orange or even purple-black, depending on the variety, but all should be smooth and shiny. Buy peppers that are firm, glossy and plump. Those with a thick flesh are juiciest and red peppers are generally sweeter than green ones. Store in a bowl like fruit and they will sweeten as they ripen. Pimiento are Spanish cooked sweet red peppers.

Also known as – capsicums

peperonata

100 ml (3½ fl oz) olive oil
1 large onion, thinly sliced
2 garlic cloves, crushed
2 large red peppers (capsicums), sliced
1 large yellow pepper (capsicum), sliced
6 firm, ripe tomatoes, seeded and chopped

heat the olive oil in a large frying pan. Add the onion, cover the pan and fry gently for 15 minutes, or until lightly golden. Add the crushed garlic and gently fry for a further 5 minutes. Add the peppers and fry for 5 minutes, stirring frequently. Finally, add the tomato and simmer for 20 minutes. Season well and serve cold as part of an antipasto-style spread or warm as an accompaniment to meat and fish. Serves 4.

stuffed peppers

175 g (6 oz) long-grain white
  white rice
315 ml (1¼ cups) chicken
  stock
6 medium red, yellow or
  orange peppers (capsicums)
50 g (⅓ cup) pine nuts
80 ml (⅓ cup) olive oil

1 large onion, chopped
125 g (½ cup) tomato passata
50 g (⅓ cup) currants
2½ tablespoons chopped
  flat-leaf (Italian) parsley
2½ tablespoons chopped mint
  leaves
½ teaspoon ground cinnamon

put the rice and stock in a saucepan and bring to the boil over medium heat. Reduce the heat to medium-low, cover and cook for 15 minutes, or until the rice is tender. Remove from the heat and set aside, covered.

bring a large saucepan of water to the boil. Cut off the tops of the peppers, reserving the lids. Carefully remove and discard the seeds and membrane from the peppers. Blanch the peppers in the boiling water (not the lids) for 2 minutes, then drain and leave upturned to dry on paper towels.

preheat the oven to 180°C (350°F/Gas 4). Gently toast the pine nuts in a small frying pan over low heat until golden brown, then remove from the pan and set aside. Increase the heat to medium and heat 2 tablespoons of olive oil in the pan. Add the onion and cook for 10 minutes, or until soft, stirring occasionally.

add the tomato passata, currants, parsley, mint, cinnamon, cooked rice and toasted pine nuts to the pan. Stir for 2 minutes, then season, to taste, with salt and pepper.

stand the peppers in a baking dish in which they fit snugly. Divide the rice mixture among the pepper cavities. Replace the lids.

pour 100 ml (3½ fl oz) boiling water into the dish and drizzle the remaining oil over the top of the peppers. Bake for 40 minutes, or until the peppers are just tender when tested with the point of a small knife. Serve warm or cold. Serves 6.

potatoes

It was some time after its arrival in late seventeenth-century Spain before the potato was allowed into the kitchen. Though not a staple food, and not even eaten often in the Eastern Mediterranean, the potato can claim a number of classic Mediterranean dishes as its own. The tortilla, a thick omelette of potatoes, onion and garlic, is a Spanish staple, and *patatas bravas* is one of that country's favourite tapas dishes. From Italy comes potato gnocchi, and the Greek cooks of Cephalonia vary the standard skordalia by using potatoes instead of bread. Elsewhere, potatoes are roasted, fried, puréed and mashed.

skordalia

500 g (1 lb 2 oz) floury potatoes, cut into 2.5 cm (1 inch) cubes
5 garlic cloves, crushed
ground white pepper, to taste
185 ml (3/4 cup) olive oil
2 tablespoons white vinegar

bring a large saucepan of water to the boil, add the potato cubes and cook for 10 minutes, or until very soft. Drain thoroughly and mash until quite smooth.

stir the garlic, 1 teaspoon salt and a pinch of white pepper into the potato, then gradually pour in the olive oil, mixing well with a wooden spoon. Stir in the vinegar and season. Serve warm or cold with crusty bread as a dip, or with grilled (broiled) meat, fish or chicken. Makes 500 ml (2 cups).

patatas bravas

1 kg (2 lb 4 oz) Desiree
  potatoes
oil, for deep-frying
500 g (1 lb 2 oz) ripe Roma
  (plum) tomatoes
2 tablespoons olive oil
1/4 red onion, finely chopped

2 garlic cloves, crushed
3 teaspoons paprika
1/4 teaspoon cayenne pepper
1 bay leaf
1 teaspoon sugar
1 tablespoon chopped flat-leaf
  (Italian) parsley, to garnish

cut the potatoes into 2.5 cm (1 inch) cubes. Rinse, then drain well and pat completely dry. Fill a deepfryer or large heavy-based saucepan one-third full of oil and heat to 180°C (350°F), or until a cube of bread dropped into the oil browns in 15 seconds. Cook the potato in batches for 10 minutes, or until golden. Drain on paper towels. Retain the oil.

score a cross in the base of each tomato. Put them into a bowl of boiling water for 20 seconds, then plunge into cold water. Drain and peel the skin away from the cross. Chop the flesh.

heat the olive oil in a saucepan over medium heat and cook the onion for 3 minutes, or until softened. Add the garlic, paprika and cayenne, and cook for 1–2 minutes until fragrant.

add the tomato, bay leaf, sugar and 90 ml (3 1/4 fl oz) water, and cook, stirring occasionally, for 20 minutes, or until thick and pulpy. Cool slightly and remove the bay leaf. Blend in a food processor until smooth, adding some water if necessary. Before serving, return the sauce to the pan and gently simmer for 2 minutes, or until heated through. Season.

reheat the oil to 180°C (350°F) and cook the potato again, in batches, for 2 minutes, or until very crisp and golden. Drain on paper towels. This second frying makes the potato extra crispy and stops the sauce soaking in immediately. Put on a platter and cover with sauce. Garnish with parsley and serve. Serves 6.

choosing potatoes

Potatoes are basically floury or waxy but some of the newer breeds are all-purpose and are difficult to categorize. Floury potatoes are low in moisture and sugar and high in starch, which makes them perfect for baking, mashing or frying but because of their low sugar content they will collapse if boiled. Examples are Spunta, Russet (Idaho) and King Edward. Conversely, waxy potatoes are high in moisture and low in starch, so hold their shape and texture when boiled. They are not suitable for making chips or mashing but are good in salads. Examples include Pink Fir Apple, Kipfler and Jersey Royal. Good 'all-round' potatoes include Desiree, Bintje, Pontiac and Sebago.

potato gnocchi with pancetta and sage

gnocchi

1 kg (2 lb 4 oz) floury potatoes, unpeeled

2 egg yolks

2 tablespoons grated Parmesan cheese

125–185 g (1–1½ cups) plain (all-purpose) flour

sauce

1 tablespoon butter

70 g (2½ oz) pancetta or bacon, cut into thin strips

8 very small sage or basil leaves

150 ml (5 fl oz) thick (double/heavy) cream

50 g (½ cup) grated Parmesan cheese

preheat the oven to 180°C (350°F/Gas 4). Prick the potatoes all over, then bake for 1 hour, or until tender. Leave to cool for 15 minutes, then peel and mash, or put through a ricer or a food mill (do not use a blender or food processor).

mix in the egg yolks and Parmesan, then gradually stir in the flour. When the mixture gets too dry to use a spoon, work with your hands. Once a loose dough forms, transfer to a lightly floured surface and knead gently. Work in enough extra flour to give a soft, pliable dough that is damp to the touch but not sticky.

divide the dough into 6 portions. Working with one portion at a time, roll out on the floured surface to make a rope about 1.5 cm (⅝ inch) thick. Cut the rope into 1.5 cm (⅝ inch) lengths. Take 1 piece of dough and press your finger into it to form a concave shape, then roll the outer surface over the tines of a fork to make deep ridges. Fold the outer lips in towards each other to make a hollow in the middle. Continue with the remaining dough.

bring a large saucepan of salted water to the boil. Add the gnocchi in batches, about 20 at a time. Stir gently and return to the boil. Cook for 1–2 minutes, or until they rise to the surface. Remove them with a slotted spoon, drain and put in a greased shallow casserole or baking dish. Preheat the oven to 200°C (400°F/Gas 6).

to make the sauce, melt the butter in a small frying pan and fry the pancetta until crisp. Stir in the sage leaves and cream. Season and simmer for 10 minutes, or until thickened. Pour the sauce over the gnocchi, toss carefully and sprinkle the Parmesan on top. Bake for 10–15 minutes, or until the Parmesan melts and turns golden. Serve hot. Serves 4.

pumpkins

Piled high on stalls or carts, these members of the gourd family are a colourful sight in markets over autumn and winter. Pumpkins have a distinct sweet flavour and are used in savoury and sweet dishes across the Mediterranean. They are boiled, steamed, roasted and mashed, used in soups and as a filling for pasta, even in a dessert. The seeds of pumpkins are dried and used in both sweet and savoury food: they are toasted and sprinkled on salads and soups, or eaten out of hand. The roasted seeds are also used to make a thick, dark brown oil with a strong flavour and aroma, which is used as a salad dressing and seasoning. Choose pumpkins that are heavy for their size and have unblemished skins. Store whole at room temperature for up to one month. Wrap cut pumpkin in plastic wrap and store in the refrigerator.

tortellini filled with pumpkin

filling

900 g (2 lb) pumpkin, peeled and cubed
125 ml (1/2 cup) olive oil
1 small red onion, chopped
100 g (3 1/3 oz) ricotta cheese
1 egg yolk, beaten
25 g (1/4 cup) grated Parmesan cheese, plus extra, to serve

1 teaspoon freshly grated nutmeg
2 tablespoons chopped sage

1 quantity fresh pasta dough (see page 36)
1 egg
2 teaspoons milk
extra virgin olive oil, to serve

preheat the oven to 190°C (375°F/Gas 5). To make the filling, put the pumpkin in a roasting tin with half the olive oil and lots of salt and pepper. Bake for 40 minutes, or until it is completely soft.

meanwhile, heat the remaining olive oil in a saucepan and gently cook the onion until soft. Put the onion and pumpkin in a bowl, draining off any excess oil, and mash well. Leave to cool, then crumble in the ricotta. Mix in the egg yolk, Parmesan, nutmeg and sage. Season well.

to make the tortellini, roll out the pasta to the thinnest setting on the machine or with a large rolling pin. Cut the pasta into 7.5 cm (3 inch) squares. Mix together the egg and milk to make an egg wash and brush lightly over the pasta. Put a small teaspoon of filling in the middle of each square and fold it over diagonally to make a triangle, pressing down the corners. Pinch together the two corners on the longer side.

cook the tortellini in small batches in a large saucepan of boiling salted water until al dente. Remove with a slotted spoon and allow to drain. Divide between 9 bowls, drizzle over some olive oil and add the extra grated Parmesan cheese. Serves 6.

rosemary

The Latin name for rosemary is *Rosmarinus officinalis*, meaning 'dew of the sea', and the herb's strong aroma and piney taste do seem to evoke images of its native Mediterranean habitat. Dating back to Roman times, rosemary has been used as much for its medicinal properties as for its aromatic flavour. Today, along with parsley, it is one of the most commonly used herbs in Italy and in French Provence, and is usually associated with roasts. If possible, use only fresh rosemary, snipping the tips off the younger, more fragrant branches. The rather coarse leaves should be either finely chopped or left on the stem, making it easy to spot them. Use with discretion, however, as its distinctive flavour can easily overpower others.

roast chicken with rosemary

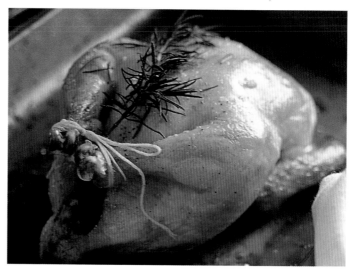

Put a rosemary sprig on top of the chicken for extra flavour.

2 rosemary sprigs
3 garlic cloves
1 teaspoon balsamic vinegar
1 x 1.5 kg (3 lb 5 oz) chicken

2 tablespoons extra virgin
  olive oil
2 tablespoons olive oil
125 ml (½ cup) chicken stock

preheat the oven to 200°C (400°F/Gas 6). Put 1 rosemary sprig, the garlic and balsamic vinegar inside the cavity of the chicken. Add a large pinch of salt and some freshly ground black pepper. Truss the chicken legs together with string.

rub the extra virgin olive oil over the chicken skin. Pour the olive oil into a roasting tin and put the chicken in the tin, breast up. Put the second sprig of rosemary on top.

transfer to the oven and roast for 1 hour, turning the chicken and basting with the pan juices every 15 minutes.

put the chicken on a warm serving plate and discard the rosemary sprig. Spoon off the fat from the roasting tin and place it over high heat on the stovetop. Add the chicken stock and deglaze the pan. Boil until reduced and thickened. Season, if necessary, then pour into a sauceboat to accompany the chicken. Serve with roast rosemary potatoes. Serves 4.

sage

This well-loved perennial herb has a long history of use in the Mediterranean, particularly for its medicinal properties. According to legend, the donkey that carried the baby Jesus to Egypt was fed dried sage to keep up its energy on the long journey. In cooking, sage has a robust flavour that holds its own with equally strong flavoured meats such as liver and pancetta. The leaves are also wonderful fried with butter and served as a simple pasta sauce. In Palestine, hand-picked and dried sage leaves, known as *miramieh*, are used in tea.

Dried sage.

salad leaves

A wide variety of lettuces and herbs, many gathered wild, are used in the Mediterranean. Wild greens are known as *horta* in Greece, the word stemming from the Greek word for 'small garden'. Salad leaves and herbs are used fresh in salads but are also cooked. In France, for example, lettuce is cooked with baby onions and peas in stock. Leaves are chosen for their flavour, texture and colour: red leaves have a bitter flavour and, like peppery green rocket (arugula), are combined with more delicate flavours; lamb's lettuce (corn salad) is valued for its slightly nutty flavour; young beet leaves are appreciated for their good green colour and earthy flavour; and crisp lettuce leaves such as cos (romaine) provide body in salads. Frisée, a type of chicory, has open, loose leaves with crisp, almost scratchy leaves. It is used to add bitter flavour and bulk to salads. Though many of the Mediterranean wild salad leaves are not available outside the area, one that is increasingly available is dandelion, now cultivated. Dandelion's name comes from the French *dents de lion*, meaning 'lion's teeth', referring to its jagged leaves. It is cooked in the same ways as spinach or is used fresh in salads such as the Roman salad *misticanza*, and dressed with a strong flavoured oil such as hazelnut or olive oil. The more familiar rocket (arugula), with its slightly bitter flavour, is used as a salad ingredient, and is a classic component of Provençal *mesclun* salad. It is also used as a pizza topping, in soups and purées or served wilted as a vegetable.

From left to right: Red- and green-leaved lettuces, rocket (arugula), frisée and dandelion.

salade aux noix

preheat the grill (broiler) and rub the bread with the cut garlic to give it flavour. Drizzle a little of the olive oil on each side of the bread and then grill (broil) until golden brown. Leave to cool.

arrange the lettuce leaves on a large platter. Mix together the remaining olive oil, walnut oil, vinegar and Dijon mustard and season to make a dressing.

put the walnuts in a small bowl and cover with boiling water. Leave for 1 minute, drain and shake dry.

cook the bacon in a frying pan until crisp, then lift out of the pan with a slotted spoon and sprinkle over the lettuce. Add the walnuts to the pan and cook for 1–2 minutes until browned, then add to the salad. Pour the dressing into the pan and heat through.

pour the dressing over the salad and toss well. Add the garlic croutons to serve. Serves 4 as a starter.

4 thin slices baguette
1 garlic clove, cut in half
80 ml (1/3 cup) olive oil
selection of mixed lettuce leaves
30 ml (1 fl oz) walnut oil
30 ml (1 fl oz) red wine vinegar
1 teaspoon Dijon mustard
70 g (2 1/2 oz) walnuts, broken into pieces
150 g (5 1/2 oz) streaky bacon, cut into small pieces

silverbeet

Though it doesn't seem to suggest ancient charm, silverbeet graced the walls of the famous Hanging Gardens of Babylon, and it has a long history of use in Arabian cooking. Silverbeet has fleshy stalks (chards) and large leaves, both of which can be eaten. Different countries of the Mediterranean tend to prefer different parts. The stalks are used in French and Italian cooking in sauces and soups, and are also sautéed, while the leaves are found in Eastern Mediterranean cooking, stuffed and added to salads, pies and tagines.

Also known as – Swiss chard

warm silverbeet and chickpea salad with sumac

250 g (9 oz) dried chickpeas
125 ml (½ cup) olive oil
1 onion, cut into thin wedges
2 ripe tomatoes
1 teaspoon sugar
¼ teaspoon ground cinnamon
2 garlic cloves, chopped

1.5 kg (3 lb 5 oz) silverbeet
 (Swiss chard)
3 tablespoons chopped mint
2–3 tablespoons lemon juice
1½ tablespoons sumac
 (see page 208)

put the chickpeas in a large bowl, cover with water and leave to soak overnight. Drain and put in a saucepan. Cover with water and bring to the boil, then simmer for 1¾ hours, or until tender. Drain thoroughly.

heat the oil in a heavy-based frying pan, add the onion and cook over low heat for 5 minutes, or until softened. Cut the tomatoes in half, scrape out the seeds and dice the flesh. Add the tomato flesh to the pan with the sugar, cinnamon and garlic, and cook for 2–3 minutes.

thoroughly wash the silverbeet and pat dry with paper towels. Trim the stems and finely shred the leaves. Add to the tomato mixture with the chickpeas and cook for 3–4 minutes, or until the silverbeet wilts. Add the mint, lemon juice and sumac, season, and cook for 1 minute. Serve immediately. Serves 4.

culinary uses

After collection, live snails are starved for a week or so to rid them of any toxins, or fed on a diet of lettuce or herbs. They are removed from their shells and cleaned, then boiled. Classically, snails are served in garlic butter; simmered in olive oils and flavoured with tomatoes and herbs; or served with a white wine sauce. Snails may be served in a dish called an *escargotière*, which is divided into sections to hold each snail. Special forks are used to remove the snail from its shell. Preparing live snails for cooking is quite complex, so those that are ready-cleaned or tinned are a good alternative. Imported varieties are sold frozen, cooked or tinned. The shells are usually sold separately, in tins or jars.

snails with garlic butter

250 ml (1 cup) white wine
250 ml (1 cup) chicken stock
3 tarragon sprigs
24 tinned snails, well drained
24 snail shells
2 garlic cloves, crushed

2 tablespoons finely chopped basil leaves
2 tablespoons chopped parsley
2 tablespoons finely chopped tarragon leaves
150 g (5½ oz) butter, at room temperature

put the wine, stock, tarragon and 125 ml (½ cup) water in a small saucepan and boil for 2 minutes. Add the snails and gently simmer for 7 minutes. Remove from the heat and leave to cool in the poaching liquid. Drain and put a snail in each shell. Preheat the oven to 200°C (400°F/Gas 6).

mix together the garlic, basil, parsley and tarragon in a small bowl. Mix in the butter and season well.

put a little garlic butter into each shell and arrange them on a snail plate or baking tray covered with a layer of rock salt. Bake for 7–8 minutes, or until the butter melts and the snails are heated through. Serve with crusty bread to mop up the garlic butter. Serves 4.

snails

There are many varieties of edible snails. They are associated with France, but snails are also found, cultivated and eaten in Spain, Algeria and Turkey. Snail flesh has a surprisingly firm texture, with a delicate, sweet flavour. The best eating varieties are the popular, but increasingly rare, large Burgundy (Roman) snail and the smaller but sweeter petit gris (the common garden snail), now more widely used.

Also known as – escargot

spinach

Originally native to Iran, this green leafy plant with slender stems is today found throughout the Mediterranean. France grows a fleshy-leaved variety with tough leaves called tetragon, which is actually an Australian and New Zealand native spinach. When young, spinach leaves are used in salads; older ones are cooked. Spinach forms a filling in pies in the Middle East, is cooked with raisins and pine nuts as a side dish in Spain, and stewed with rice in Greece. Spinach needs to be used within one or two days of purchasing and stored with the roots attached in the refrigerator in a plastic bag. Mediterranean varieties of spinach are often sold under the name English spinach.

spinach with garlic and chilli

250 g (9 oz) baby English spinach leaves
2 tablespoons olive oil
1 garlic clove, crushed
1 red chilli, finely chopped
2 tablespoons cream
cayenne pepper

wash the spinach thoroughly and shake it dry, leaving a little water clinging to the leaves. If you are using frozen spinach, defrost it completely and drain it very well—squeeze it with your hands to get rid of excess moisture.

heat the oil in a frying pan, add the garlic and chilli and cook for a few seconds, being careful not to burn them. Add the spinach and stir it through the oil. Put a lid on the pan for a minute to create some steam. Remove the lid and turn up the heat. Stir the spinach, turning it over frequently until all the liquid has evaporated, then season well. Drizzle with the cream and dust with cayenne pepper. Serves 2.

thyme

thyme-flavoured semi-dried tomatoes

16 Roma (plum) tomatoes
3 tablespoons thyme, chopped
2 tablespoons olive oil

preheat the oven to 160°C (315°F/Gas 2–3). Quarter the tomatoes lengthways and lay skin-side-down on a rack in a baking tray.

sprinkle with 1 teaspoon each of salt and freshly ground black pepper and the thyme and bake for 2½ hours. Check occasionally to make sure the tomatoes don't burn. Toss in the oil and cool before packing into sterilized jars and sealing. Refrigerate for 24 hours before serving as part of an antipasto plate. Makes 64 slices.

note: To sterilize the storage jars, preheat the oven to 120°C (250°F/ Gas ½). Wash the jar and lid in hot soapy water and rinse with hot water. Put in the oven for 20 minutes, or until fully dry. The tomatoes can be kept in sterilized jars in the refrigerator for up to 7 days.

This hardy little plant has its home in the hills of the Mediterranean and the Middle East, releasing its aroma into the air about it. There are many varieties and all have small leaves that can be used as a flavouring in casseroles, stews and soups. Its rich, aromatic flavour also makes it good in stuffings and slow-cooked food and roasts, combining especially well with meats such as lamb and rabbit. In its dried form, thyme's flavour intensifies and is an essential part of spice mixes such as *za'atar*, which is also the Arabic word for wild thyme.

tomatoes

The tomato is another ingredient that appears quintessentially Mediterranean but is actually native to South America. But so thoroughly has the tomato been assimilated that it's now difficult to imagine Italian cuisine, in particular, without it. The tomato arrived in Naples in the sixteenth century and originally was seen as a medicinal plant only. A generation passed before it began to appear on the table.

Today, Italy and Turkey grow many varieties in various shapes, sizes and colours. Most varieties are red, although others are pink or yellow. The best flavoured ones are those that are vine-ripened. In cooking, the tomato's uses are seemingly endless. Tomatoes go with a wide range of ingredients, and can be pulped, puréed, roasted, baked, grilled (broiled) or stuffed. For immediate use, tomatoes should be firm and bright coloured, with no wrinkles and a strong tomato smell. Buy in small quantities (unless making sauce), or buy some greener than others.

types of tomatoes

cherry These come in various sizes but essentially are a tiny variety of tomato. Some are red, others are yellow and some are pear-shaped and yellow. They are used in salads or whole or halved in stews and pasta sauces.

beef steak These are larger tomatoes, either smooth and rounded or more irregular and ridged. They can be used for stuffing or in salads.

roma Also known as plum or egg, these tomatoes are commercially used for canning and drying. They have few seeds and a dry flesh, which makes them ideal for use in sauces and purées. A good variety is San Marzano.

round The most common tomato, they are commercially bred to be round and red. They can be bought on the vine or vine-ripened; there are also yellow- and orange-coloured varieties.

spanish red gazpacho

score a cross in the base of each tomato. Put them into a bowl of boiling water for 20 seconds, then plunge into cold water. Drain and peel the skin away from the cross. Cut the tomatoes in half and scoop out the seeds with a teaspoon. Chop the tomatoes.

soak the bread in cold water for 5 minutes, then squeeze out any excess liquid. Put the bread in a food processor with the tomato, pepper, garlic, chilli, sugar and vinegar, and process until combined and smooth.

with the motor running, add the oil to make a smooth, creamy mixture. Season with salt and freshly ground black pepper. Refrigerate for at least 2 hours. Add a little extra vinegar, if desired.

mix the ingredients for the garnish in a bowl. Pour the soup into bowls and add 2 ice cubes to each. Serve the garnish in separate bowls. Serves 4.

1 kg (2 lb 4 oz) vine-ripened tomatoes
2 slices day-old white Italian bread, crust removed, broken into pieces
1 red pepper (capsicum), seeded, roughly chopped
2 garlic cloves, chopped
1 small fresh green chilli, chopped, optional
1 teaspoon sugar
2 tablespoons red wine vinegar
2 tablespoons extra virgin olive oil
8 ice cubes

garnish
½ Lebanese (short) cucumber, seeded, finely diced
½ red pepper (capsicum), seeded, finely diced
½ green pepper (capsicum), seeded, finely diced
½ red onion, finely diced
½ ripe tomato, diced

simple tomato sauce

125 g (4½ oz) Roma
  (plum) tomatoes
3 basil leaves
2 garlic cloves, crushed
1 tablespoon tomato passata
2 teaspoons extra virgin
  olive oil

core the tomatoes and purée in a food processor with the basil leaves (or chop the tomatoes and basil very finely and stir together). Stir in the garlic, tomato passata and olive oil and season well. Leave for at least 30 minutes to allow the flavours to blend. Use on pizzas, toss through pasta or serve with arancini. Makes 200 ml (7 fl oz).

sauce vierge

700 g (1 lb 9 oz) tomatoes
170 ml (²/₃ cup) extra virgin olive oil
3 tablespoons lemon juice
2 garlic cloves, crushed
6 black olives, pitted and finely chopped
1 tablespoon each of chives, parsley and tarragon,
  finely chopped

score a cross in the base of each tomato, put into boiling water for 20 seconds and then plunge into cold water. Drain, and peel the skin away from the cross. Remove the seeds and chop the flesh roughly. Put in a bowl and add the olive oil, lemon juice and garlic. Stir well. Set aside for 2 hours. Just before serving, stir in the chopped olives and herbs. Serve with fish such as tuna, salmon or turbot, or over pasta such as ravioli. Makes 435 ml (1 ³/₄ cups).

provençal ratatouille

score a cross in the base of each tomato, put into boiling water for 20 seconds and then plunge into cold water. Drain, and peel the skin away from the cross. Chop roughly.

heat the oil in a frying pan. Add the onion and cook over low heat for 5 minutes. Add the peppers and cook, stirring, for 4 minutes. Remove from the pan and set aside.

fry the eggplant until lightly browned all over and then remove from the pan. Fry the zucchini until browned and then return the onion, peppers and eggplant to the pan. Add the tomato paste, stir well and cook for 2 minutes. Add the tomato, sugar, bay leaf, thyme and basil, stir well, cover and cook for 15 minutes. Remove the bay leaf, thyme and basil.

mix together the garlic and parsley and add to the ratatouille at the last minute. Stir through and serve. Serves 4.

4 tomatoes
2 tablespoons olive oil
1 large onion, diced
1 red pepper (capsicum), diced
1 yellow pepper (capsicum), diced
1 eggplant (aubergine), diced
2 zucchini (courgettes), diced
1 teaspoon tomato paste (purée)
1/2 teaspoon sugar
1 bay leaf
3 thyme sprigs
2 basil sprigs
1 garlic clove, crushed
1 tablespoon chopped flat-leaf (Italian) parsley

zucchini

These members of the marrow family are usually dark green in colour, though light green and yellow varieties of various shapes and sizes are also found in the Mediterranean. Though delicately flavoured, zucchini are versatile and combine with a range of ingredients such as egg and cheese, herbs like mint and dill, rice, sultanas and pine nuts. Popular in the cooking of Greece, Italy and the Middle East, young zucchini are sliced thinly, dressed in oil and lemon juice and eaten raw in salads. Larger ones are sliced, coated in batter and deep-fried, or hollowed-out, stuffed and baked. The flowers are eaten, too, usually stuffed then baked or fried. Zucchini need to be used soon after purchase.

Also known as – courgettes

vegetable tian

60 ml (¼ cup) olive oil
500 g (1 lb 2 oz) zucchini
  (courgettes), thickly sliced
  on the diagonal
4 garlic cloves, crushed
pinch nutmeg
650 g (1 lb 7 oz) tomatoes
2 red onions, chopped
60 ml (¼ cup) white wine
20 g (⅔ cup) chopped
  flat-leaf (Italian) parsley
125 g (4½ oz) Gruyère
  cheese, grated
a few small thyme sprigs

preheat the oven to 180°C (350°F/Gas 4). Grease a 15 x 25 cm (6 x 10 inch) ovenproof dish with melted butter or oil. Heat half the oil in a large frying pan and add the zucchini and half the garlic. Cook, stirring, over low heat for 8 minutes until just beginning to soften. Season well with salt, pepper and nutmeg. Spread evenly into the dish.

score a cross in the base of each tomato. Put into boiling water for 20 seconds then plunge into cold water. Peel the skin away from the cross. Chop roughly. Cook the onion in the remaining oil over low heat for 5 minutes, stirring often. Add the remaining garlic, tomato, wine and parsley. Cook, stirring, for 10 minutes until the liquid has evaporated.

sprinkle the cheese over the zucchini and evenly spread the tomato mixture over the top. Scatter with thyme sprigs and bake for about 20 minutes, or until heated through. Serves 4.

A *tian* is the French word for a shallow earthenware dish and the food it contains. Originally, this was a Provençal dish of gratinéed vegetables but today may be a range of dishes.

Long slender zucchini from Sicily in Italy (left) and small round ball-like ones from France (right).

deep-fried zucchini flowers

check the zucchini flowers are clean and aren't hiding any insects. Trim the stems to about 2.5 cm (1 inch).

to make the batter, sift the flour into a bowl and stir in ¼ teaspoon salt. Mix in the oil with a wooden spoon, then slowly add 80–100 ml (2½–3½ fl oz) warm water to make a smooth thick batter. Whisk the egg whites until stiff peaks form, then fold gently into the batter.

fill a deep-fryer or deep pan one-third full with oil and heat to about 180°C (350°F), or until a cube of bread dropped in the oil fries golden brown in 15 seconds. If the oil starts to smoke, it is too hot.

dip the zucchini flowers into the batter, coating them completely. Fry in batches until golden brown, turning over once. Drain on paper towels, sprinkle with salt and serve with lemon wedges. Serves 4.

12 zucchini (courgettes) flowers
oil, for deep-frying
lemon wedges, to serve

batter
50 g (1¾ oz) plain (all-purpose) flour
2 teaspoons olive oil
3 egg whites

Carefully put the zucchini flowers into the oil, holding them at the end.

note: Like many deep-fried foods, these zucchini flowers will become soggy if you let them sit for too long before serving. If you want to prepare them a little in advance, keep them warm on a tray lined with crumpled greaseproof paper in a low oven.

from branch and vine

almonds

Perhaps more familiar to us in their blanched, flaked or ground form, packaged and ready for purchasing from supermarkets, these pale, sweet-textured nuts are the seeds of a white-blossomed tree native to the Mediterranean and Central Asia. There are two varieties of almonds: a bitter, poisonous one and the (not surprisingly) more commonly used sweet variety. Mediterraneans have found uses for the bitter almond, mainly in confectionery (in marzipan, for example) and as a flavouring in liqueurs such as amaretto. The sweet almond is a noted feature of Arabian-influenced cooking of the region.

culinary uses

Sweet almonds are used in soups and stews, combining especially well with chicken and duck, and with grains such as couscous and semolina. In sweet dishes they appear in fruit compotes, cakes, syrupy pastries and creamy puddings such as *mahallabia*, eaten all over the Eastern Mediterranean and Middle East. They are a classic stuffing for figs and dates and are made into a Middle Eastern drink, almond horchata, which is traditionally served at celebrations.

almond horchata

500 g (1 lb 2 oz) blanched whole almonds
1/2 lemon
1 cinnamon stick
2 tablespoons sugar

grind the almonds in a food processor, or with mortar and pestle, with 1 litre (4 cups) warm water to form a very thick paste. Spoon into a large bowl. Cut the half lemon into slices and add to the paste, along with the cinnamon stick and 500 ml (2 cups) warm water. Stir well, cover and leave at room temperature for at least 2 hours. Strain the liquid through cheesecloth or muslin, add the sugar and serve chilled. Serves 4.

mahallabia

500 ml (2 cups) milk
75 g (2 1/2 oz) caster (superfine) sugar
2 tablespoons cornflour (cornstarch)
2 tablespoons ground rice
75 g (2 1/2 oz) ground blanched almonds
1 teaspoon rose water
2 tablespoons flower blossom honey
2 tablespoons shelled pistachio nuts, chopped

put the milk and sugar in a saucepan and heat over medium heat, stirring until the sugar has dissolved.

combine the cornflour and ground rice with 60 ml (1/4 cup) water and mix to a paste. Add to the milk and cook, stirring occasionally, over low heat for 20 minutes. Add the almonds and cook for 15 minutes, then add the rose water. Spoon into shallow serving dishes and refrigerate for 1 hour. Serve drizzled with a little honey and sprinkled with pistachios. Serves 4.

buying and preparing

Young almonds are hard to come by, but if you do, eat them straight out of their soft, green husk—a favourite street snack in the Mediterranean. When buying the mature almonds, if possible choose whole almonds still in the shell or in their skins. To remove the skins (to blanch), soak the almonds in boiling water for 2 minutes, then drain and slip off the skins with your fingers. Chop the blanched almonds while they are still soft and damp. Almonds can also be lightly toasted in the oven at 180°C (350°F/Gas 4) for 10 minutes, or until golden, to give them a deeper flavour. To grind, use a food processor or mortar and pestle. Add a little sugar to help absorb the oil and prevent an oily paste forming.

apricots

Originally from northern China, where they grew wild more than 2000 years ago, apricots were first introduced to the Middle East and Mediterranean along with other exotics as part of the ancient silk trade between East and West. As with many other ingredients that arrived in the Mediterranean this way, its culinary uses reflect its early passage westward. For example, it is often included in lamb and rice dishes and tagines of Turkey and Morocco that hark back to the Persian tradition of combining fruit with meat. Moroccans also stuff fresh apricots with ground almonds, another legacy of the Persians. Elsewhere, apricots are used in tarts and pastries, poached in aromatic syrups, made into jam, and last, but certainly not least, eaten fresh when in season. Varieties include white, orange and pink ones.

orchard fruit compote

90 g (¼ cup) honey
½ teaspoon ground ginger
1 cinnamon stick
3 cloves
pinch ground nutmeg
750 ml (3 cups) dessert wine
  such as Sauternes
1 lemon
10 dried apricots

6 pitted prunes
5 dates, seeded and halved
3 dried peaches, halved
1 lapsang souchong tea bag
2 golden delicious apples
2 beurre bosc pears
410 g (1²/₃ cups) Greek-style
  natural yoghurt

put the honey, ginger, cinnamon, cloves, nutmeg and wine in a saucepan. Peel a large piece of zest from the lemon and add to the pan. Squeeze the juice from the lemon to give 60 ml (¼ cup) and add to the pan. Bring to the boil, stirring, then simmer for 20 minutes.

meanwhile, put the apricots, prunes, dates and peaches in a large heatproof bowl. Cover with boiling water, add the tea bag and leave to soak. Peel and core the apples and pears, and cut into pieces about the same size as the dried fruit. Add to the honey syrup and simmer for 8–10 minutes until tender. Drain the dried fruit and remove the tea bag, then add the dried fruit to the syrup and cook for a further 5 minutes.

remove all the fruit from the pan with a slotted spoon and put in a serving dish. Return the pan to the heat, bring to the boil, then reduce the heat and simmer for 5 minutes, or until the syrup has reduced by half. Pour over the fruit compote and chill for 30 minutes. Serve with the yoghurt alongside. Serves 4.

dried apricots

In summer, it is still possible to see flat rooftops in Turkey and Syria covered with apricots, left out in the sunshine to dry naturally. Most commercially dried apricots are chemically treated to preserve the golden apricot colour but the naturally sun-dried ones, which are much darker in colour, have a fuller flavour. Dried apricots are eaten as snacks, added to sweet and savoury couscous dishes and poached in aromatic syrups as a simple dessert. In the Eastern Mediterranean, a chewy snack is made from the fruit that has been puréed and dried, then cut into strips.

cherries

A relation of the plum, peach and apricot, cherries are native to the Eastern Mediterranean and Western Asia. There are three main types: sweet, sour and hybrids. Sweet cherries can be eaten fresh or cooked; sour cherries are usually cooked in pies, added to jams and liqueurs or used as an accompanying sauce to savoury dishes such as lamb meatballs; and hybrids like Duke cherries (known as *Royale* in France) can be used for both eating and cooking. *Mahlab*, the kernel of the black cherry, is found in Turkish and Syrian cooking. The kernels are ground to a powder and used primarily to add a nutty flavour to breads and biscuits.

Clafoutis is a classic French harvest dish. Seasonal cherries are mixed with a batter pudding, though other berries can be used. It is traditional to leave the stones in the cherries when making a clafoutis, as they add a bitter, almost almond-like flavour during cooking, but it's best to point this out to guests when serving the pudding.

cherry clafoutis

60 g (2¼ oz) unsalted butter, melted, plus extra
500 g (1 lb 2 oz) fresh cherries, or 720 g (1 lb 9 oz) jar of cherries, drained
90 g (¾ cup) plain (all-purpose) flour
2 eggs, lightly beaten
90 g (⅓ cup) caster (superfine) sugar
250 ml (1 cup) milk
60 ml (¼ cup) thick (double/heavy) cream
icing (confectioners') sugar, for dusting

preheat the oven to 180°C (350°F/Gas 4). Grease a 1.5 litre (6 cup) baking dish with a little of the melted butter. Pit the cherries, if you wish, and spread the fruit into the dish in a single layer.

sift the flour into a large bowl, add the eggs and whisk until smooth. Add the sugar, milk, cream and melted butter, whisking until just combined. Do not overbeat.

pour the batter over the cherries and bake for 30–40 minutes, or until a skewer comes out clean when inserted into the centre. Dust generously with icing sugar before serving. Serve warm, straight from the oven. Serves 4–6.

Chestnuts grow in the mountainous areas of the Mediterranean and are in season in late autumn. They are used in soups and stews, as well as in cakes and creams, but their most popular use is also the simplest— cooked on portable roasters in the street or marketplace, and eaten out of the shell. In Italy and France, chestnuts are also ground into flour or dried for year-round use. To use, dried chestnuts are soaked in water, then boiled in milk for use in soups or sweet desserts. If fresh chestnuts are required for a recipe but aren't available, substitute vacuum-packed, frozen or tinned ones instead.

chestnut, pancetta and cabbage soup

cook the cabbage in 1.5 litres (6 cups) boiling salted water for about 10 minutes. Drain, reserving the water. Rinse the cabbage in cold water if too hot to handle, then chop more finely.

heat the oil in a large saucepan, add the onion and pancetta and cook over moderately high heat until the onion is soft and the pancetta lightly browned. Add the garlic and rosemary and cook for a few minutes more. Break up the chestnuts a little and add to the pan with the cabbage. Stir to combine the flavours, season, then add the wine. Bring to the boil and cook for a couple of minutes. Finally, add the cabbage water and simmer for about 15 minutes.

purée half of the soup, leaving the remainder as it is, for extra texture. Combine together again, then serve hot with a drizzle of extra virgin olive oil over the top. Serves 4.

chestnuts

100 g (3½ oz) cavolo nero or
  Savoy cabbage, roughly
  chopped
2 tablespoons olive oil
1 large onion, finely chopped
185 g (6¼ oz) pancetta, diced
3 garlic cloves, crushed
10 g (¼ oz) rosemary,
  chopped
300 g (10½ oz) cooked
  peeled chestnuts
150 ml (5 fl oz) red wine
drizzle of extra virgin
  olive oil

dates

Distant oases of date palms shimmering in the desert heat seem the stuff of movies but for the Bedouin of North Africa, their significance cannot be underestimated. The date palm is known to them as the 'tree of life', and has been cultivated for over 5000 years. It is essential not only for its sweet, luxurious fruit but also for the shade it provides and the fronds for weavings.

The Bedouin diet was simple, and dates were an important part. Dates were ideal travelling food for the Bedouin, as they could be dried, but they also provided much-needed sugar. Fermented milk, wild herbs and the occasional piece of meat were the other mainstays of a spartan diet. In the Middle East in general, dates are highly esteemed for their taste and nutritional value. They are widely associated with prosperity and longevity.

orange-scented date crescents

185 g (heaped 1 cup) chopped pitted dates
3 teaspoons finely grated orange zest
2 teaspoons orange flower water or orange juice
125 g (4½ oz) unsalted butter, cubed and softened
125 g (heaped ½ cup) caster (superfine) sugar
1 egg
250 g (2 cups) plain (all-purpose) flour, sifted
1 teaspoon baking powder
sugar, to sprinkle

put the dates and 1 tablespoon water in a small pan. Stir over low heat for 2–3 minutes, or until the dates are soft. Remove from the heat and stir in 1 teaspoon of the grated orange zest and 1 teaspoon of the orange flower water. Set aside to cool.

line 2 baking trays with baking paper. Beat the butter, caster sugar and the remaining orange zest and orange flower water until creamy. Add the egg and beat until fully combined.

mix in the combined flour and baking powder until a smooth dough forms. Cover with plastic wrap and refrigerate for 30 minutes. Put half the dough between 2 sheets of baking paper and roll out to a rectangle 5 mm (¼ inch) thick. Refrigerate again if the dough is too soft. Preheat the oven to 180°C (350°F/Gas 4.)

cut out ten 6 cm (2½ inch) circles from the dough with a fluted cutter. Put 1 teaspoon of date filling onto each circle and fold over to form a crescent, gently pressing the edges to seal. The pastry should be well filled with the mixture. Repeat with the remaining dough.

put the crescents on the trays, brush the tops with water and sprinkle with the sugar. Bake for 10–15 minutes, or until just turning golden. Cool on a wire rack. Makes about 25.

varieties and uses for dates

These life-sustaining trees are abundant across North Africa and the Middle East, and countless local varieties of the fruit exist, including medjool, halawy and the highly prized deglet noor. Unripe dates are green, turning pale honey to brown as they ripen, though colour, texture and flavour vary with variety.

Fresh dates are boiled to a pulp to make *dibbis* (date syrup), and used in some sweet and savoury dishes. Dried dates are more widely used, however. They are added to cakes or biscuits, stuffed with pistachios, almonds or rose-scented almond paste, and are used in stews, tagines, couscous and pilafs.

Fresh dates are often sold in bunches, still on their thin branch. Dried dates are sold loose or in boxes. Choose fresh dates with skin that is translucent when held to the light, and dried ones that are moist-looking. Fresh dates need to be stored at room temperature, and dried dates in an airtight container in a cool, dark place.

figs

One of the most ancient of cultivated plants, figs have a distinguished culinary and cultural history in the Mediterranean. The fig leaves were mentioned in the Bible story of Adam and Eve, the Greeks regarded the fruit as a symbol of fertility and a gift from the gods, and the Egyptians left them in tombs to provide sustenance for the deceased on his or her journey to the next life. Figs are also recorded as growing in the famous Hanging Gardens of Babylon, where they were covered in hot sand as a means of preserving them.

selecting and using figs

The best figs are those that are left to ripen on the tree: small, soft and pear-shaped, they have a sweet, heady pulpy flesh full of tiny edible seeds. Figs are grown today in Turkey, Greece, North Africa, southern Italy and Sicily and range in colour from pale green and golden yellow to brown, red and purple. Varieties include Smyrna, Caprifig and San Pedro. Fresh figs are usually treated simply—wrapped in prosciutto and grilled (broiled) or eaten with a creamy cheese—while dried figs are used in compotes, stews or stuffed with nuts. Both fresh and dried are delicious baked with honey. When buying, make sure figs are ripe, soft and unblemished and use on the day of purchasing. Dried figs, if stored in an airtight container, will last indefinitely.

Today's figs are descendants of the wild fig tree, which may have been cultivated as long ago as 4000BCE in the Mediterranean. Highly unusual, each fruit is actually hundreds of minute fruits, encased in an outer shell. Fresh figs are brief luxuries; dried figs are valued for their year-round sweetness and are used as sweetmeats.

figs in honey syrup

100 g (3½ oz) blanched whole almonds
12 whole fresh figs (about 750 g/1 lb 10 oz)
125 g (heaped ½ cup) sugar
115 g (⅓ cup) honey
2 tablespoons lemon juice
6 cm (2½ inch) sliver of lemon zest
1 cinnamon stick
250 g (1 cup) Greek-style natural yoghurt

preheat the oven to 180°C (350°F/Gas 4). Put the almonds on a baking tray and bake for 5 minutes, or until light golden. Leave to cool. Cut the stems off the figs and make a small crossways incision 5 mm (¼ inch) deep on top of each. Push a blanched almond into the base of each fig. Roughly chop and reserve the remaining almonds.

put 750 ml (3 cups) water in a large saucepan, add the sugar and stir over medium heat until the sugar dissolves. Increase the heat and bring to the boil. Stir in the honey, lemon juice, lemon zest and cinnamon stick. Reduce the heat to medium, add the figs to the pan and simmer gently for 30 minutes. Remove with a slotted spoon and put on a large serving dish.

boil the liquid over high heat for about 15–20 minutes, or until thick and syrupy. Remove the cinnamon and lemon zest. Cool the syrup slightly and pour over the figs. Sprinkle with the reserved almonds and serve warm or cold with yoghurt. Serves 4.

grapes

Perhaps no fruit is more evocative of the Mediterranean's Classical age than the grape. First brought to the region by the intrepid sea-going Phoenicians, grapes were cultivated by the ancient Egyptians, Greeks and Persians. During the ancient Roman era, grape vines were encouraged to intertwine with the olive trees, thus firmly establishing their place in the cuisines and economies of the region.

Though mainly appreciated as a table fruit, fresh grapes are an essential part of the well-known chilled Andalusian almond and garlic soup, *ajo blanco*.

ajo blanco

1 loaf (200 g/7 oz) day-old white Italian bread, crust removed
155 g (1 cup) whole blanched almonds
3–4 garlic cloves, chopped
125 ml (½ cup) extra virgin olive oil
80 ml (⅓ cup) sherry or white wine vinegar
310–375 ml (1¼–1½ cups) vegetable stock
2 tablespoons olive oil, extra
75 g (2¾ oz) day-old white Italian bread, extra, crust removed, cut into 1 cm (½ inch) cubes
200 g (7 oz) small seedless green grapes

soak the bread in cold water for 5 minutes, then squeeze out any excess liquid. Chop the almonds and garlic in a processor until well ground. Add the bread and process until smooth.

with the motor running, add the oil in a steady slow stream until the mixture is the consistency of thick mayonnaise. Slowly add the sherry and 310 ml (1¼ cups) of the stock. Blend for 1 minute. Season with salt. Refrigerate for at least 2 hours. The soup thickens on refrigeration so you may need to add stock or water to thin it.

when ready to serve, heat the extra oil in a frying pan, add the bread cubes and toss over medium heat for 2–3 minutes, or until golden. Drain on paper towels. Serve the soup very cold. Garnish with the grapes and bread cubes. Serves 4–6.

dried grapes

Currants, raisins and sultanas are all dried grapes. Currants are small black grapes; sultanas are dried white grapes; and raisins vary according to the variety but are traditionally muscatel grapes. All three are used in cakes and biscuits, with couscous, in stuffings and sauces.

hazelnuts

hazelnut and chocolate cake

140 g (1 cup) skinned hazelnuts
3 tablespoons cocoa powder
60 g (½ cup) plain (all-purpose) flour
30 g (¼ cup) self-raising flour
185 g (1 cup) soft brown sugar
250 g (9 oz) unsalted butter, softened
4 eggs, separated
icing (confectioners') sugar

toast the hazelnuts under a hot grill (broiler), turning them so they brown on all sides. Leave them to cool, then put in a food processor and process until fine (don't overprocess or they will become oily), or chop finely with a knife. Transfer to a bowl with the cocoa powder and sifted flours. Preheat the oven to 180°C (350°F/Gas 4).

lightly grease and flour a 20 cm (8 inch) cake tin. Beat together the sugar and butter until very creamy. Add the egg yolks one at a time, mixing well after each addition. Add the hazelnut mixture and stir together. Whisk the egg whites in a clean, dry glass bowl until stiff peaks form, then fold into the hazelnut mixture.

pour the mixture into the tin and bake for 50 minutes, or until a skewer inserted into the centre comes out clean. Rest for 15 minutes, then cool on a wire rack. Dust with icing sugar before serving. Serves 8.

Medieval records note that hazelnuts were favoured by gourmets; in earlier times it was believed that the wood of the tree contained magical properties. Today, hazelnuts tend to be viewed in humbler ways but are still appreciated for their sweet flavour. They are roasted and eaten whole, ground and used in sweet dishes or biscuits, added to fish dishes or used in savoury sauces such as *salsa romesco* from Catalonia. They are also used in an alternative version of *tarator*, the garlic, vinegar and bread sauce usually made with walnuts. In desserts, hazelnuts are a classic companion of chocolate, as shown in this rustic French cake.

lemons

The lemon is an indispensable part of Mediterranean cuisines, particularly so in the Arabian- and Persian-inspired cooking of the region. Lemon juice is used in soups such as the well-known Greek soup *avgolemono*, in sauces, in countless dips and appetizers, and for providing flavour when roasting and stewing meat, vegetables or poultry. The grated zest adds tartness to sauces such as gremolata and to dressings, and lemon wedges are squeezed over cooked or raw vegetables and barbecued or fried seafood, meat or cheese. As well, the whole lemon is dried, pickled or preserved, and the peel is preserved in sugar and used as a sweetmeat. In sweet dishes, lemons are classic flavourings for ice cream, gelato, soufflés and tarts. Finally, on a hot Mediterranean day, there is not much that can surpass the refreshing tang of chilled home-made lemonade.

avgolemono soup with chicken

1 onion, halved
2 cloves
1 carrot, cut into chunks
1 bay leaf
500 g (1 lb 2 oz) chicken
   breast fillets

75 g (⅓ cup) short-grain
   white rice
3 eggs, separated
3 tablespoons lemon juice
2 tablespoons chopped
   flat-leaf (Italian) parsley
4 thin lemon slices, to garnish

stud the onion with the cloves and put into a large saucepan with 1.5 litres (6 cups) water. Add the carrot, bay leaf and chicken and season with salt and freshly ground black pepper. Slowly bring to the boil, then reduce the heat and simmer for 10 minutes, or until the chicken is cooked.

strain the stock into a clean saucepan, reserving the chicken and discarding the vegetables. Add the rice to the stock, bring to the boil, then reduce the heat and simmer for 15 minutes, or until the rice is tender. Meanwhile, tear the chicken into shreds.

whisk the egg whites in a clean, dry bowl until stiff peaks form, then beat in the yolks. Slowly beat in the lemon juice. Gently stir in about 150 ml (5 fl oz) of the hot (not boiling) stock and beat thoroughly. Add the egg mixture to the stock and heat gently, but do not let it boil otherwise the eggs may scramble. Add the chicken and season with salt and ground black pepper.

set aside for 2–3 minutes to allow the flavours to develop, then sprinkle the soup with the parsley. Garnish with the lemon slices. Serves 4 (or 6 as a starter).

citrus tart

to make the pastry, sift the flour and a pinch of salt into a large bowl. Make a well in the centre and add the butter, egg yolk and icing sugar. Work them together with your fingertips, then slowly incorporate the flour. Bring together into a ball—you may need to add a few drops of cold water. Flatten the ball slightly, cover with plastic wrap and refrigerate for 20 minutes.

preheat the oven to 200°C (400°F/Gas 6). Lightly grease a shallow 20 cm (8 inch) loose-bottomed flan tin.

roll the pastry out between 2 sheets of baking paper to an even thickness to fit the base and side of the tin. Put in place, then trim the edge. Chill for 10 minutes. Line the pastry with crumpled baking paper, fill with baking beads or rice and bake for 10 minutes, or until cooked. Remove the paper and beads or rice and bake for 6–8 minutes, or until the pastry looks dry all over. Cool the pastry and reduce the oven to 150°C (300°F/Gas 2).

whisk the eggs, yolks and sugar together, add the cream and juice and mix well. Strain into a jug and add the zest. Put the flan tin on a baking tray on the middle shelf of the oven and carefully pour in the filling. Bake for 40 minutes, or until just set—it should wobble in the middle when the tin is firmly tapped. Cool before removing from the tin.

wash and scrub the lemons well. Slice very thinly. Combine the sugar and 200 ml (7 fl oz) of water in a small frying pan and stir over low heat until the sugar has dissolved. Add the lemon slices and simmer over low heat for 40 minutes, or until the peel is very tender and the pith looks transparent. Lift out of the syrup and drain on baking paper. If serving the tart immediately, cover the surface with the lemon slices. If not, keep the slices covered and decorate the tart when ready to serve. Serve with whipped cream, if desired. Serves 6–8.

pastry

- **125 g (1 cup) plain (all-purpose) flour**
- **75 g (2½ oz) unsalted butter, softened**
- **1 egg yolk**
- **2 tablespoons icing (confectioners') sugar, sifted**

filling

- **3 eggs**
- **2 egg yolks**
- **185 g (heaped ¾ cup) caster (superfine) sugar**
- **125 ml (½ cup) cream**
- **185 ml (¾ cup) lemon juice**
- **1½ tablespoons finely grated lemon zest**
- **2 small lemons**
- **160 g (⅔ cup) sugar**

olives and olive oil

choosing and using olives

Olives differ in colour according to their stage of ripeness. Mostly, however, olives are classed as either green or black. Green ones are immature olives and are hard and very bitter. Black olives are fully mature and plump. Both types are inedible straight from the tree and need to be cured. In parts of the Mediterranean, the wild bitter green olives are considered by some to be a delicacy, but most olives are cured, then preserved in oil or brine with flavourings added. If possible, buy loose olives and ask to taste one first—it's the best way to guarantee the quality—and choose fresh plump olives; dried ones should be wrinkled but still shiny and healthy looking.

Apart from being an essential part of a selection of appetizers, olives are at home in stews and pasta sauces, in pastes such as Provençal tapenade and in salads and added to breads. Eastern Mediterranean cooks tend not to use olives in cooking.

It is quite remarkable that the olive tree—always dry and parched-looking, seemingly grimly clinging to life on rocky and barren soils—is one of the three cornerstones of Mediterranean cooking and culture (the other two being wheat and vine). But it is true: the tree, which is native to the Eastern Mediterranean, was first cultivated as early as 3000BCE in Syria and Palestine, and its bounty has never long been absent from the tables and kitchens across the region.

olive types

italian olives The glossy black Gaeta olives from Liguria are considered to be among the finest of Italy's eating olives. Others to look for are the salty black olives from Lazio and large Sicilian green ones.

kalamata olives Hailing from Kalamata in the southern Peloponnese, these almond-shaped olives are among Greece's best due to their fruity, rich flavour and firm flesh. Packed in either olive oil or wine vinegar to accentuate their robust taste, they are often found on a mezze plate, and in salads, sauces and breads.

niçoise olives These small and ripe olives range in colour from purple and brown to black. Cured in brine and often packed in olive oil, they are an integral part of Provençal cuisine, where they are eaten as a table olive and also added to beef stews, poultry stuffing, savoury tarts such as pissaladière and to salads such as Niçoise.

spanish olives These are served in different guises in every tapas bar in Spain. Well-known ones include Sevillanas, Mansanillas and Gordals, which are mostly served marinated. Others are stuffed with almonds, anchovies or pimientos, or stuffed and crumbed then deep-fried.

marinated olives

150 g (5½ oz) Kalamata olives
150 g (5½ oz) good-quality green olives
185 ml (¾ cup) extra virgin olive oil
2 rosemary sprigs

2 teaspoons thyme leaves
2 small red chillies, seeded
several strips lemon zest
2 garlic cloves, bruised
½ teaspoon fennel seeds
2 thyme sprigs, extra

put the olives, oil, rosemary, thyme, chillies, lemon zest, garlic and fennel in a large saucepan and warm over low heat. Transfer to a bowl and marinate overnight at room temperature.

remove the olives from the oil with a slotted spoon and discard the herbs, reserving the oil. Add the extra thyme to the olives before serving. Makes 300 g (10½ oz).

tapenade

process all the ingredients together in a food processor until they form a smooth consistency. Season with freshly ground black pepper. Spoon into a sterilized, warm jar, seal and refrigerate for up to 2 weeks. Makes 375 ml (1½ cups).

notes: To prepare a sterilized storage jar, preheat the oven to 120°C (250°F/Gas ½). Wash the jar and lid in hot soapy water and rinse with hot water. Put the jar in the oven for 20 minutes, or until fully dry. Do not dry with a tea towel.

If refrigerated, the olive oil may solidify, making it white. This will not affect the flavour of the dish. Bring to room temperature before serving and the oil will return to a liquid state.

400 g (14 oz) Kalamata olives, pitted
2 garlic cloves, crushed
2 anchovy fillets in oil, drained
2 tablespoons capers in brine, rinsed and squeezed dry
2 teaspoons chopped thyme
2 teaspoons Dijon mustard
1 tablespoon lemon juice
60 ml (¼ cup) olive oil
1 tablespoon brandy, optional

This Provençal olive, anchovy and caper paste was invented in Marseilles only in the nineteenth century, but it has quickly established itself as a classic appetizer. It is delicious served with fresh or toasted bread and makes an excellent stuffing for hard-boiled eggs.

The term 'à la niçoise' refers to dishes typical of Nice and its surrounding area that contain tomatoes, olives, anchovies and garlic. A debate rages over what should feature in a *salade niçoise*—apart from egg, purists prefer to use only raw ingredients.

salade niçoise

4 small new potatoes (about 300 g/10½ oz)
12 small green beans, topped, tailed and halved
4 tablespoons olive oil
200 g (7 oz) tuna steak, cubed
1 garlic clove, crushed
½ teaspoon Dijon mustard
1 tablespoon white wine vinegar
a couple of handfuls of green lettuce leaves
6 cherry tomatoes, halved
8 Niçoise olives
1 tablespoon capers, drained
2 hard-boiled eggs, cut into wedges
4 halved anchovies
lemon wedges

cook the potatoes in boiling salted water for about 10 minutes, or until they are just tender. Drain, cut them into wedges, then put into a bowl. Cook the beans in boiling salted water for 3 minutes, then drain and refresh under cold running water for a minute (this will stop them cooking any further). Add them to the potatoes.

heat 1 tablespoon of the olive oil in a frying pan and, when it is hot, add the tuna cubes and cook for 3 minutes, or until they are browned on all sides. Add the cubes to the potatoes and beans.

whisk together the garlic, mustard and vinegar, then add the remaining oil in a thin, steady stream, whisking until smooth. Season well. You can also do this by putting all the dressing ingredients in a screw-top jar (with the lid on) and shaking it for a minute.

cover the base of a large bowl with the lettuce leaves. Scatter the potatoes, beans, tuna, tomatoes, olives and capers over the leaves, then drizzle with the dressing. Decorate with the egg wedges and anchovies. Squeeze some lemon juice over the salad. Serves 2.

flavours and health benefits

Olive oil is a perfect example of the way in which an ingredient or dish will be found throughout the Mediterranean, seemingly the same but actually differing slightly but surely from one region to another. French oils are known for their light, floral qualities, the Spanish oils for being sweet or aromatic, and the Greek oils for their robust, bold flavours. Colour is no indication of quality—the best way to discover which is your favourite variety is by tasting and comparing.

Apart from its many culinary uses, olive oil also comes with numerous health benefits: it is cholesterol-free, and actually helps reduce 'bad' cholesterol; is high in 'good' monounsaturated fats; and is high in vitamin E. Generally, the better the olive oil, the greater its health benefits.

olive oil

Anyone who has ever dipped a piece of bread into a bowl containing nothing more than some good-quality olive oil and a dash of balsamic vinegar and been amazed at how good it is, will understand the Mediterranean love of good olive oil. Connoisseurs of the oil discuss it in much the same way that wine connoisseurs discuss their favourite beverage. Like wine, the flavour, colour and taste of olive oil varies according to the type of fruit used and the climate, soil and area of cultivation. Generally, green olives give grassy, green oils, while ripe black olives produce rich, yellow oils. Less ripe olives produce green oil that pales after three months and is considered superior. However, riper olives yield more oil. Some olive trees are grown to produce olives for eating and some for oil—they are not harvested from the same trees.

From left to right: extra light olive oil, pure olive oil from Greece, virgin olive oil from Spain and extra virgin olive oil from Italy.

types of olive oil

Olive oils can be divided into four major groups, which are distinguished by their level of acidity.

extra virgin olive oil This is the highest quality oil, made from the first pressing of olives, with the lowest acidity level at less than 1 per cent. This oil has an intense, fruity flavour. It can only be extracted mechanically or manually cold pressed, without using heat or chemicals, so the oil is not altered. This oil is reserved for making salad dressings or drizzled over tomatoes, bocconcini and basil leaves or on food such as pasta where its flavour can be best appreciated.

virgin olive oil This has a good flavour and is treated and extracted in the same way as extra virgin olive oil. However, it has an acidity level of less than 2 per cent. It is used in much the same way as extra virgin olive oil is.

olive oil Also known as pure olive oil, this is a blend of unrefined virgin olive oil and refined virgin olive oil, and has an acidity level of less than 3.3 per cent. The use of heat to aid extraction contributes to the higher level of acidity. It can be used in cooking.

light olive oil This is made from the filtered combination of refined olive oil with very small amounts of virgin olive oil. Despite popular belief, it isn't light in kilojoules (calories), as it has exactly the same amount as other oils. It is lighter than other olive oils in texture and taste, making it ideal for baking. It has a high smoking point so is also excellent for deep-frying.

basic vinaigrette

2 tablespoons lemon juice
4 tablespoons extra virgin
   olive oil
2 teaspoons finely chopped
   onion or 1 finely chopped
   French shallot
1 tablespoon chopped
   flat-leaf (Italian) parsley

make the dressing by combining all the ingredients. Season with salt and freshly ground black pepper. Makes 185 ml (3/4 cup).

basic mayonnaise

2 egg yolks
1 teaspoon Dijon mustard
450 ml (16 fl oz) olive oil
2 tablespoons lemon juice

beat the egg yolks, then add the mustard and whisk for 1 minute. Slowly add the olive oil in a thin stream while continuing to beat. When the mayonnaise begins to thicken, start adding the oil more rapidly, still beating well after each addition. When all the oil has been added, beat in the lemon juice and some salt and pepper. Store covered in the refrigerator for up to 4 days. Makes approximately 450 ml (16 fl oz).

oranges

Many houses and buildings in Spain feature internal courtyards and patios adorned with orange trees, a custom dating back more than 1000 years to the era of Arab rule in Spain. One of the first examples of this is *El Patio de Los Naranjos*, the Courtyard of the Oranges built in AD976 in Córdoba, and constructed by the Arab rulers to recreate in Spain the environments and foods of their homelands. Originally, only the bitter orange was cultivated in the Mediterranean. It was used as a perfume and in cooking; medieval cookbooks feature it in a tangy sauce for fish. It wasn't until the late fifteenth century that sweet oranges arrived from China with Portuguese traders. Today oranges, and their relatives kumquats and clementines, are readily available.

types of oranges

bitter Seville is the best-known variety of the bitter orange. It has a thick rind, tough membrane and lots of seeds, and is usually reserved for making marmalade and jellies. The aromatic oils extracted from the skin are used to make Grand Marnier, Cointreau and Curaçao.

blood These have lots of red pigment in the flesh and skin. They are rich, sweet and aromatic but their season is short. Sicily is a big grower of blood oranges; Jaffa, originally from Palestine, are a related variety.

navel So called because of a navel-like depression at the base. These oranges have a slightly pebbly skin and bright orange colour and are nearly always seedless. Good for desserts or eating fresh.

sweet These oranges have smoother, firmer skin than the navel and more seeds. They are ideal for juicing. Varieties include Valencia.

carrot and orange salad

2 oranges
2 carrots, grated
½ red onion, sliced
100 g (²/₃ cup) pitted black olives
2 tablespoons chopped coriander (cilantro) leaves
2 tablespoons orange juice
3 tablespoons good-quality olive oil

cut a thin slice from each end of both oranges. Using a small sharp knife, slice off the skin and pith, removing as much pith as possible. Slice down the side of a segment between the flesh and the membrane. Repeat on the other side and lift the segment out. Do this over a bowl to catch the juice. Repeat with all the segments.

put the orange segments in the bowl of juice, and add the grated carrots. Add the onion, olives and coriander. Mix well. Whisk the juice and olive oil together, then add to the salad and gently mix. Serves 4.

culinary uses

Today, the bitter orange is reserved mainly for use in marmalades or in specific dishes such as duck à l'orange. Its oils are important in liqueurs and its blossoms are distilled to make orange flower water. Throughout the Mediterranean, the various sweet oranges are eaten fresh, added to raw vegetable salads, used in sorbets and granitas, squeezed for their juice, or valued for their aromatic zest, which is used in savoury dishes such as meat and fish stews and soups, and also in desserts and baking. Peeled whole oranges are poached in syrups or boiled and puréed for cakes such as Spanish *tarta de naranja*.

When buying, choose oranges that feel heavy and have tight skin. Store at room temperature for a day or so, then store in the refrigerator after this time.

clementines in brandy

wash enough small clementines to fill a 2 litre (8 cup) jar. Dissolve 1 kg (2 lb 4 oz) sugar in 1 litre (4 cup) water, bring to the boil and simmer for 5 minutes. Prick the fruit all over with a needle, then add the fruit to the syrup. Simmer for 1 hour, remove the fruit from the syrup and put in the jar. Simmer the syrup until thick, then add 500 ml (2 cups) brandy. Allow to cool, then pour over the fruit. Leave the fruit to infuse for 1 week before eating. Makes 2 litres (8 cups).

macerated oranges

4 oranges
1 teaspoon grated lemon zest
3 tablespoons caster (superfine) sugar
1 tablespoon lemon juice
2 tablespoons Cointreau or Maraschino (optional)

cut a thin slice off the top and bottom of the oranges. Using a small sharp knife, slice off the skin and pith, removing as much pith as possible. Slice down the side of a segment between the flesh and the membrane. Repeat on the other side and lift the segment out. Do this over a bowl to catch the juice. Repeat with all the segments. Squeeze out any juice remaining in the membranes.

put the segments on a shallow dish and sprinkle with the lemon zest, sugar, lemon juice and saved orange juice. Toss carefully. Cover and refrigerate for 4 hours. Toss again. If you wish, add the liqueur just before serving. Serves 4.

spanish orange and almond cake

grease and lightly flour a 23 cm (9 inch) springform cake tin, tipping out any excess flour. Wipe 2 of the oranges with a damp cloth to remove any dirt. Put them into a saucepan full of water and boil for 2 hours, topping up the water as it evaporates. Remove the oranges.

preheat the oven to 180°C (350°F/Gas 4). Cut the cooked oranges into quarters and place in a food processor. Process until smooth, then allow to cool.

put the egg yolks, orange flower water and caster sugar in a large bowl and beat until smooth, then stir in the orange purée and mix well. Whisk the egg whites in a clean, dry bowl until firm peaks form.

add the ground almonds and baking powder to the orange mixture, stir together well, then carefully fold in the egg whites. Pour into the prepared cake tin and cook for 1 hour. Cover the cake with foil if it is browning too quickly. Cool the cake in the tin before transferring it to a serving plate.

meanwhile, to make the syrup, put the orange juice, sugar and Sauternes in a saucepan over medium heat and stir until the sugar is dissolved. Reduce the heat and simmer for about 20 minutes, or until reduced by half and slightly syrupy, skimming off any scum that forms on the surface. The syrup will thicken as it cools.

peel the remaining 3 oranges and remove all pith and sinew. Cut each orange into thin slices. Decorate the cake with orange slices and drizzle with the syrup. Serve with cream if you like. Serves 6–8.

5 large sweet oranges
6 eggs, separated
1 tablespoon orange flower water
250 g (1 cup) caster (superfine) sugar
300 g (3 cups) ground almonds
1 teaspoon baking powder
cream, to serve (optional)

orange syrup
500 ml (2 cups) fresh orange juice, strained
185 g (3/4 cup) caster (superfine) sugar
60 ml (1/4 cup) Sauternes

peaches

The Mediterranean summer brings with it juicy white and orange peaches. The best and only way to determine which is the season's best is to try both.

Even a brief glance at Mediterranean food reveals layers of history. A Sicilian word for peach, *pérsichi,* actually means 'Persian', and this fruit, though probably originally from China, did arrive in Italy via Persia. Italy is still the primary grower and consumer of peaches in the Mediterranean; among the various varieties, white-fleshed peaches are considered to be the best for eating. In cooking, the fragrant, sweet, juicy fruit is used in sorbets and tarts and as a purée.

peach and campari sorbet

100 g (3 1/2 oz) caster (superfine) sugar
100 ml (3 1/2 fl oz) Campari, grappa or brandy
1.5 kg (3 lb 5 oz) ripe peaches
juice of 2 large lemons

heat the sugar and Campari in a small saucepan over low heat until the sugar has dissolved.

blanch the peaches in boiling water, refresh in cold water, then peel. Cut the flesh off the stones and chop. Purée the peaches in a food processor or blender, or push the flesh through a sieve. Pour the purée into a bowl (you should have about 1 litre/4 cups), add the Campari and lemon juice and mix thoroughly. Taste a little to check the balance between sweetness and bitterness. If too sweet, add more fruit purée or lemon juice; if too bitter, add more sugar dissolved in water.

churn in an ice cream machine according to the manufacturer's instructions. Alternatively, pour into a metal or plastic freezer box and freeze, whisking every 30 minutes to break up the ice crystals and give a creamy texture. Once set, freeze until ready to serve. Serves 6–8.

pears

This teardrop-shaped fruit, with its juicy white flesh, is a popular ingredient in Spanish and French cooking. Most varieties eaten today are the results of crosses developed in the seventeenth and eighteenth century in Europe and America, as growers tried to develop a variety that was free of the tiny, hard grains that made pears gritty. Varieties include Conference, Beurre Bosc, William Bartlett and Comice.

poached pears in saffron citrus syrup

1 vanilla bean, split lengthways
½ teaspoon saffron threads
185 g (¾ cup) caster (superfine) sugar
2 teaspoons grated lemon zest
4 pears, peeled
whipped cream, to serve (optional)
biscotti, to serve (optional)

put the vanilla bean, saffron threads, sugar, lemon zest and 500 ml (2 cups) of water in a large saucepan and mix together well. Heat over low heat, stirring constantly, until the sugar has dissolved. Bring to the boil, then reduce to a gentle simmer.

add the pears and cook, covered, for 12–15 minutes, or until tender when tested with a metal skewer. Turn the pears over with a slotted spoon halfway through cooking. Once cooked, remove the pears from the syrup with a slotted spoon.

remove the lid and bring the syrup to the boil. Cook for 10 minutes, or until the syrup has reduced by half and thickened slightly. Remove the vanilla bean and drizzle the syrup over the pears. Serve with whipped cream and a couple of pieces of biscotti. Serves 4.

culinary uses

The Spanish use pears in a spiced sauce that is traditionally served with duck, a dish known as *pato con peras*. In French cooking, pears feature in tarts, desserts and compotes, and are also poached with spices and wine. Pears are also classic accompaniments to cheese and cured meats such as prosciutto.

pine nuts

There are many species of pine tree, but only a few produce seeds big enough to warrant harvesting for food. In the Mediterranean, Italy has traditionally been the key centre for pine nut production; a labour-intensive process. The 'nut', actually the kernel, is found inside the pine cone, which must be heated to release the nuts. The nuts must then be extracted from their hard shell before going to market. Pine nuts have a rich texture with a sweet 'piney' taste. They may be eaten raw but the flavour is enhanced when roasted or fried. Because the nuts are high in oil, they burn quickly when heated. For the same reason, they also go rancid quickly, so buy them in small quantities.

culinary uses

Pine nuts are extensively used in both sweet and savoury Middle Eastern dishes, combining well with ingredients such as lamb, rice, spinach, honey, raisins and eggplant (aubergine). They are an essential part of stuffings, pastries and cakes, often appearing in the sweet-sour combinations that are so typical of Arabian-influenced cooking. Elsewhere, cooks in both the Languedoc region of southern France and Lebanon make an omelette featuring pine nuts, and Italian pesto would not be the same without these creamy nuts.

roast chicken stuffed with pine nuts, rice and sultanas

preheat the oven to 180°C (350°F/Gas 4). Pour half the butter into a large frying pan, then add the onion and cook for 5 minutes over medium heat until the onion is transparent. Stir in the allspice.

add the rice and nuts to the pan, then cook for 3–4 minutes over medium-high heat. Add the sultanas, stock and 60 ml (¼ cup) of water. Bring to the boil, then reduce the heat and simmer for 8–10 minutes, until the water is absorbed. Allow to cool.

rinse the cavity of the chicken with cold water and pat dry inside and out with paper towels. When the stuffing is cool, spoon it into the cavity. Truss the chicken with string, then put in a deep baking dish. Rub ½ teaspoon salt and ¼ teaspoon freshly ground black pepper into the skin using your fingertips.

pour the rest of the butter over the chicken, then add the stock to the baking dish. Roast for 2 hours 10 minutes, basting every 25 minutes with juices from the pan. Allow the chicken to rest for 15 minutes before carving. Serve with the stuffing. Serves 4–6.

note: To clarify butter, melt it in a saucepan over low heat, then remove from the heat and let the milk solids drop to the base. Only use the yellow liquid part of the butter. Discard the white milk solids at the base of the pan.

stuffing

- **60 g (2¼ oz) clarified butter or ghee, melted**
- **1 onion, chopped**
- **1 teaspoon ground allspice**
- **65 g (⅓ cup) long-grain white rice**
- **30 g (¼ cup) chopped walnuts**
- **50 g (⅓ cup) pine nuts**
- **60 g (½ cup) sultanas**
- **125 ml (½ cup) chicken stock**

- **1.6 kg (3 lb 8 oz) chicken**
- **170 ml (⅔ cup) chicken stock**

pistachios

pistachio nut crème brûlée

500 ml (2 cups) cream
35 g (¼ cup) finely chopped pistachio nuts
½ vanilla bean, halved lengthways
½ teaspoon grated orange zest
125 g (heaped ½ cup) caster (superfine) sugar
5 egg yolks
pistachio biscotti (optional), to serve

preheat the oven to 140°C (275°F/Gas 1). Put the cream, pistachio nuts, vanilla bean, orange zest and 50 g (1¾ oz) of the sugar in a pan over medium heat and stir to dissolve the sugar, then slowly bring to the boil. Remove from the heat and leave to infuse for 10 minutes.

whisk the egg yolks and 50 g (1¾ oz) of the sugar together in a bowl. Strain the cream mixture into a jug, then add to the egg mixture, stirring continuously.

ladle the egg custard into six 125 ml (½ cup) ramekins and put in a baking dish. Carefully pour in enough cold water to come halfway up the side of the ramekins, then put in the oven and cook for 1 hour, or until the custard has set and is only just wobbly. Remove from the oven and transfer to a wire rack to cool, then refrigerate for 4 hours.

preheat the grill (broiler) to very hot. Sprinkle 1–2 teaspoons of the remaining sugar over the top of each brûlée. Put the brûlées in a roasting tin full of ice, then put the tin under the grill for 4 minutes, or until the tops have caramelized. Remove the ramekins from the roasting tin and dry around the outside edges with a tea towel.

refrigerate for 1–2 hours only, then serve with a couple of pieces of pistachio biscotti if you like and some fresh fruit. Serves 6.

This yellow-green nut, encased in a hard, pale shell, is much prized in the Mediterranean, particularly in Turkey. As the nuts mature, the shells open slightly, revealing the nuts inside. Pistachios have a delicate flavour and are eaten roasted and salted, or used in salads, stuffings and pâtés. They are also added to and sprinkled over cakes and syrupy pastries, and used to flavour ice creams.

pomegranates

Encountering this ancient fruit for the first time is something of a voyage of discovery: the size of a large apple, it has a thick, tough reddish skin that encloses hundreds of edible seeds, each encased in translucent-red juicy pulp, and surrounded by a bitter white pith. The fruit was highly regarded in ancient Greek and Roman, Persian and Islamic traditions.

culinary uses

Sour and sweet pomegranate varieties exist: the sour ones were originally used as a souring agent before lemons arrived, and are still seen in marinades and tangy sorbets. The seeds and juice of the sweet pomegranate are used in fruit salads and drinks and the seeds make an excellent garnish on sweet and savoury dishes.

sweet saffron rice

1 teaspoon saffron threads
110 g (½ cup) medium-grain white rice
250 g (heaped 1 cup) caster (superfine) sugar
2 tablespoons rose water
3 tablespoons toasted pine nuts, chopped
3 tablespoons pistachios, chopped
pomegranate seeds and extra pistachios, to garnish

gently crush the saffron threads between your fingers and soak in 2 tablespoons of boiling water for 30 minutes. Add 1.25 litres (5 cups) water to a large saucepan and bring to the boil, then add the rice. Reduce to a simmer and cook, stirring occasionally, for 20 minutes. Stir in the sugar, rose water and the saffron with the soaking liquid and simmer for another 10 minutes. Add the nuts, and gently simmer for 10 minutes more. The mixture should be thick and soupy. If it is too thick, add a little more water. Serve either hot or cold. Garnish with pomegranate seeds and pistachios and serve with yoghurt. Serves 6.

using pomegranates

These fruit have only a relatively short season in autumn, so buy them when you can. Choose ones that are heavy for their size, with smooth skin that gives slightly when pressed. If you are after the fresh juice, cut the fruit in half with a sharp knife and scoop out the tangy-sweet seeds, then separate them from the white pith—a time consuming exercise. Gently press to extract the juice. Otherwise, use pomegranate concentrate, a perfectly good alternative.

quinces

A fragrant relative of the apple, quinces were held sacred by the ancient Greeks who considered them the fruit of Aphrodite, goddess of love. Golden when ripe, and often coated in a soft grey down, their flesh is firm, dryish and rarely softens sufficiently to eat raw. However, when baked in foil, stewed or poached, the flesh becomes meltingly soft, can turn a golden pink and the delicate flavour and perfume is enhanced. Thus transformed, it becomes easy to see why quinces have long been symbols of love, happiness and fertility.

culinary uses

Quinces contain large amounts of pectin, so are particularly good for making jams, preserves and pastes such as Spanish *membrillo*. The French make quince into a clear jelly called *cotignac*, and the Italians make a similar paste known as *cotognata*. However, quinces do have other uses. In the Arabian-influenced parts of the Mediterranean, they are added to savoury dishes such as Moroccan lamb tagines and are also poached with sugar and spices for lovely aromatic desserts. When buying quinces choose the smoother, larger varieties as these are easier to prepare and less wasteful. Quinces will keep for several months.

membrillo

wash 3 large quinces, put in a saucepan, cover with water and simmer for 30 minutes, or until tender. Drain. Peel and core the quinces then push them through a sieve or potato ricer. Weigh the fruit pulp, place in a heavy-based saucepan and add the same weight of sugar. Cook over low heat, stirring occasionally with a wooden spoon, for 3½–4½ hours, or until very thick. Pour into a shallow 28 x 18 cm (11 x 7 inch) tin lined with plastic wrap. Allow to cool. Quince paste can be kept for several months in a tightly sealed container. Serve with cheese (try the salty Spanish cheese manchego), on toast or with game such as pheasant.

poached quinces on brioche

2 large quinces
345 g (1½ cups) caster (superfine) sugar
1 vanilla bean
1 cinnamon stick
1 cardamom pod
8 slices brioche
butter, for brioche
ground cinnamon and sugar, to serve

peel the quinces, core and cut into quarters. Pour 350 ml (12½ fl oz) water into a saucepan, add the sugar and spices and bring to the boil. When the sugar has dissolved add the quinces, cover and simmer for 2–3 hours, or until very tender. Remove the quinces and vanilla and simmer the cooking liquid to a syrup, then strain. Toast the brioche, butter, sprinkle with cinnamon and sugar and top with poached quinces. Drizzle some syrup over the top and serve hot or cold. Serves 8.

walnuts

Walnuts are thought to have originated in ancient China or Persia. In many countries of the Mediterranean, the word for walnut is also the general word for nut and, indeed, walnuts do seem multi-purpose, appearing in all sorts of dishes, from sauces to elaborate pastries.

culinary uses

Walnuts are especially popular in Turkish, Syrian and Italian cooking. Their uses are numerous: in sweet dishes they feature in cakes, biscuits, breads and pastries such as baklava; and in savoury dishes appear in salads, stuffings, pasta sauces, dips, pâtés and a French walnut soup. The green walnuts are pickled in spiced vinegar and served with meat or cheese, and in Italy they are used to make a digestif called nocino. While the shells are still soft, the immature green walnuts can be eaten whole. In the Middle East, half-ripe walnuts are preserved in sugar syrup. Walnuts are also ground into flour or pressed to produce a richly flavoured, but expensive, oil.

Tarator, a garlicky nut sauce, is eaten from Turkey to Egypt. It is served as a dip with bread, or served over fish, chicken or fried vegetables.

walnut tarator

250 g (9 oz) shelled walnuts
80 g (1 cup) fresh white breadcrumbs
3 garlic cloves
60 ml (¼ cup) white wine vinegar
250 ml (1 cup) olive oil
chopped flat-leaf (Italian) parsley, to garnish

finely chop the walnuts in a blender or food processor. Set aside ½ teaspoon of the walnuts for a garnish. Add the breadcrumbs, garlic, vinegar and 3 tablespoons water to the rest and blend well.

with the motor running, gradually add the olive oil in a thin steady stream until smooth. Add a little more water if the sauce appears to be too thick. Season to taste, then transfer to a serving bowl, cover and refrigerate. Combine the reserved walnuts and parsley and sprinkle on top before serving. Serve with seafood, chicken, fried vegetables or bread. Serves 8.

selecting and using walnuts

Walnuts in the shell are far superior in taste to those shelled and packaged. When buying walnuts in the shell, choose ones that are free of cracks and holes. Store in a cool dry place for up to 3 months. Shelled walnuts should be plump and crisp when you buy them. Store in an airtight container in the refrigerator for around 6 months. After toasting walnuts, leave them until they are completely cold before chopping or grinding or they will become oily.

tagliatelle with walnut sauce

lightly toast the walnuts in a dry frying pan over moderately high heat for 2 minutes, or until browned. Set aside to cool for 5 minutes.

put the walnuts in a food processor with the parsley and blend until finely chopped. Add the butter and mix together.

gradually add the olive oil in a thin, steady stream, keeping the motor running. Add the garlic, Parmesan cheese and the cream. Season with salt and black pepper.

cook the pasta in a large saucepan of boiling salted water until *al dente*. Drain, then toss through the sauce to serve. Serves 4.

200 g (7 oz) shelled walnuts
20 g (3/4 oz) roughly chopped parsley
50 g (13/4 oz) butter
200 ml (7 fl oz) extra virgin olive oil
1 garlic clove, crushed
35 g (1/3 cup) grated Parmesan cheese
100 ml (31/2 fl oz) thick (double/heavy) cream
400 g (14 oz) tagliatelle

catch of the day

anchovies and sardines

Fresh anchovies can come as a surprise to many of us who half believe that anchovies only exist in tinned or bottled forms. Each year in spring, however, along the coasts of Italy, France, Spain and especially Turkey, there is much excitement at the start of the anchovy fishing season. Sardines, too, take their place on Mediterranean menus at this time. Anchovies and sardines are both members of the herring family, and are classic staples of easy summer cooking. Abundant, cheap and versatile, they are eaten fresh, marinated, cooked or salted and preserved. The herring family also includes tiny whitebait. These juvenile fish come from a variety of families, depending on where they are fished, though they are usually from the herring family.

These tiny whitebait specimens are juvenile fish. They are fried and eaten whole as snacks.

anchovies

Most anchovies are tinned or bottled, preserved in either salt or oil. Anchovies preserved in salt have a far superior flavour and texture than those in oil, and are also larger and left whole. However, they are not always available. If buying anchovies in oil, choose ones preserved in olive oil, rather than vegetable oil, for their fuller flavour. If using salt-preserved anchovies, wash the salt off under running water or soak in milk for 15 minutes. Remove the fillets from the bone using your fingers.

culinary uses

Fresh anchovies are usually simply prepared: grilled (broiled), fried or marinated, or even eaten raw with just a little lemon juice squeezed over. Fresh or preserved anchovies feature in a number of pastes and sauces, such as *anchoïade*, and are also served with pasta, pizza and on *pissaladière*, the well-known onion tart from Nice. Traditionally this featured pissala, an anchovy paste, hence its name.

marinated fresh anchovies

400 g (14 oz) very fresh anchovies
60 ml (¼ cup) olive oil
1 tablespoon extra virgin olive oil
3 tablespoons lemon juice
2 garlic cloves, crushed
2 tablespoons finely chopped parsley
2 tablespoons finely chopped basil
1 small red chilli, seeded and chopped

fillet the anchovies by running your thumbnail or a sharp knife along the backbone, then pulling the head upwards. The head, bones and guts should all come away together, leaving you with the fillets. Carefully wash under cold water and pat dry with paper towels. Put the fillets in a shallow serving dish.

mix all the remaining ingredients together with some salt and pepper and pour over the anchovies. Cover with plastic wrap and marinate in the refrigerator for at least 3 hours before serving. Serve with some bread to mop up the juices. The dish can be kept refrigerated for up to 3 days. Serves 4.

anchoïade

85 g (3 oz) anchovy fillets in oil **1 teaspoon thyme leaves**
2 garlic cloves **3 teaspoons chopped parsley**
14 black olives, pitted **olive oil**
1 small tomato **8 slices baguette**

put the anchovy fillets (with their oil), garlic, olives, tomato, thyme, 1 teaspoon chopped parsley and a generous grinding of black pepper in a mortar and pestle or food processor and pound or mix until you have a coarse paste. Add a little extra olive oil if the paste is very thick—it should have a spreadable consistency.

preheat the grill (broiler) and lightly toast the baguette slices on both sides until golden brown. Spread the anchoïade over the baguette and sprinkle with the remaining parsley. Serves 4.

This pungent anchovy paste hails from the south of France and is a typical feature of Provençal cooking. It can be served as a dip, used as a pasta topping or sauce, or spread on bread, fish and chicken and then grilled (broiled).

sardines

Small oily-fleshed fish, sardines have a distinctive strong flavour and can vary considerably in size. Different varieties of sardine are caught all over the world but some of the best are found in the Mediterranean. Superb summer fish, sardines are often barbecued outdoors over coals, which allows the skin to develop a wonderful crispiness, and the smell to seduce passerbys. Sardines are also excellent stuffed—a favourite technique of French, Italian and Moroccan cooks. The French also use sardines in a layered dish, known as a *tian*, which is a speciality of the Côte Niçoise. Sardines are best eaten very fresh as their flesh deteriorates quite quickly.

barbecued sardines

8 fresh sardines
2 tablespoons olive oil
3 tablespoons lemon juice
½ lemon, halved and thinly sliced
lemon wedges

slit the sardines along their bellies and remove the guts. Rinse well and pat dry. Use scissors to cut out the gills.

mix together the oil and lemon juice and season generously with salt and black pepper. Brush the inside and outside of each fish with the oil, then put a few lemon slices into each cavity.

put the sardines onto a preheated chargrill pan (griddle) or under a very hot grill (broiler) and cook, basting with the remaining oil, for 3 minutes each side until cooked. Serve with lemon wedges. Serves 4.

moroccan stuffed sardines

100 g (½ cup) long-grain white rice
2 tablespoons olive oil
25 g (1 oz) dried apricots, chopped into
　small pieces
25 g (1 oz) raisins
1 tablespoon flaked toasted almonds
1 tablespoon chopped parsley
1 tablespoon chopped mint
grated zest of 1 orange
2 tablespoons freshly squeezed orange juice
1 teaspoon finely chopped preserved lemon rind
1 teaspoon ground cinnamon
½ teaspoon harissa (see page 206)
16 whole large sardines, butterflied
16 large fresh or preserved vine leaves
250 ml (1 cup) Greek-style natural yoghurt, to serve

cook the rice in boiling water until it is tender. Drain and transfer to a bowl. Add the olive oil, the apricots, raisins, almonds, parsley, mint, orange zest and juice, preserved lemon, cinnamon and the harissa. Season with salt and freshly ground black pepper, and mix together.

divide the stuffing among the sardines, folding the 2 fillets of each fish together to enclose the rice mixture (save any extra stuffing to serve with the sardines). Bring a pan of water to the boil and, in batches, blanch the vine leaves for 30 seconds at a time. Pat dry on crumpled paper towels. If you are using preserved vine leaves, rinse and dry them. Wrap a vine leaf firmly around each sardine and secure with a toothpick. Use 2 toothpicks per roll if necessary.

preheat a grill (broiler) or barbecue. Cook the sardines for 6 minutes, turning them over halfway through. Serve each one with a dollop of yoghurt and any extra rice stuffing. Makes 16.

1 Mix together all the stuffing ingredients, using a light action.

2 Fold the fillet over, taking care not to press too hard.

3 Wrap a vine leaf around the fillet and secure with a toothpick.

the cod family

Cod itself is usually available salted, not fresh, in the Mediterranean. Other members of the cod family are more likely to feature as fresh fish, including hake (particularly favoured in Spain), pollack, whiting and ling. These fish have flaky white flesh with little fat and so form an essential part of the fish pies, stews and soups that are found all along the Mediterranean coast. They are also eaten as cutlets and fillets, such as in the Greek *plaki* dishes, which consist of fish and vegetables baked together. A similar style of dish from Turkey, *pilakisi*, is served cold. Most fish in the cod family can be substituted for each other in recipes.

everyday fresh fish

Mediterranean recipe books often do not specify a particular fish, or if they do, give half a dozen or more to chose from. This is because fish is customarily bought fresh from markets and shoppers will be guided by what is available and appealing on the day. Fish are seasonal creatures, and supplies will vary according to spawning seasons and fishing patterns. Thus recipes will allow for flexibility as regards the choice of fish. The following pages serve as an introduction only to some of the more typical fish, cooking techniques and dishes of the Mediterranean.

greek-style baked fish with tomato and onion

60 ml (¼ cup) olive oil
2 onions, finely chopped
1 small celery stalk, finely chopped
1 small carrot, finely chopped
2 garlic cloves, chopped
400 g (14 oz) tin chopped tomatoes
2 tablespoons tomato passata
¼ teaspoon dried oregano

½ teaspoon sugar
55 g (2 oz) one-day old white bread
500 g (1 lb 2 oz) cod fillet or steak, or any other white fish such as snapper
3 tablespoons chopped flat-leaf (Italian) parsley
1 tablespoon lemon juice

preheat the oven to 180°C (350°F/Gas 4). Heat 2 tablespoons of oil in a heavy-based frying pan. Add the onion, celery and carrot and cook over low heat for 10 minutes, or until soft. Add the garlic, cook for 2 minutes, then add the chopped tomato, passata, oregano and sugar. Simmer for about 10 minutes, stirring occasionally, until reduced and thickened. Season to taste.

to make the breadcrumbs, chop the bread in a food processor for a few minutes until fine crumbs form.

arrange the fish in a single layer in a large baking dish. Stir the chopped parsley and the lemon juice into the sauce. Season the sauce with salt and freshly ground black pepper, then pour over the fish. Scatter the breadcrumbs all over the top and drizzle with the remaining oil. Bake for 20 minutes, or until the fish is just cooked. Serves 4.

inshore fish

As their name suggests, these fish live relatively close to the shore and include a number of well-known species such as John Dory, monkfish, red mullet, sea bass and sea bream, as well as the Mediterranean's most elusive fish, the spiny scorpion fish rascasse. Inshore fish generally have a delicate flavour and are best cooked on the bone, as the fillets are usually small due to the amount of waste (bones). As with most fish, the method of fishing is important, as fish that have been caught by hand, rather than line trawled, are far less likely to have been bruised in the process. In the case of inshore fishing, however, small boats have the advantage over bigger ones, and they are more likely to use hand lines, thus sparing the fish.

monkfish

This dramatically ugly fish is usually sold as a tail because this is where the meat is (in France the monkfish tail is referred to as a *gigot*—leg of lamb—due to its shape). The tail is skinned, then grilled (broiled) or roasted. The Spanish are fond of monkfish, known there as *rape*, and add it to paella and stews, or cook it with sherry and garlic. Its most famous use is in the flamboyant Catalan stew *zarzuela*, whose name aptly means operetta. This dish is an excellent introduction to the cooking of Catalan, in Spain's northeast, as it involves both sofrito and picada, two classic elements of the region's cooking. A sofrito is a flavour base for soups and stews. It means literally to 'under-fry' and the mixture should be sweated rather than coloured. The picada is an almond and garlic paste, always worked in at the end of the cooking.

catalan zarzuela

to make the sofrito base, heat the oil in a large flameproof casserole dish on the stovetop. Add the onion and cook, stirring, for 5 minutes, without letting it brown. Add the tomato, tomato paste and 125 ml (½ cup) water and gently stir for a further 10 minutes. Stir in another 125 ml (½ cup) water, season and set the dish aside.

to make the picada sauce, finely chop the bread, toasted almonds and garlic in a food processor or by hand. With the motor running, or continuously stirring, very gradually add the oil to form a paste.

preheat the oven to 180°C (350°F/Gas 4). Cut the lobster tail into rounds through the membrane that separates the shell segments, then set aside. Cut the fish fillets into bite-sized pieces and lightly coat them in flour. Heat the oil in a large frying pan and fry the fish in batches over medium heat for 2–3 minutes, or until cooked and golden brown all over. Transfer to the casserole dish with the sofrito.

add a little oil to the pan if necessary, add the squid and cook, stirring, for 1–2 minutes. Remove and add to the fish. Cook the lobster and prawns for 2–3 minutes, or until just pink, then add to the casserole. Add the wine to the pan and bring to the boil. Reduce the heat, add the mussels, cover and steam for 4–5 minutes. Add to the casserole, discarding any unopened mussels.

pour the brandy into the pan, ignite and when the flames have died down, pour over the seafood. Mix, cover and bake for 20 minutes. Stir in the picada sauce and cook for another 10 minutes, or until warmed through—do not overcook, or the seafood will toughen. Sprinkle with the parsley. Serves 4–6.

sofrito base
- 1 tablespoon olive oil
- 2 onions, finely chopped
- 2 large tomatoes, peeled, seeded and chopped
- 1 tablespoon tomato paste (purée)

picada sauce
- 3 slices white bread, crusts removed
- 1 tablespoon almonds, toasted
- 3 garlic cloves
- 1 tablespoon olive oil

- 1 raw lobster tail (weighing about 400 g/14 oz)
- 750 g (1 lb 10 oz) monkfish fillets, skinned
- plain (all-purpose) flour, seasoned with salt and black pepper
- 2–3 tablespoons olive oil
- 125 g (4½ oz) squid, cleaned and cut into rings
- 12 large prawns (shrimp)
- 125 ml (½ cup) dry white wine
- 12–15 mussels, cleaned
- 125 ml (½ cup) brandy
- 3 tablespoons chopped parsley

the mediterranean fish stew

There are numerous wonderful fish stews found throughout the Mediterranean, bouillabaisse being just one. The Greeks make *kakavia*, named after the three-legged cooking pot taken by ancient Ionians on their fishing expeditions; from Liguria comes *zuppa di pesce*; *caldillo de perro* (dog's broth) hails from Cádiz; and *brodetto*, another fish broth, is found all along Italy's coasts. Customarily, *kakavia* is made on the boat, the fishermen having brought with them a mixture of onions, tomatoes, potatoes, lemons and various flavourings, with bread to mop up the juices. The fish will be a mixture of whatever small, unmarketable fish is caught that day. Today, these stews seem anything but a simple meal, championing as they do the use of a great many different fish and shellfish, but they still carry a real sense of the Mediterranean with them. In all, improvisation is the key, with subtlety in the cooking: a good cook will manage to combine the flavours without masking any.

Conger eel is a seawater eel with a meaty texture and flavour. Tail cutlets are bony and usually made into soup, but middle or neck cut sections are good for baking and roasting.

rascasse

This is a sweet, firm-fleshed fish that is rarely found outside the Mediterranean, but is said to impart the true flavour of bouillabaisse, the famous fisherman's soup from the south of France and, in particular, from Marseille. Indeed, cooks in Marseille believe that it is not worth making the soup without it. Given that a properly made bouillabaisse should contain up to seven different types of fish, it's hard to believe that excellent results won't still occur, but rascasse is described as having a special, unique taste and smell. It is worth noting that if you do find a fishmonger who stocks rascasse, ask him or her to fillet it for you as the spines are poisonous.

bouillabaisse

rouille
- 1 small red pepper (capsicum)
- 1 slice white bread, crusts removed
- 1 red chilli
- 2 garlic cloves
- 1 egg yolk
- 80 ml (⅓ cup) olive oil

soup
- 18 mussels
- 1.5 kg (3 lb 5 oz) mixed firm white fish fillets such as sea bass, red mullet, snapper, monkfish, rascasse, John Dory or eel, skin on
- 2 tablespoons oil
- 1 fennel bulb, thinly sliced
- 1 onion, chopped
- 750 g (1 lb 10 oz) ripe tomatoes
- 1.25 litres (5 cups) fish stock or water
- pinch saffron threads
- bouquet garni
- 5 cm (2 inch) piece of orange zest

to make the rouille, preheat the grill (broiler). Cut the pepper in half, remove the seeds and membrane and put, skin-side-up, under the hot grill until the skin blackens and blisters. Leave to cool before peeling away the skin. Roughly chop the pepper.

soak the bread in 3 tablespoons water, then squeeze dry with your hands. Put the pepper, chilli, bread, garlic and egg yolk in a mortar or food processor and pound with a pestle or mix together. Gradually add the oil in a thin stream, pounding or mixing until the rouille is smooth and has the texture of thick mayonnaise. Cover and refrigerate the rouille until needed.

Cut the various fish fillets into even-sized, chunky pieces.

to make the soup, scrub the mussels and remove their beards. Discard any mussels that are already open and don't close when tapped on the work surface. Cut the fish into bite-sized pieces.

heat the oil in a large saucepan and cook the fennel and onion over medium heat for 5 minutes, or until golden.

score a cross in the base of each tomato. Put into boiling water for 20 seconds, then plunge in cold water. Drain and peel the skin away from the cross. Chop the tomatoes, discarding the cores. Add to the pan and cook for 3 minutes. Stir in the stock, saffron, bouquet garni and orange zest, bring to the boil and boil for 10 minutes. Remove the bouquet garni and either push the soup through a sieve or purée in a blender. Return to the cleaned pan, season and bring back to the boil.

reduce to a simmer and add the fish and mussels. Cook for 5 minutes, or until the fish is tender and the mussels have opened. Discard any mussels that haven't opened in this time. Serve with the rouille and bread or lift out the fish and mussels and serve separately. Serves 6.

migratory fish

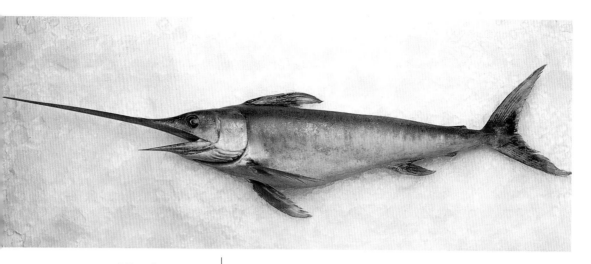

swordfish

Fishermen from southern Italy, Sardinia and Sicily have a long history of hunting swordfish, traditionally chasing these big predator fish each year at spawning time in sleek boats, the men lying in wait with harpoons. Worryingly, today's mass fishing has resulted in a serious decline in swordfish numbers—and of predator fish generally—which needs to be considered when choosing fish. Traditionally, this mild-flavoured, meaty fish has been served with strong flavours such as olives and capers, and prepared on skewers for kebabs or in Italian *involtini*.

note: To prevent wooden skewers from burning during cooking, soak them in cold water for 20 minutes before using.

involtini of swordfish

1 kg (2 lb 4 oz) swordfish, skin removed, cut into four 4 x 5 cm (1½ x 2 inch) pieces
3 lemons
80 ml (⅓ cup) olive oil
1 small onion, chopped
3 garlic cloves, chopped
2 tablespoons chopped capers
2 tablespoons finely chopped pitted Kalamata olives
35 g (⅓ cup) grated Parmesan cheese
120 g (1½ cups) fresh white breadcrumbs
2 tablespoons chopped flat-leaf (Italian) parsley
1 egg, lightly beaten
24 bay leaves
2 small white onions, quartered and separated into pieces
lemon wedges, to serve

cut each swordfish piece horizontally into 4 slices to give 16 slices altogether. Put each piece between 2 pieces of plastic wrap and roll gently with a rolling pin to flatten the fish without tearing it. Cut each piece in half to give 32 pieces altogether.

wipe clean the lemons, then peel the zest from them with a vegetable peeler and cut it into 24 even pieces. Squeeze the lemons until you have 60 ml (¼ cup) juice.

heat 2 tablespoons olive oil in a frying pan, add the onion and garlic, and cook for 2 minutes, or until soft and translucent. Put in a bowl with the capers, olives, Parmesan, breadcrumbs and parsley. Season, add the egg and mix to bind.

divide the stuffing among the fish pieces and, with oiled hands, roll up the fish to form neat parcels. Thread 4 rolls each onto 8 skewers, alternating with the bay leaves, lemon zest and onion.

mix the remaining oil with the lemon juice. Barbecue or grill (broil) the skewers for 3–4 minutes each side, basting with the oil and lemon mixture. Serve with lemon wedges. Serves 4.

moroccan tuna skewers
with chermoula

800 g (1 lb 12 oz) tuna steaks, cut into 3 cm (1¼ inch) cubes
2 tablespoons olive oil
½ teaspoon ground cumin
2 teaspoons finely grated lemon zest

chermoula

½ teaspoon ground coriander
3 teaspoons ground cumin
2 teaspoons paprika
pinch cayenne pepper
4 garlic cloves, crushed
15 g (½ cup) chopped flat-leaf (Italian) parsley
25 g (½ cup) chopped coriander (cilantro)
80 ml (⅓ cup) lemon juice
125 ml (½ cup) olive oil

if using wooden skewers, soak them in cold water for at least 20 minutes to prevent them from burning during cooking.

put the tuna in a shallow non-metallic dish. Combine the oil, cumin and lemon zest and pour over the tuna. Toss to coat, then cover and marinate in the refrigerator for 10 minutes.

meanwhile, to make the chermoula, put the coriander, cumin, paprika and cayenne pepper in a small frying pan and cook over medium heat for 30 seconds, or until fragrant. Combine with the remaining chermoula ingredients and set aside.

thread the tuna onto the skewers. Lightly oil a chargrill pan (griddle) or barbecue and cook the skewers for 1 minute on each side for rare or 2 minutes for medium. Serve the skewers on a bed of couscous with the chermoula drizzled over the tuna. Serves 4.

tuna

The highly prized migratory bluefin tuna passes through the Straits of Gibraltar to spawn in the Mediterranean Sea and thus provides the basis for a long-standing tuna industry around the Spanish Andalusian coast and the waters around Sicily and Turkey. Fresh tuna has a dark meaty flesh that is delicious both raw and cooked. The better tasting red flesh indicates that the tuna was caught by hand, killed and bled quickly, while muddy-brown flesh means the fish drowned and so probably was caught by net. Tuna is eaten raw in tuna carpaccio; skewered and barbecued; grilled (broiled) as a steak and topped with the Sicilian version of ratatouille, *caponata*; or added to salads such as Niçoise salad.

octopus, squid and cuttlefish

These cephalopods, meaning heads with feet, are very popular summer foods in Italy, Greece, Tunisia and Spain. Octopus, in particular, is one of the classic culinary pleasures of Mediterranean coastal life and is simply cooked on a chargrill pan (griddle), stewed or braised and added to fresh, light salads. Squid, the most versatile of the three species, is generally served deep-fried, sometimes stuffed first, or stewed with onions and tomatoes. In Greece squid is stewed with wine and herbs, while the Italians and Spanish tend more towards grilling (broiling) it, accompanying it with a salsa verde or picada sauce. From Italy, too, comes risotto nero, which features the squid or cuttlefish ink. Cuttlefish, known as *sepia* in Spain, is cooked there *a la plancha*, on a hot plate, flavoured with sea salt, parsley and garlic. All three species appear on antipasto seafood platters.

preparing and using

octopus Buy small octopus if you can find them—they are far more tender than the large ones. If only large are available, tenderize them by beating with a rolling pin before cooking. In some coastal regions, you can see octopus being tenderized in a cement mixer. Otherwise, long boiling will also do the trick.

squid and cuttlefish Available both whole and as cleaned tubes, squid come in varying sizes; cuttlefish are about 25 cm (10 inches) long. If buying squid or cuttlefish for their ink, check before buying as it may not be available. Instead, buy sachets of ink from fishmongers and delicatessens—they are easier to use and have a long shelf life.

note: The general rule for cooking these cephalopods is that they should either be cooked for a very short time or for a very long time, but nothing in between, as that causes the seafood to toughen. Barbecuing, chargrilling (griddling) or frying take only minutes, otherwise stew for 1 hour or more.

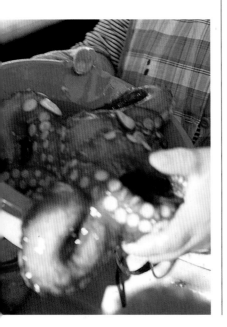
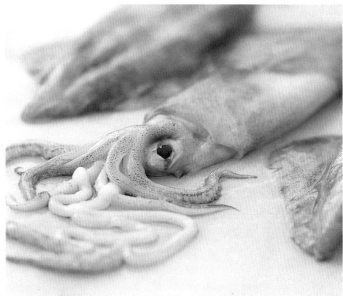

chargrilled octopus

16 small octopus (about 1.5 kg/3 lb 5 oz)
170 ml (²/₃ cup) extra virgin olive oil
4 thyme sprigs
2 bay leaves
2 garlic cloves, crushed
lemon wedges, to serve

clean the octopus by slitting the head and pulling out the innards. Cut out the eyes and hard beak and rinse. Skin the octopus tentacles and make small diagonal cuts along their length, cutting about a third of the way through the tentacle. Put in a bowl and pour over the oil. Add the thyme, bay leaves and garlic and toss well. Cover with plastic wrap and marinate in the refrigerator overnight. Leave 4 wooden skewers to soak in water for 20 minutes.

heat the chargrill pan (griddle) or a barbecue. Drain the excess oil from the octopus and thread onto the skewers. Cook for 5–7 minutes on each side or until the octopus is golden and the tip of a knife slips through a tentacle. Season with salt and pepper and drizzle with some extra virgin olive oil if you like. Leave for a few minutes and then serve with lemon wedges. Serves 4.

Marinate the octopus in the fresh herbs, overnight if possible.

shellfish

This term refers to any aquatic animal covered by a shell. In the Mediterranean, common shellfish include clams; mussels; scallops; oysters; crustaceans such as lobsters and prawns (shrimp); and sea urchins. It is interesting to note that many of the recipes for fish and shellfish in the Mediterranean can be divided roughly into two sorts—those quick, simple recipes involving grilling (broiling) or frying, and the more elaborate ones that may ask for half a dozen different fish and various flavourings. Plentiful fish such as clams, mussels, salted cod, sardines and anchovies belong to 'cucina povera', while lobsters, scallops and seasonal fish are more likely to be seen in the dishes of the wealthier townsfolk.

clams

There are many species of clams available in the Mediterranean (interchangeable in most recipes), but they are generally classified as either hard- or soft-shelled. Certain species are only found locally, such as the smooth-shelled clams, *telline* in France, and the hard-shelled razor clam, *navaja*, popular in Spain. Clams are eaten with pasta, in tapas dishes such as *almejas a la marinera*, and in stews and broths.

almejas a la marinera

1 kg (2 lb 4 oz) clams
2 large, ripe tomatoes
2 tablespoons olive oil
1 small onion, finely chopped
2 garlic cloves, crushed

1 tablespoon chopped flat-leaf (Italian) parsley
pinch nutmeg
80 ml (1/3 cup) dry white wine

soak the clams in salted water for 1 hour to release any grit. Rinse under running water and discard any open clams.

score a cross in the base of each tomato. Put in a bowl of boiling water for 20 seconds, then plunge into cold water. Drain and peel away from the cross. Cut the tomatoes in half, scoop out the seeds and chop.

heat the oil in a flameproof casserole and cook the onion over low heat for 5 minutes. Add the garlic and tomato and cook for 5 minutes. Stir in the parsley and nutmeg. Add 80 ml (1/3 cup) water. Add the clams and cook over low heat until they open. Discard any that don't open. Add the wine and cook over low heat for 3–4 minutes, gently stirring, until the sauce thickens. Serve with bread. Serves 4.

mussels

Sometimes referred to as 'poor man's oyster', mussels are nevertheless full of flavour. Mussels attach themselves to rocks or, if farmed mussels, to bags or ropes, gripping with their tough brown fibres known as the 'beard'. Farmed mussels take up to two years to mature. The French consume great amounts of these shellfish, mostly farmed ones grown on wooden posts in the northeast of the country, and dishes such as *moules marinières* and *moules frites* are now famed the world over. Mussels are also stuffed, and added to soups and seafood salads.

moules marinières

2 kg (4 lb 8 oz) mussels
50 g (1¾ oz) butter
1 large onion, chopped
½ celery stalk, chopped
2 garlic cloves, crushed
400 ml (14 fl oz) white wine

1 bay leaf
2 thyme sprigs
225 ml (7½ fl oz) thick
  (double/heavy) cream
2 tablespoons chopped
  parsley

scrub the mussels and remove their beards. Discard any that are open already and don't close when tapped on the work surface. Melt the butter in a large saucepan and cook the onion, celery and garlic, stirring occasionally, over moderate heat until the onion is softened but not browned.

add the wine, bay leaf and thyme to the saucepan and bring to the boil. Add the mussels, cover the pan tightly and simmer over low heat for 2–3 minutes, shaking the pan occasionally. Use tongs to lift out the mussels as they open, putting them into a warm dish. Discard any that haven't opened after 3 minutes.

strain the liquid through a fine sieve into a clean saucepan, leaving behind any grit or sand. Bring to the boil and boil for 2 minutes. Add the cream and reheat the sauce without boiling. Season well. Serve the mussels in individual bowls with the liquid poured over. Sprinkle with the parsley and serve with plenty of bread. Serves 4.

buying and using clams and mussels

When buying clams or mussels, look for ones with tightly closed shells. Discard any that are dead (the shell should close if tapped). Before cooking, soak the clams or mussels in salted water for at least 1–2 hours to purge the shellfish of any grit. Both only require gentle and brief cooking, otherwise they will be tough and chewy. Once cooked, discard any that haven't opened.

Above, from left to right: prawn (shrimp), lobster, clams and mussels.

prawns

Tapas, little dishes to accompany a drink, are served in bars throughout Spain, ranging from the simple to the exquisite. Prawns lend themselves perfectly to this sort of eating and Spain offers a number of dishes that feature them. Two favourites are *gambas al pil pil*, prawns with chilli and garlic, and *gambas al ajillo*, garlic prawns, both of which are traditionally served in the dish in which they are prepared in, a small cast iron or glazed terracotta pot. Prawns are also barbecued and served with romesco sauce and added to salads and antipasto platters.

Fresh prawns should always have a pleasant sea smell and a nice sheen or gloss. The shells should be quite firm to the touch. Avoid any that smell of ammonia, or have dark discolouration around the head and legs, as these are early signs of deterioration.

Also known as – shrimp

spanish garlic prawns

20 large raw prawns (shrimp)
60 ml (¼ cup) olive oil
85 g (3 oz) butter
½ red chilli, finely chopped
10 garlic cloves, crushed
60 ml (¼ cup) white wine
3 tablespoons chopped parsley

peel and devein the prawns, leaving the tails intact if you like. Put the olive oil in a large frying pan and add the butter, chilli and half the garlic. Cook, stirring, for 3 minutes. Add the prawns and sprinkle with the remaining garlic.

cook for 3 minutes or until the prawns are pink. Turn the prawns over, add the wine and cook for another 4 minutes. Add the parsley, season well with salt and pepper and serve with bread. Serves 4.

scallops

These pretty little creatures are associated with the legend of St James (St Iago in Spanish) and pilgrims to the Saint's cathedral in Santiago de Compostela in Spain traditionally wore the shells as badges on their journey. Though fresh scallops are more expensive than frozen, they have a beautiful mild flavour and are well worth the cost. When buying fresh scallops, look for plump, moist ones with a creamy-white translucent flesh. If the roe is attached, it should be plump and brightly coloured.

scallops with goat's cheese and crispy prosciutto

4 thin slices prosciutto
16 scallops on shells, thoroughly cleaned and roes removed
2–3 tablespoons extra virgin olive oil
1 tablespoon chopped flat-leaf (Italian) parsley
100 g (3½ oz) goat's cheese, crumbled
2 tablespoons good-quality aged balsamic vinegar

cook the prosciutto under a hot grill (broiler) until crisp, then drain on paper towels and break into small pieces.

put the scallops on two baking trays. Combine the oil and parsley in a small bowl and season with sea salt and freshly ground black pepper. Brush the scallops with the oil mixture.

cook the scallops in batches under a hot grill (broiler) for 2–3 minutes, or until they are tender. Do not overcook.

top the scallops with the crumbled goat's cheese and prosciutto, then drizzle with balsamic vinegar. Carefully transfer the scallops from the trays to serving plates lined with rock salt—the shells will be very hot. Serves 4 as a starter.

mixed seafood platter

There is little that surpasses a selection of seafood, either fresh or fried, to begin a special meal with. Frying fish and shellfish is almost an art form in Andalucia in Spain, and is also a hallmark of southern Italian cooking. Vary the selection according to availability but try to stick to Mediterranean varieties. Though demanding some effort, a dish like this captures the Mediterranean in one, indulgent sweep.

fritto misto di mare

250 g (9 oz) baby squid
12 large raw prawns (shrimp)
8 small octopus
16 scallops, cleaned
12 fresh sardines, gutted and heads removed
250 g (9 oz) firm white fish fillets such as ling, cod
  or snapper, skinned and cut into large cubes

oil, for deep-frying
lemon wedges

garlic and anchovy sauce

125 ml (½ cup) extra virgin olive oil
2 garlic cloves, crushed
3 anchovy fillets, finely chopped
2 tablespoons finely chopped parsley
pinch chilli flakes

batter

210 g (1⅔ cups) plain (all-purpose) flour
80 ml (⅓ cup) olive oil
1 large egg white

preheat the oven to 140°C (275°F/Gas 1). Clean the squid by pulling the heads and tentacles out of the bodies, along with any innards. Cut the heads off below the eyes, just leaving the tentacles. Discard the heads and set the tentacles aside. Rinse the bodies, pulling out the clear quills, and cut the bodies into rings. Peel and devein the prawns, leaving the tails intact.

clean the octopus by slitting the head and pulling out the innards. Cut out the eyes and hard beak and rinse. If the octopuses seem a bit big, cut them into halves or quarters.

to make the sauce, warm the oil in a frying pan. Add the garlic, anchovy, parsley and chilli flakes. Cook over low heat for 1 minute, or until the garlic is soft but not browned. Serve warm or chilled.

to make the batter, sift the flour into a bowl and stir in ¼ teaspoon salt. Mix in the oil with a wooden spoon, then gradually add 315 ml (1¼ cups) tepid water, changing to a whisk when the mixture becomes liquid. Continue whisking until the batter is smooth and thick. Stiffly whisk the egg white and fold into the batter. Heat the oil in a deep-fryer or deep frying pan to 190°C (375°F), or until a piece of bread fries golden brown in 10 seconds when dropped in the oil.

dry the seafood on paper towels so the batter will stick. Working with one type of seafood at a time, dip the pieces in batter. Shake off the excess batter, then carefully lower the fish into the oil. Deep-fry for about 3 minutes, depending on the size of the pieces. Drain on paper towels, then transfer to the oven. Do not crowd the seafood. Keep warm while you fry the remaining seafood. Serve the seafood immediately with the lemon wedges and the sauce. Serves 4.

Buy direct from the fishmarkets prawns and whatever firm white fish looks good on the day, for example snapper, cod or sea bream.

whole-cooked fish

culinary uses

Mediterranean fish is baked whole in a number of ways—with vegetables such as peppers (capsicums) and potatoes; stuffed with dried dates and spices; or marinated in a coriander or tahini spice paste. In Morocco, whole fish is often cooked in an earthenware tagine set over charcoal, with saffron, ginger, cinnamon and other spices added, creating a wonderfully aromatic dish. In Spain and Italy, vast quantities of salt are used to form a fully sealed crust around the fish. The salt seals in the moisture and steams the fish, without making it salty.

A number of fish in the Mediterranean lend themselves to being cooked whole as their firm, lean flesh holds together well. Examples are snapper and grouper, both reef fish, and red mullet, sea bass and sea bream, all inshore fish. Sea bass is large enough to feed several people and contains relatively few bones, so is generally considered suitable for special occasions. Sea bream is also highly valued, both for its excellent flavour and its beautiful golden markings.

fish baked in salt

1.8 kg (4 lb) whole fish such as sea bass, grouper, blue-eye, scaled and cleaned
2 lemons, sliced
4 thyme sprigs
1 fennel bulb, thinly sliced
3 kg (6 lb 8 oz) rock salt

preheat the oven to 200°C (400°F/Gas 6). Rinse the fish and pat dry inside and out with paper towel. Put the lemon, thyme and fennel inside the cavity.

pack half the salt into a large baking dish and put the fish on top. Cover with the remaining salt, pressing down until the salt is packed firmly around the fish.

bake the fish for 30–40 minutes, or until a skewer inserted into the centre of the fish comes out hot. Carefully remove the salt from the top of the fish to one side of the pan. Peel the skin away, ensuring that no salt remains on the flesh. Serve hot or cold with aïoli or your choice of accompaniment. Serves 4–6.

red mullet

This is a prized fish in the Mediterranean, an appreciation that goes back to Roman times. There are two varieties: one striped, the other mottled, though these days stocks of both are sadly depleted and the days of the big two-pounders are over, at least for now. The lovely red skin retains its colour when cooked, making it attractive for grilling (broiling) whole. Red mullet is traditionally cooked with its liver intact and its delicate flesh combines well with Moroccan flavourings such as chermoula or preserved lemon, with a nutty tarator sauce, bitter chicory, or with herbs such as rosemary and oregano.

whole red mullet with fennel

2 fennel bulbs
2 tablespoons butter
2 tablespoons extra virgin olive oil, plus extra, for brushing
1 onion, chopped
1 garlic clove, crushed
4 red mullet, gutted and scaled
1 lemon, quartered
2 teaspoons chopped oregano or ½ teaspoon dried oregano
lemon wedges, to serve

preheat the oven to 190°C (375°F/Gas 5) and lightly grease a large shallow ovenproof dish. Finely slice the fennel, reserving the feathery green fronds.

heat the butter and olive oil in a large frying pan and gently cook the fennel, onion and garlic for 12–15 minutes until softened but not browned. Season with salt and pepper.

stuff each fish with a heaped tablespoon of the fennel mixture and a quarter of the fennel fronds. Brush with extra virgin olive oil, squeeze a lemon quarter over each one and season well.

spoon the remainder of the cooked fennel into the dish and sprinkle with half of the oregano. Arrange the fish, side by side, on top. Sprinkle the remaining oregano over the fish and cover the dish loosely with foil. Bake for 25 minutes, or until just cooked through. Serve with lemon wedges. Serves 4.

Lightly brush the prepared fish with good-quality olive oil.

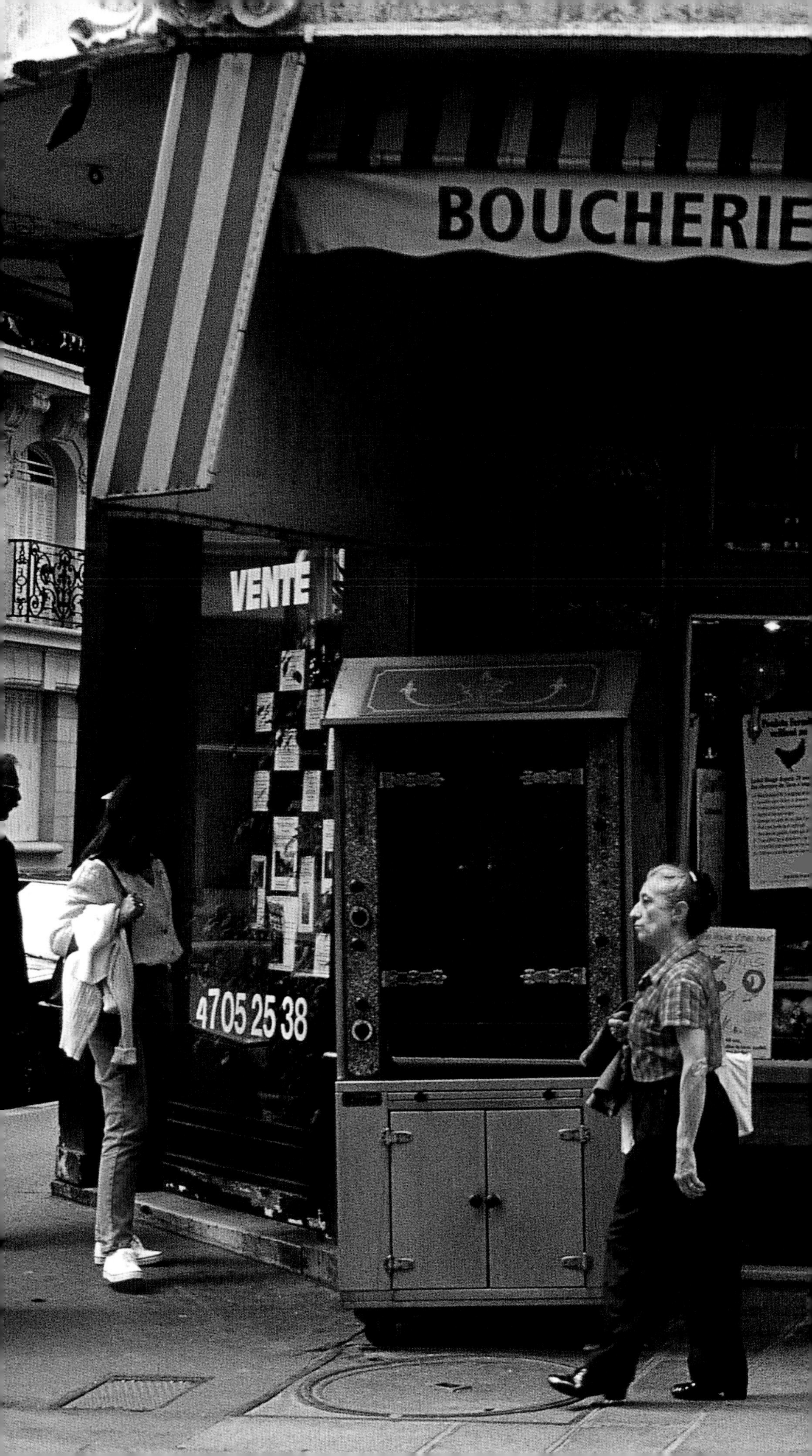
BOUCHERIE
VENTE
47 05 25 38

select cuts

beef

With only limited land suitable for raising cattle, beef does not form a large part of the Mediterranean diet. It is common in the cooking of only a few areas: southern France, northern Italy and parts of Spain. Even in these areas it has generally been used carefully and sparingly. For example, in numerous small dishes, such as in stuffed tomatoes and rice croquettes; in meatballs; and in various pasta fillings or sauces, such as Bolognese sauce. Luxurious dishes have developed, however, and from Provence hails one such dish, *boeuf en daube*. This warming winter dish gets its name from the *daubière*, the squat earthenware dish in which it was traditionally cooked.

boeuf en daube

1.5 kg (3 lb 5 oz) chuck steak, cut into 3 cm (1¼ inch) cubes
2 tablespoons olive oil
1 small onion, sliced
375 ml (1½ cups) red wine
2 tablespoons chopped flat-leaf (Italian) parsley
1 tablespoon chopped rosemary
1 tablespoon chopped thyme
2 bay leaves
250 g (9 oz) speck, rind removed, cut into 1 x 2 cm (½ x ¾ inch) pieces
400 g (14 oz) tin crushed tomatoes
250 ml (1 cup) beef stock
500 g (1 lb 2 oz) baby carrots
45 g (⅓ cup) pitted Niçoise olives

put the cubed beef, 1 tablespoon of the oil, the onion, 250 ml (1 cup) of wine and half the herbs in a bowl and combine. Cover with plastic wrap and marinate in the refrigerator overnight.

drain the beef, reserving the marinade. Heat the remaining oil in a heavy-based saucepan and brown the beef and onion. Set aside.

add the speck to the saucepan and cook for 3–5 minutes, until crisp. Return the beef and onion to the pan with the remaining wine and marinade and cook, scraping the residue from the base of the pan for 2 minutes, or until the wine has slightly reduced. Add the tomato and stock and bring to the boil. Reduce the heat and add the remaining herbs. Season well, cover and simmer for 1½ hours.

add the carrots and olives to the saucepan and cook, uncovered, for 30 minutes, or until the meat is tender. Season, if necessary. Serves 6.

Ranging from the scrawny to the lovingly plump, chickens bring a raucous presence to markets across the Mediterranean. They have been domesticated in the region since ancient Roman times and, though expensive until relatively recently, have been eaten by rich and poor alike, as either regular or special occasion fare. Mediterraneans until recently have largely been spared the unsatisfactory state of meat from intensively reared chickens—the meat is usually firm and full of flavour and in rural areas in particular most chicken will be corn-fed.

chicken

spanish-style chicken casserole

2 tablespoons light olive oil
750 g (1 lb 10 oz) chicken
   thighs
750 g (1 lb 10 oz) chicken
   drumsticks
1 large onion, chopped
2 garlic cloves, crushed
2 teaspoons sweet paprika
1 red pepper (capsicum), sliced

200 ml (7 fl oz) dry sherry
400 g (14 oz) tin peeled
   tomatoes
2 tablespoons tomato paste
   (purée)
165 g (3/4 cup) pitted and
   halved green olives
1 teaspoon sweet paprika,
   extra

preheat the oven to 180°C (350°F/Gas 4). Heat the oil in a large frying pan, add the chicken in batches and cook over medium heat for 3–4 minutes, or until browned. Transfer to a 4 litre (16 cup) flameproof casserole dish. Add the onion, garlic, paprika and red pepper to the frying pan and cook for 5–8 minutes, or until softened. Add the sherry and cook for 2 minutes, or until slightly reduced. Add the tomato and tomato paste, stir well and cook for a further 2 minutes. Pour the tomato mixture over the chicken and add 250 ml (1 cup) water.

bake, covered, for 1 hour 15 minutes, then uncovered for 15 minutes more. Add the olives and leave for 10 minutes. Garnish with the extra paprika and serve with rice. Serves 4.

culinary uses

Chicken is used in a multitude of dishes, from soups and pies to paella and casseroles. The flavourings in a chicken dish can reveal much about the origins of the recipe: chicken with figs, for example, is a speciality of Greece; in Morocco preserved lemon and olives are typical companions, as are almonds, pine nuts and raisins; while sherry is a famed Andalusian ingredient. In southern France and Italy, garlic, rosemary and tarragon are more typical. Chickens are prepared in various ways—roasted, fried and slow-cooked in tagines and stews. In the Eastern Mediterranean, chickens are often split down the middle and grilled (broiled) over coals outdoors or cooked as kebabs and eaten in pitta bread wraps with sumac sprinkled over.

circassian chicken

2 teaspoons paprika

¼ teaspoon cayenne
     pepper

1 tablespoon walnut oil

4 chicken breasts, on the
     bone

4 chicken wings

1 large onion, chopped

2 celery stalks, roughly
     chopped

1 carrot, chopped

1 bay leaf

4 parsley sprigs

1 thyme sprig

6 peppercorns

1 teaspoon coriander seeds

250 g (9 oz) walnuts, toasted

2 slices white bread, crusts
     removed

1 tablespoon paprika, extra

4 garlic cloves, crushed

put the paprika and the cayenne pepper in a small dry frying pan and heat over low heat for about 2 minutes, or until aromatic, then add the walnut oil to the pan and set aside until ready to use.

put the chicken in a large saucepan with the onion, celery, carrot, bay leaf, parsley, thyme, peppercorns and coriander seeds. Add 1 litre (4 cups) of water and bring to the boil. Reduce the heat to low and simmer for 15–20 minutes, or until the chicken is tender. Remove from the heat and allow to cool in the stock. Remove the chicken and return the stock to the heat. Simmer for 20–25 minutes, or until reduced by half. Strain, skim off the fat and reserve the stock. Remove the chicken skin and shred the flesh into bite-sized pieces. Put the flesh into a bowl, season well and ladle some stock over it to moisten it. Set aside.

reserve a few of the walnuts to use as a garnish and blend the rest in a food processor to form a rough paste. Mix the bread with 125 ml (½ cup) stock, add to the food processor and mix in short bursts for several seconds. Add the extra paprika, the garlic and some salt and pepper and process until smooth. Gradually add 250 ml (1 cup) warm chicken stock until the mixture is of a consistency smooth enough to pour, adding a little more stock if necessary.

mix half the sauce with the chicken, then transfer to a serving platter. Pour the rest over to cover, then sprinkle with spiced walnut oil and the remaining walnuts. Serve at room temperature. Serves 6.

Circassian chicken, *çerkez tavuğu*, hails from the culinary legacy of the Circassian women from the North Caucasus who were part of the Sultan's harem during the days of the Ottoman Empire. It is now a much-loved classic of Turkish cuisine.

culinary uses

Apart from Morocco, pigeon is also a favourite of Egyptians, who raise the birds for food and as carrier birds. They serve it stuffed with pine nuts, raisins and grains such as freekeh. Duck is popular throughout the Mediterranean for its dark, moist and richly flavoured meat. Fruit is often used to balance its richness: in eastern areas it is served with a walnut and pomegranate sauce and in Spain it is combined with pears. In France it is used in a variety of dishes such as duck à l'orange and duck confit. Cooks in Greece specialize in quail, protecting its delicate flesh by wrapping it in vine leaves, then baking or barbecuing it. Rabbit is mostly farmed these days, and has a milder flavour than wild rabbit or hare, which is always wild. It is most commonly found in the cooking of Spain, Provence and North Africa.

quails wrapped in vine leaves

4 rosemary sprigs	**1 tablespoon balsamic vinegar**
4 quails	**2 teaspoons brown sugar**
2 tablespoons olive oil	**4 large vine leaves**

preheat the oven to 180°C (350°F/Gas 4). Stuff a rosemary sprig into each quail and then gently tie its legs together. Tuck the wings behind the back.

heat the olive oil in a large frying pan and add the quails. Brown them all over and then add the vinegar and sugar. Cook, allowing the sauce to bubble, for a few minutes. Remove from the heat.

blanch the vine leaves in boiling water for 15 seconds and then wrap one leaf around each quail. Put the wrapped quail in a roasting tin, seam-side-down, and bake for 15 minutes. Serves 4.

game

While chicken has become everyday fare in much of the Mediterranean, other birds and game still retain their status as rare and occasional treats only. This group includes duck and geese, pigeon, quail, pheasant, venison and rabbit, even wild boar. The dishes they appear in often contain precious spices, require involved cooking methods and take some effort and skill to perfect. One legendary example of this is Morocco's pigeon pie, *bisteeya*, which, even in its home country, is understood to be a dish for specialist cooks only.

buying and storing game

Duck is available whole (head on or off), portioned, fresh and frozen. When selecting a fresh duck, look for those that have an adequate layer of fat beneath the breast skin and have pearly, creamy white skin. Always thaw frozen ducks and other poultry in the refrigerator, uncovered and placed on paper towels. Do not cook partially thawed meat. Buy wild rather than farmed pigeon, if possible, for their more robust flavour. When storing pigeon, remove any packaging, wrap in greaseproof paper and refrigerate. Wash and gently pat dry before cooking. Quail perish rapidly, so store for 2 or 3 days only.

duck breast with walnut and pomegranate sauce

4 large duck breasts
1 onion, finely chopped
250 ml (1 cup) fresh
   pomegranate juice
2 tablespoons lemon juice
2 tablespoons soft brown
   sugar
1 teaspoon ground cinnamon
185 g (1½ cups) chopped
   walnuts
pomegranate seeds
   (optional), to garnish

preheat the oven to 180°C (350°F/Gas 4). Score each duck breast 2 or 3 times on the skin side with a sharp knife. Cook in a non-stick frying pan over high heat, skin-side-down, for 6 minutes, or until crisp and it has rendered most of its fat. Transfer to a baking dish.

remove all but 1 tablespoon of fat from the frying pan. Add the onion to the pan and cook over medium heat for 2–3 minutes, or until soft and translucent. Add the pomegranate and lemon juice, sugar, cinnamon and 125 g (1 cup) of the walnuts and cook for 1 minute. Pour over the duck breasts and bake for 15 minutes.

transfer the duck to a serving dish and rest for 5 minutes. Skim any excess fat from the sauce. Slice the duck and serve with some sauce. Garnish with the pomegranate seeds and the remaining chopped walnuts. Serves 4.

note: If fresh pomegranate juice isn't available, combine 60 ml (¼ cup) pomegranate concentrate with 185 ml (¾ cup) water.

pigeon with raisins and pine nuts

4 pigeons or squabs, spatchcocked
200 ml (7 fl oz) balsamic vinegar
2 tablespoons olive oil
1 large red onion, finely sliced
50 g (⅓ cup) pine nuts
2 garlic cloves, crushed
40 g (¼ cup) raisins
2 rosemary sprigs, chopped
100 ml (3½ fl oz) red wine or water

put the pigeons in a large bowl with the balsamic vinegar, making sure each piece is coated, and marinate in the refrigerator for at least 4 hours. Drain the pigeons, reserving the vinegar.

heat the olive oil in a frying pan and cook the onion and pine nuts until the onion is soft and translucent and the pine nuts golden brown. Add the garlic, raisins and rosemary and cook for 2 minutes. Pour in the reserved vinegar and the wine or water and cook for 10 minutes over medium heat. Season and set aside.

grill (broil) the pigeons for 5–10 minutes on each side until the skin is browned and the flesh cooked through (pull a leg away from the body to check if it is cooked). Transfer the pigeons to a serving dish.

scrape the juices left in the grill (broiler) pan into the sauce. Bring the sauce back to the boil and pour it over or alongside the pigeons. Serve at once, with gnocchi. Serves 4.

note: When grilling (broiling) the pigeons, the heat must be high enough to cook them through and brown the skin, but not so hot that they burn before they are properly cooked. Pigeon can be served a little pink if you prefer—it does not have to be as well cooked as chicken.

Marinate the pigeons in balsamic vinegar for a rich, golden brown colour when cooked.

lamb

Shish and döner kebabs, moussaka, roast lamb, kofta, lamb tagine, rack of lamb with herb crust—these are just some of the world-famous lamb dishes that have emerged from the Mediterranean. Sheep and goat rearing may be a natural consequence of the terrain—cattle are not suited to the often hilly, rocky land—but it is difficult to think of an area that has better exploited its natural state of affairs.

religious significance

As meat was historically scarce and expensive, lamb is traditionally associated with religious feast days and other special times. At occasions such as births, funerals, weddings and the blessing of a house, it was customary in Muslim parts of the Mediterranean to ritually slaughter a whole sheep. Both Jews and Muslims mark the biblical story of Abraham's (Ibrahim's) near-sacrifice of his son Isaac (Isma'il) with special dishes that feature lamb. For Christians, lamb is enormously significant as the symbol of Christ and, during Easter, the most important religious festival for Orthodox Greeks, an entire lamb, including its entrails, will be spit roasted as part of the celebrations.

outdoor cooking

A love of outdoor cooking is shared by all Mediterraneans, but particularly so in the east of the region, where the fat-tailed sheep is found, originally introduced by the Arabs. Its meat is lean and the fat, which is stored in the sheep's tail, is used for basting the cooking meat. Kebabs are classic street food, and in Turkey, where evidence dates sheep back to the Bronze Age, the smell of roasting meat wafts through the air from vying stalls. Shish kebabs are said to have originated with the Turkish Ottoman Empire, when hungry soldiers threaded chunks of meat onto their swords and cooked them over open fires. The döner kebab, *shawarma* in Arabic, consists of layers of lamb threaded onto a vertical rotating spit, which is then sliced off as it cooks.

Older lamb, which needs long cooking times to tenderize it, is ideally suited to slow spit roasting, braising in stews or pounding and grinding into mincemeat; quick grilling (broiling) over intense heat is best for young, tender lamb.

paprika lamb kebabs with greek skordalia

**1 kg (2 lb 4 oz) lamb backstraps or eye of loin fillets, cut into
    2.5 cm (1 inch) cubes**
1 tablespoon sweet paprika
1 tablespoon hot paprika
125 ml (½ cup) lemon juice
125 ml (½ cup) olive oil
3 large (750 g/1 lb 10 oz) floury potatoes, cut into large cubes
3–4 garlic cloves, crushed with a pinch of salt
300 g (10½ oz) English spinach leaves
lemon wedges, to serve

soak 12 wooden skewers in water for at least 20 minutes. Thread
6 lamb cubes onto each, then put in a non-metallic dish large enough
to hold all the skewers in one layer.

combine the sweet and hot paprika, 80 ml (⅓ cup) lemon juice and
60 ml (¼ cup) olive oil in a small non-metallic jug. Pour over the
skewers. Season. Cover and refrigerate.

to make the skordalia, boil the potato cubes for 20 minutes, or until
tender. Drain and put in a food processor with the garlic and about
1 tablespoon of the lemon juice. With the motor running, slowly add
the remaining oil in a thin stream and continue blending for about
60 seconds, or until all the oil is incorporated—avoid overprocessing as
it will become gluey. Season. Set aside to serve at room temperature.

heat a chargrill pan (griddle) or barbecue and brush the surface with
oil. Cook the lamb kebabs for 3–4 minutes each side for medium-rare,
or 5–6 minutes for well done.

wash the spinach and add to a saucepan with just the water clinging
to the leaves. Cook, covered, over medium heat for 1–2 minutes, or
until wilted. Remove and sprinkle over the remaining lemon juice. Serve
the kebabs with the skordalia, spinach and lemon wedges. Serves 4.

Tagines are cooked throughout North Africa, but those of Morocco are particularly famed. Tagine refers both to the dish, a type of stew, and to the conical earthenware cooking pot in which it is traditionally prepared. Tagines are characterized by their mix of sweet and savoury flavours, often combining honey, orange flower water or fruit such as prunes, preserved lemons or quinces with meats such as lamb, chicken or pigeon.

lamb tagine

1 tablespoon ground cumin
1 teaspoon ground ginger
1 teaspoon paprika
1/2 teaspoon ground turmeric
1/2 teaspoon ground cinnamon
2 garlic cloves, crushed
80 ml (1/3 cup) olive oil
1.5 kg (3 lb 5 oz) diced lamb
  shoulder
2 onions, sliced
500 ml (2 cups) beef stock
2 tomatoes, peeled and
  chopped

1/2 teaspoon saffron threads
1 carrot, cut into matchsticks
25 g (1/2 cup) chopped
  coriander (cilantro)
155 g (1 cup) pitted Kalamata
  olives
1 teaspoon finely chopped
  rinsed preserved lemon rind
370 g (2 cups) instant
  couscous
60 g (21/4 oz) butter
11/2 tablespoons honey

put the cumin, ginger, paprika, turmeric, cinnamon, crushed garlic, 2 tablespoons oil and 1 teaspoon salt in a large bowl. Mix together, add the lamb and toss to coat. Cover and refrigerate for 2 hours.

heat the remaining oil in a large casserole dish over medium heat, add the lamb in batches and cook for 5–6 minutes, or until browned. Return the meat to the dish, add the onion and cook for 1–2 minutes. Add the stock, tomato, saffron, carrot and coriander. Bring to the boil, then reduce the heat to low and cook, covered, for 1 hour. Add the olives and preserved lemon and cook, uncovered, for 30 minutes.

put the couscous in a large heatproof bowl. Add 375 ml (1 1/2 cups) boiling water and leave to stand for 3–5 minutes. Stir in the butter and fluff up with a fork. Season with a little salt. Spoon into deep bowls, top with the tagine and drizzle with the honey. Serves 4.

note: Only use the rinsed rind of preserved lemons. Discard the flesh and pith, which have a bitter, unpleasant taste.

lamb kofta

1 kg (2 lb 4 oz) minced
   (ground) lamb
1 onion, finely chopped
2 garlic cloves, finely chopped
2 tablespoons finely chopped
   flat-leaf (Italian) parsley
2 tablespoons finely chopped
   coriander (cilantro) leaves
1/2 teaspoon cayenne pepper
1/2 teaspoon ground allspice
1/2 teaspoon ground ginger
1/2 teaspoon ground
   cardamom
1 teaspoon ground cumin
1 teaspoon paprika

tomato sauce
2 tablespoons olive oil
1 onion, finely chopped
2 garlic cloves, finely chopped
2 teaspoons ground cumin
1/2 teaspoon ground
   cinnamon
1 teaspoon paprika
2 x 400 g (14 oz) tins
   chopped tomatoes
2 teaspoons harissa
4 tablespoons chopped
   coriander (cilantro) leaves

preheat the oven to 180°C (350°F/Gas 4). Lightly grease 2 baking trays. Put the lamb, onion, garlic, herbs and spices in a bowl and mix well. Season with salt and pepper. Roll tablespoons of mixture into balls and put on the trays. Bake for 20 minutes, or until browned.

meanwhile, for the tomato sauce, heat the oil in a large saucepan, add the onion and cook over medium heat for 5 minutes, or until soft. Add the garlic, cumin, cinnamon and paprika and cook for 1 minute, or until fragrant. Stir in the tomato and harissa and bring to the boil. Reduce the heat and simmer for 20 minutes. Add the meatballs and simmer for 10 minutes, or until cooked. Stir in the coriander, season and serve immediately with pitta bread. Serves 4.

offal

It is sometimes easy to forget that the Mediterranean hasn't always been a land of plenty. Offal dishes, although often associated with religious festivals such as Easter, were historically regarded as poor people's food. When an animal was slaughtered little was wasted: liver, heart, brains and kidneys, as well as intestines, feet, eyes, tongue, testicles and stomach (tripe) were all eaten. Eating habits are changing but offal such as liver, brains and kidneys are still widely eaten. Liver and brains are poached, sautéed, grilled (broiled) and fried. Kidneys are popular in Spain fried in sherry and served as a tapas dish; this similar dish hails from Lombardy in France.

Cook the lamb kidneys briefly until browned all over.

kidneys turbigo

8 lamb kidneys
60 g (2¼ oz) butter
8 chipolata sausages
12 small pickling or pearl onions or shallots
125 g (4½ oz) button mushrooms, sliced
1 tablespoon plain (all-purpose) flour
2 tablespoons dry sherry

2 teaspoons tomato paste (purée)
250 ml (1 cup) beef stock
2 tablespoons chopped parsley

croutes
oil, for brushing
2 garlic cloves, crushed
12 slices baguette, cut on an angle

trim, halve and cut the white membrane from the kidneys with scissors. Heat half the butter in a frying pan and cook the kidneys for 2 minutes to brown all over. Remove. Add the chipolatas to the pan and cook for 2 minutes until well browned. Remove and cut in half on the diagonal.

lower the heat and add the remaining butter to the frying pan. Cook the onions and mushrooms, stirring, for 5 minutes, or until golden brown.

mix together the flour and sherry to make a smooth paste. Add the tomato paste and stock and mix until smooth.

remove the frying pan from the heat and stir in the stock mixture. Return to the heat and stir until boiling and slightly thickened. Season well. Return the kidneys and chipolatas to the sauce. Lower the heat, cover and simmer for 25 minutes, or until cooked. Stir occasionally.

meanwhile, to make the croutes, preheat the oven to 180°C (350°F/Gas 4). Mix together the oil and garlic and brush over the bread slices. Place on a baking tray and bake for 3–4 minutes. Turn over and bake for a further 3 minutes, or until golden brown. Sprinkle the kidneys with parsley and serve with the croutes. Serves 4.

pork

One of the oldest and most important meats worldwide, except in areas where Jewish or Muslim communities predominate, pigs were first domesticated in China approximately 5000 years ago. Pork is widely consumed in France, and is also an important part of the cooking of Italy and the interior of Spain. It lends itself to simple, hearty fare: in Spain it is cooked in stews, often combined with beans; the French add it to their quintessential winter dish, *cassoulet*, or flavour it with ingredients such as capers, sage, apples or prunes; and in Italy it is also prepared simply, cooked in Marsala or sauce *pizzaiola*, a speciality of Naples. Young sucking pig is stuffed with herbs and roasted as porchetta in Italy, the meat sold as slices and often eaten in bread rolls.

pork chops pizzaiola

using scissors or a knife, cut the pork fat at 5 mm (¼ inch) intervals around the rind. Brush the chops with 1 tablespoon of the olive oil and season well. Score a cross in the base of each tomato. Put in boiling water for 20 seconds then plunge in cold water. Drain and peel the skin away from the cross and chop the tomatoes.

heat 2 tablespoons of the oil in a saucepan over low heat and add the garlic. Soften without browning for 1–2 minutes, then add the tomato and season. Increase the heat, bring to the boil and cook for 5 minutes, or until thick. Stir in the basil.

heat the remaining oil in a large frying pan with a tight-fitting lid. Brown the chops in batches over medium-high heat for 2 minutes on each side. Put in a slightly overlapping row down the centre of the pan and spoon the sauce over the top, covering the chops completely. Cover the pan and cook over low heat for about 5 minutes. Sprinkle with parsley to serve. Serves 4.

- **4 pork chops**
- **4 tablespoons olive oil**
- **600 g (1 lb 5 oz) vine-ripened tomatoes**
- **3 garlic cloves, crushed**
- **3 basil leaves, torn into pieces**
- **1 teaspoon finely chopped flat-leaf (Italian) parsley**

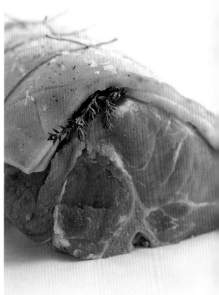

the perfumed apothecary

aniseed

Aniseeds are the seeds from a bush related to hemlock and are of Middle Eastern origin. They have an intense liquorice flavour, which is used to advantage across the Mediterranean primarily in the making of spirits: Pernod and pastis in France, ouzo in Greece, raki in Turkey and arak in Syria, Lebanon and Jordan. Aniseeds are also valued as digestives and are added to teas and tisanes. They are used in moderation to add sweet, interesting undertones to stuffings for fish, and in breads and cakes. It is best to buy aniseeds in small quantities as needed, as they quickly lose their potency.

A number of varieties of cardamom can be found across the Mediterranean, including brown and white, but the green pods are the most common. Their use goes back to ancient Egyptian times, and they are still popularly called the 'queen of spices'. The whole pod or the whole or ground seeds are used, primarily in the cooking of Turkey and other Eastern Mediterranean countries. They are used to impart a strong, sweet aroma and flavour to both sweet and savoury dishes such as tagines and stews, rice dishes, biscuits, puddings and ice cream. Perhaps of greatest fame, however, is their use in Turkish coffee, where their addition brings an aromatic sweetness to the rich brew.

cardamom

turkish coffee

2 tablespoons very finely ground Arabic coffee beans
2 teaspoons caster (superfine) sugar
1 cardamom pod

put all the ingredients in a small saucepan (or in a Turkish coffee pot, an *ibrik*, if you have one) with 250 ml (1 cup) cold water. Stir over medium heat until the coffee starts to rise to the surface. Remove from the heat immediately. Spoon the froth into 2 small cups and return the pan to the heat. When the coffee starts to rise to the top again, remove the pan from the heat and fill the cups with coffee. The key to successful Turkish coffee is the froth; it is said that if the froth is missing from the coffee, so too, is the honour of the host. Serves 2.

cinnamon

At the height of the spice trade during the Middle Ages, the desire for spices by wealthy Europeans grew to such a fervour pitch that it has since been labelled a 'spice orgy'. Historians tell of King Ferdinand of Spain (1452–1516), who grew so concerned at the large amounts of silver changing hands for cinnamon and pepper that he tried to encourage the use of locally grown garlic instead. Luckily for us, he wasn't entirely successful.

culinary uses

A member of the laurel plant family native to Sri Lanka, cinnamon is the inner bark dried and sold as quills or sticks. It is a spice much-prized by Spanish cooks, who use it in ice creams and sweet puddings, such as *crema catalana*, but also in savoury dishes, a reflection of their Moorish heritage. Similarly, throughout North Africa and the Eastern Mediterranean, cinnamon is vital to many spice mixes, including Morocco's famed *ras el hanout*, and in Turkey, Lebanon and Syria it and allspice are almost exclusively used among spices to flavour meat. Cinnamon is also available ground or powdered.

ensuring freshness

As with most spices, the flavour and freshness of cinnamon will fade over time, though whole sticks will retain their flavour better than ground cinnamon. If a recipe specifically asks for ground cinnamon, grind the sticks yourself (a small clean grinder will do the job perfectly well); otherwise, buy in small quantities only as needed.

crema catalana

1 litre (4 cups) milk
1 vanilla bean
1 cinnamon stick
zest of 1 small lemon, sliced into strips
2 strips orange zest, 4 x 2.5 cm (1½ x 1 inch)

8 egg yolks
125 g (heaped ½ cup) caster (superfine) sugar
4 tablespoons cornflour (cornstarch)
3 tablespoons soft brown sugar

put the milk, scraped vanilla bean, cinnamon stick and lemon and orange zest in a saucepan and bring to the boil. Simmer for 5 minutes, then strain and set aside.

whisk the egg yolks with the caster sugar in a bowl for 5 minutes, or until pale and creamy. Add the cornflour and mix well. Slowly add the warm milk mixture to the egg and whisk continuously. Return to the saucepan and cook over low to medium heat, stirring constantly, for 5–10 minutes, or until the mixture is thick and creamy. Do not boil as it will curdle. Pour into six 250 ml (1 cup) ramekins and refrigerate for 6 hours, or overnight.

when ready to serve, sprinkle evenly with brown sugar and grill (broil) for 3 minutes, or until caramelized. Serves 6.

cumin seeds

This annual herb is indigenous to the Eastern Mediterranean and parts of North Africa. The seeds, whole and ground, have a hot, pungent taste—a characteristic flavour of much of North African cooking. Cumin is used in couscous, rice dishes and stews, particularly those with pulses; is added to sausages for a spicy edge; and is found in numerous spice mixes including Egyptian *dukka*. The Moroccans make it into a paste to be rubbed onto meat, usually lamb, which is then slowly roasted on an outdoor spit for as many as 4 hours, resulting in a very tender piece of meat. This style of cooking is known as *mechoui*, and is a communal, enjoyable event.

maximizing flavour

Cumin seeds are generally lightly dry-roasted before using to release their aroma. As with many spices, the older the cumin is, the less flavour it has; this is particularly true of pre-ground cumin. For best flavour, buy whole seeds and dry-roast them yourself, then grind, if necessary for the recipe. To dry-roast: put in a frying pan and toss over medium heat for a few minutes.

mechoui lamb with cumin and paprika

2.25 kg (5 lb) leg of lamb
70 g (2½ oz) butter, at
**   room temperature**
3 garlic cloves, crushed
2 teaspoons ground cumin

3 teaspoons ground coriander
1 teaspoon paprika
1 tablespoon cumin seeds,
**   extra, for dipping**

preheat the oven to 220°C (425°F/Gas 7). With a sharp knife, cut small deep slits into the top and sides of the lamb. Mix the butter, garlic, spices and ¼ teaspoon salt in a bowl until a smooth paste forms.

with the back of a spoon, rub the paste all over the lamb, then use your fingers to spread the paste evenly, making sure all the lamb is covered.

put the lamb bone-side-down in a deep baking dish and place on the top shelf of the oven. Bake for 10 minutes, then baste and return to the oven. Reduce the temperature to 160°C (315°F/Gas 2–3). Bake for 3 hours 20 minutes, basting every 20–30 minutes. Carve the lamb into chunky pieces. Mix the cumin seeds with 1½ teaspoons salt and serve on the side for dipping the meat into. Serves 6.

lavender

This pretty herb is most popular in Provençal cooking. It is a member of the mint family, as is rosemary, and can sometimes be used in recipes that feature that herb; it is also good with citrus. Lavender is most commonly seen in *herbes de Provence*, a classic blend of dried herbs widely used in southern French cooking. Blends vary, but always contain thyme, lavender, savory and rosemary. Marjoram, oregano, sage, fennel and basil may also be included. The herb blend is added to meat, creamy pasta dishes, soups and salad dressings. It can be bought ready-made from delicatessens. The fresh herb is used in custards, ice creams and as a decoration; when using fresh lavender, the sweet English lavender is best.

lavender ice cream

8 stems English lavender (or 4–6 if the lavender is in full flower, as it will have a stronger flavour)
600 ml (2½ cups) thick (double/heavy) cream
1 small piece lemon zest
170 g (¾ cup) sugar
4 egg yolks, lightly whisked

wash and dry the lavender, then put in a saucepan with the cream and lemon zest. Heat until almost boiling, then add the sugar. Stir to dissolve. Strain through a fine sieve, then gradually pour onto the egg yolks in a bowl, return to the pan and stir continuously over low heat until thick enough to coat the back of a spoon—do not let it boil.

pour the mixture into a chilled metal tray to cool, covering the surface with a layer of plastic wrap to prevent a skin forming. Once cool, churn in an ice cream machine, following the manufacturer's instructions.

if making by hand, freeze until frozen around the edges but not in the centre, then whisk with electric beaters to break down any ice crystals. Return to the freezer and repeat this process at least twice more. The finished ice cream should be light not icy. Serves 6–8.

marzipan

The origins of marzipan have been hotly disputed, with everyone from the Castilians of Spain to an order of nuns in Jerusalem laying claim to its invention. However, historians suggest it can most feasibly be traced back to the Arabs, who are well known for their love of sweets (in turn, gained from the Persians), and it probably first arrived in Europe with returning Crusaders. Whatever marzipan's origins, its use is widespread throughout the Mediterranean, and people of all persuasions—Jews, Christians and Muslims—all delight in this almond-based treat.

culinary uses

Marzipan was originally made from sugar, ground almonds and rose water and was regarded as a great delicacy, sometimes served covered in gold leaf. For a long time only apothecaries were allowed to produce and sell marzipan and it was not until the eighteenth century that confectioners took over its production. Making marzipan is not easy—particularly the miniature fruit, animal and vegetable shapes it comes in. For general baking purpose, marzipan is used as a tart filling, to stuff dates and sweetmeats, or is rolled out into thin sheets to decorate and cover fruit cakes, such as Sicilian cassata. Linked to Sicily as early as 1409, this over-the-top ricotta cake is generally considered a speciality of Sicilian nuns, who serve it as part of their Easter celebrations. Interestingly, however, Sicilian Jews also have a long history of making the cake, which they serve at their religious festivals.

buying and storing

Marzipan is sold from delicatessens in block form; wrap any unused marzipan in plastic wrap and store in an airtight container in the refrigerator for 1 month or freeze for up to 6 months.

sicilian cassata

use plastic wrap to line a 20 cm (8 inch) round cake tin with sloping sides (such as a moule à manqué). Cut the cake into 5 mm (¼ inch) slices to line the tin, reserving enough pieces to cover the top at the end. Fit the slices of cake carefully into the tin, making sure there are no gaps, and trim the sponge flush with the top of the tin. Brush the Marsala over the cake in the tin, covering it as evenly as possible and reserving a little for the top.

put the ricotta in a bowl and beat until smooth. Add the sugar and natural vanilla extract and mix well. Mix in the candied fruit and chocolate. Spoon the mixture into the mould, smooth the surface and then cover with the remaining slices of cake. Cover completely with plastic wrap and press the top down firmly. Refrigerate the cassata for at least 2 hours, then unmould onto a plate.

knead enough green food colouring into the marzipan to tint it light green. Roll out the marzipan in a circle until it is large enough to completely cover the top and side of the cassata. Melt the jam in a saucepan with 1 tablespoon of water and brush over the cassata. Position the marzipan over the top, smoothing it over the side to get rid of any folds. Trim it to fit around the edge.

mix the icing sugar with a little hot water to make a smooth icing that will spread easily. Either pipe or drizzle it over the top decoratively. Serve immediately. Makes 1 x 20 cm (8 inch) cake.

25 cm (10 inch) round sponge or Madeira (pound) cake
4 tablespoons sweet Marsala
350 g (12 oz) ricotta cheese
80 g (⅓ cup) caster (superfine) sugar
½ teaspoon natural vanilla extract (essence)
100 g (3½ oz) mixed candied fruit, finely chopped
50 g (1¾ oz) dark chocolate, chopped
green food colouring
250 g (9 oz) marzipan
2 tablespoons apricot or strawberry jam
90 g (¾ cup) icing (confectioners') sugar

1 Line the tin with cake pieces, making sure there are no gaps.

2 Cover the cassata with a layer of marzipan, smoothing it down.

3 Drizzle or pipe the icing in a crosshatch pattern over the cake.

mastic

Mastic is a resin collected from the mastic tree, a relative of the pistachio tree. The tree is found throughout the Mediterranean, but curiously only those on the Greek Island of Chios produce the chewy resin. Its collection is laborious: once a year incisions are made in the tree, which allow the resin to escape, in teardrop-shaped crystals. It is then either collected while it runs down the tree, or is left to dry on the ground, to be gathered and cleaned later.

culinary uses

This resin has an earthy flavour and is gently aromatic. It is used for flavouring (and for giving an interesting chewy edge) to ice cream, milk puddings and Turkish delight. It is also used in a Greek liqueur called Mastika. It was probably the original chewing gum—the source of the verb 'masticate'—and has remarkable medicinal qualities. It is an excellent breath freshener, has antibacterial and fungicidal properties and is reputedly effective in treating stomach aches and ulcers, diabetes and cholesterol problems. Mastic is sold in the form of hard, semi-transparent crystals. The crystals scraped straight off the tree are more expensive (and cleaner) than those left to dry on the ground. Store in an airtight container in a cool place away from direct sunlight.

A number of flower essences are used in Mediterranean cooking, principally rose water and orange flower water, both made from a distillation of their blossoms. The popularity of orange flower water is widespread—from Spain and Morocco across to the Eastern Mediterranean—and it is used to perfume pastries, biscuits, puddings, syrups and fruit salads, as well as drinks. It can be bought in bottles from specialist stores and will last for around two years. Only use the amount specified in a recipe as the flavour can be overpowering.

easter walnut cakes

200 g (7 oz) unsalted butter, softened
125 g (heaped ½ cup) caster (superfine) sugar
2 tablespoons orange flower water
250 g (2 cups) plain (all-purpose) flour, sifted

walnut filling

50 g (1¾ oz) walnuts, chopped
60 g (¼ cup) caster (superfine) sugar
1 teaspoon ground cinnamon

preheat the oven to 160°C (315°F/Gas 2–3). Grease 2 baking trays and line with baking paper.

cream the butter and sugar in a small bowl until light and fluffy. Transfer to a large bowl. Using a metal spoon, fold in the orange flower water and flour until well combined. Using your hands, press the mixture until it comes together in a stiff dough.

to make the walnut filling, combine all the ingredients in a bowl and mix well. Roll heaped tablespoons of dough into balls. Press a hollow in the centre with your thumb. Place 1 teaspoon of filling into each hollow. Place on the trays and flatten slightly without folding any dough over the filling. Bake for 15–20 minutes, or until golden. Cool on a wire rack and serve. Makes about 28.

orange flower water

orchid root

Like saffron and rose petals, dried orchid root, or *sahlab*, does seem more at home in the long-ago past when camel trains from the East brought heady spices to revive the gloomy diet of Western Europeans in the Middle Ages. Indeed, it is hard to get nowadays, even in the Middle East, its home. But its appeal remains, possibly stemming from its reputed aphrodisiac qualities—the botanical name *orchis* actually means 'testicle' in Greek.

The dried roots are small and bulb-shaped, and are sometimes sold threaded on strings like necklaces, or are ground into a fine, white powder. The dried root is rarely exported but the powdered form can sometimes be found in specialist stores. It is mainly used in the cooking of Turkey, Lebanon and Syria, and its most popular use is in a hot, milky sweet drink, known as *salep* in Turkey, often garnished with chopped pistachios and sprinkled with cinnamon. In the south of Turkey it is also made into an ice cream; elsewhere it is used as a thickening agent.

paprika

This spice powder is made by grinding the dried pods of a sweet red pepper (capsicum) called pimento. These peppers were introduced to Turkey from South America, and from Turkey travelled to Hungary where they were made into paprika. There are several varieties, including sweet, hot and smoked, which are determined by the type of pepper used and whether or not the seeds have been added. Paprika is most common in the cooking of Turkey and North Africa. It is also a key ingredient in the Spanish tapas dish, *patatas bravas*.

turkish poached eggs with yoghurt

preheat the oven to 150°C (300°F/Gas 2). Melt one-third of the butter in a heavy-based frying pan, add the onion and cook over low heat for 15 minutes, or until golden brown. Remove from the pan and allow to cool slightly. Transfer to a small bowl and add the yoghurt and some salt, to taste. Combine well.

divide the yoghurt mixture among 4 ovenproof ramekins, each about 7.5 cm (3 inches) in diameter and 4 cm (1½ inches) deep. Put the ramekins on a tray in the oven to heat gently.

meanwhile, fill a large deep frying pan three-quarters full of water, add a pinch of salt and bring to a gentle simmer. Gently break the eggs one at a time into a small bowl or large spoon and slide the eggs into the water. Reduce the heat so that the water barely moves. Cook for 2–3 minutes, or until the eggs are just set. Remove with a slotted spoon and pat off any excess water using paper towels. Place an egg in each ramekin and season with salt and pepper.

melt the remaining butter in a small saucepan and add the paprika. Drizzle over the eggs and serve at once. Serves 4.

60 g (2¼ oz) butter
1 onion, thinly sliced
250 g (1 cup) Greek-style
  natural yoghurt
4 large eggs
1 teaspoon hot paprika

note: This easy dish is perfect for a light supper or brunch. Instead of, or as well as, the onions, you can use 2 crushed garlic cloves cooked gently in the butter for 1 minute, or until softened.

roses

Ever since Cleopatra made Mark Antony wade through rose petals strewn knee-high around her bed, roses have been synonymous with luxury. Their uses in cooking are no less so. The ancient Romans and Persians made wine scented with roses and the Turkish Ottomans created sumptuous pastries and puddings that were perfumed with the petals and the distilled rose water. Today, Turkish cooks use the petals to produce scented jams, sorbets and milk puddings such as *mahallabia* and, further to the west, the dried buds appear in the spice mixes of Tunisia and Morocco, including *ras el hanout*, meaning 'top of the shelf'. The dried buds and petals can be bought from markets in Turkey and other countries of the Eastern Mediterranean, and are also sold infused in ingredients such as sugar syrup, wine, honey, oil, vinegar and water. Rose water is often added to a bowl of water as a delightful hand wash, used in salads and rice desserts, and, of course, added to Turkish delight. All rose petals are edible as long as they haven't been sprayed with any chemicals; rose water is available in bottles.

turkish delight

1 kg (4 cups) sugar
125 g (1 cup) cornflour (cornstarch)
1 teaspoon cream of tartar
2 tablespoons rose water
red food colouring
40 g (⅓ cup) icing (confectioners') sugar
2 tablespoons cornflour (cornstarch), extra

pour 625 ml (2½ cups) water into a large, heavy-based saucepan and bring to the boil. Add the sugar and stir until thoroughly dissolved. Remove from the heat.

in a large bowl, blend the cornflour and cream of tartar with 250 ml (1 cup) cold water. Gradually add the blended cornflour to the syrup, then return the saucepan to medium heat and stir until the mixture boils.

reduce the heat and cook very slowly for 45 minutes, stirring often. During this time, the colour will change from cloudy to clear and golden and the mixture will thicken.

add the rose water and a few drops of food colouring, then pour onto a lightly oiled 30 x 20 cm (12 x 8 inch) tray and leave to set. When firm and cool, cut into 2.5 cm (1 inch) squares and toss in the combined icing sugar and extra cornflour. Makes 25 pieces.

Turkish delight is the Western name for *rahat lokum*, meaning 'rest for the throat'. The sweet is made by slowly boiling a mixture of syrup and cornflour (cornstarch), sometimes with honey, fruit juice or mastic until gummy and gel-like. The mixture is often flavoured with orange or rose water or mint, or may include nuts such as pistachios or almonds. The set mixture is cut into squares and rolled in icing (confectioners') sugar.

saffron

In the medieval world, certain foods were considered to have magical qualities, and saffron, with its rich golden colour, was thought to bestow wellbeing. Saffron comes from the dried stigmas of autumn crocus flowers, and is the most expensive spice in the world. Each flower consists of just three stigmas, which must be hand-picked, then dried— an extraordinarily labour-intensive process. Fortunately, saffron's flavour is pungent and aromatic, and its colour intense, so only a little is needed at a time.

using and buying

Saffron is used to give flavour and colour to dishes such as paella, risotto, pilaf, tagines and bouillabaisse, as well as ice creams and custards. The best saffron comes from Spain, Iran and Kashmir, and is available in both powdered and thread form (the whole stigma). Powdered forms are often adulterated, so buy threads if possible. Beware: there is no such thing as cheap saffron. Store in a cool, dry cupboard away from the light.

saffron pasta with garlic prawns and preserved lemon

put the wine and saffron in a small saucepan and boil for 3 minutes, or until reduced by half. Remove from the heat. Cook the pasta in a large saucepan of boiling water for 2–3 minutes, or until *al dente*. Drain and keep warm.

heat the oil and 25 g (1 oz) of the butter in a large frying pan and cook the prawns in batches over high heat for 3 minutes, or until pink and tender. Cut into thirds, then transfer to a plate and keep warm.

add the garlic and remaining butter to the same pan and cook over medium heat for 3 minutes, or until golden. Add the wine and stir to remove any sediment from the bottom of the pan. Add the preserved lemon, lemon juice, spring onion, lime leaves and stock and bring to the boil, then reduce the heat and simmer for 2 minutes.

return the prawns to the frying pan and heat through. Serve the pasta in mounds, then top with some of the prawns and sauce and sprinkle with snipped fresh chives. Serves 4.

125 ml (1/2 cup) dry white wine
pinch saffron threads
500 g (1 lb 2 oz) fresh saffron pasta
1 tablespoon virgin olive oil
125 g (41/2 oz) butter
750 g (1 lb 10 oz) raw prawns (shrimps), peeled and deveined
3 garlic cloves, crushed
1/2 preserved lemon, rinsed, pith and flesh removed, cut into thin strips
1 tablespoon lemon juice
4 spring onions (scallions), thinly sliced
4 lime leaves, thinly shredded
125 ml (1/2 cup) chicken stock
2 tablespoons snipped chives

sesame

The sesame plant probably originated in India or China but has been present in the Eastern Mediterranean since ancient times. The sesame seeds are usually cream in colour, but may also be yellow, reddish or black, depending on the variety. They are oil-rich, so are most prevalent in the cooking of those areas of the Mediterranean lacking in olive trees, the main source of oil for the region. The seeds can be used raw, but are usually toasted to release a nutty, slightly sweet flavour. Sesame seeds are used in spice mixes such as *dukka* and *za'atar*; are sprinkled liberally on breads such as Egyptian *semit* (bread rings); and are used in confectionery. The oil is made from the crushed seeds and is amber-yellow or dark brown. It has a very strong flavour and aroma, and is used as a salad dressing and for frying.

tahini

This is a thick oily paste extracted from husked white sesame seeds. The name comes from the Arab word *tahana*, meaning to 'grind' or 'crush'. The seeds are husked by crushing and soaking, they are then dried and lightly roasted before being ground to a thick paste or cream. In Eastern Mediterranean countries and in Greece, tahini is an essential part of the dips served as appetizers. For example, it is mixed with ground chickpeas to make hummus, and with puréed eggplant (aubergine) to make baba ghannouj. When blended with garlic and lemon, tahini is used as a tangy dressing for roast vegetables or as an ingredient in the Greek sweetmeat, *halvah*. Tahini can be made at home by grinding the sesame seeds in a mortar and pestle or food processor until smooth, or is commercially available as both a dark and light paste (the latter is usually of better quality).

storage

Because of their high oil content, sesame seeds quickly become rancid. Purchase in small amounts or store in the refrigerator for up to 3 months. Once opened, tahini will generally keep for 4–6 weeks in the refrigerator.

baked fish with tahini sauce

preheat the oven to 200°C (400°F/Gas 6). Lightly grease a large baking dish. Make 3 diagonal cuts on each side of the fish through the thickest part of the flesh to ensure even cooking. Combine the garlic, harissa and olive oil in a small dish. Put 2 teaspoons in the fish cavity and spread the remainder over both sides of the fish, rubbing it into the slits. Put 2 lemon slices in the cavity of the fish.

arrange the onion in a layer in the baking dish. Top with the tomato, thyme and remaining lemon slices. Put the fish on top and bake, uncovered, for about 25–30 minutes, or until the fish flesh is opaque.

meanwhile, to make the tahini sauce, heat the olive oil in a small saucepan over low heat. Add the garlic and cook over medium heat for 30 seconds, then add the tahini, lemon juice and 125 ml (½ cup) water and stir until combined. Add more water, if necessary, to make a smooth, but fairly thick sauce. Cook for 2 minutes, then remove from the heat and stir in the chopped coriander. Season with salt and pepper. Transfer the onion and tomato to a serving dish. Put the fish on top and season with salt. Pour some of the sauce over the fish and the rest in a serving dish on the side. Serves 4.

- **1 kg (2 lb 4 oz) whole white-fleshed fish such as snapper or bream, scaled and cleaned**
- **3 garlic cloves, crushed**
- **2 teaspoons harissa**
- **2 tablespoons olive oil**
- **1 lemon, thinly sliced**
- **1 onion, thinly sliced**
- **2 large firm, ripe tomatoes, sliced**
- **4 thyme sprigs**

tahini sauce

- **2 teaspoons olive oil**
- **1 garlic clove, crushed**
- **3 tablespoons light tahini**
- **2½ tablespoons lemon juice**
- **1½ tablespoons chopped coriander (cilantro) leaves**

spice mixes

At the heart of Mediterranean cooking are its flavourings—aromatic and vibrant herbs, spices, marinades and pastes. The use of fresh and dried herbs is more characteristic of southern French and Italian cooking, while spices play an essential role in those Mediterranean cuisines with Arabian and Persian heritages. A carefully blended spice should suggest various levels of flavour and aroma—no single ingredient should dominate. *Baharat*, for example, common in the Middle East, is a mixture of black pepper, cassia, cloves, cumin, cardamom, nutmeg, paprika and coriander, sometimes also with *loomi* (dried Omani limes) added. It has been variously described as round and deep, sweet with a bitter edge, pungent yet fruity—something for everyone. The following are just some of the more typical and useful spice mixes, which can be easily made at home.

chermoula

For newcomers to Mediterranean spice mixes, Morocco's chermoula is a good starting place. It is not as hot as some, as the dried spices are balanced by the presence of fresh herbs. It is popular as a marinade for fish, which is often left to marinate overnight, then fried, grilled (broiled) or baked. It is also served with vegetables and meat.

80 ml (⅓ cup) virgin olive oil
3 tablespoons chopped coriander (cilantro) leaves
2 tablespoons chopped flat-leaf (Italian) parsley
2 tablespoons chopped preserved lemon rind
2 tablespoons lemon juice
2 garlic cloves, chopped
1 small red chilli, seeded and finely chopped
1 teaspoon ground cumin
½ teaspoon paprika

process the ingredients to a coarse purée, then season with salt. Makes approximately 100 ml (3½ fl oz).

4 tablespoons sesame seeds
3 tablespoons coriander seeds
2 tablespoons cumin seeds
60 g (½ cup) roasted, chopped hazelnuts

put the spices and nuts in a shallow frying pan and add salt and pepper. Dry-fry until aromatic, then remove from the heat and allow to cool. Using either a food processor or a mortar and pestle, grind the ingredients to a coarse powder. Makes approximately 100 g (1½ cups).

dukka

This much-loved old spice mix is widely eaten in Egypt, where it is sold in paper cones at street stalls and used as a dip for bread. At home, it is served in small dishes, alongside bread and bowls of olive oil, for easy dipping, as part of the mezze table or for breakfast. Its ease and simplicity are its strength—serve it as a dip for hard-boiled eggs for an excellent and unusual appetizer.

ras el hanout

Meaning 'top of the shelf', this Moroccan spice mixture can include anywhere from 10 to 30 different spices—some say up to 100—and vendors fiercely guard their own special recipe. Typically, it includes aniseed, allspice, cloves, cayenne pepper, cinnamon, cardamom, cumin, dried rosebuds or petals, galangal, ginger, mace, nutmeg, orris root and various peppers. Green Spanish fly (*Lytta vesicatoria*), believed to be an aphrodisiac, was another traditional ingredient. Ras el hanout is a great all-purpose spice, with a balanced, warm flavour. It is used with rice and couscous, meat and game dishes. Buy ready-made or make this simple home-made version yourself.

7 g (⅕ oz) turmeric
15 g (½ oz) allspice berries
30 g (1 oz) black peppercorns
1½ nutmegs
1 clove
10 cardamom pods
1 cinnamon stick
1 teaspoon cayenne pepper
3 dried rosebuds

grind all the ingredients in a spice blender until fine, then sieve the mixture and store in a tightly sealed jar. Flavour will fade over time. Makes approximately 55 g (2 oz).

making and storing harissa

Commercial harissa can be purchased from delicatessens but it is a pale imitation of the real thing, which is remarkably easy to make. In Tunisia, harissa is normally bought freshly made from spice shops, prepared with a mortar and pestle. Home-made harissa should be stored in the refrigerator where it will last for 2–6 months.

spicy harissa

This spicy paste blend is a popular accompaniment for many North African dishes, in particular those from Tunisia. It is traditionally served with couscous, but is also used as a flavouring in soups, tagines, with lamb or merguez sausages and just about anywhere aromatic heat and red colour are required. It can also be mixed with a little olive oil and served with flatbread. Harissa can be fiery hot or milder and more aromatic. *Tabil*, also from Tunisia, is a similar mix, with the exception that it contains no paprika or cumin, so is even hotter.

125 g (4½ oz) dried red chillies, stems removed
1 tablespoon dried mint
1 tablespoon ground coriander
1 tablespoon ground cumin
1 teaspoon ground caraway seeds
10 garlic cloves, chopped
125 ml (½ cup) olive oil

roughly chop the chillies. Put in a bowl, cover with boiling water and soak for 1 hour. Drain, put in a food processor (or use a mortar and pestle) and add the mint, spices, garlic, 1 tablespoon of the oil and ½ teaspoon salt. Process for 20 seconds, scrape down the side of the bowl, then process for another 30 seconds. Add 2 tablespoons oil and process again. Repeat the process until a thick paste forms.

spoon the paste into a clean, sterilized jar, cover with a thin layer of olive oil and seal. Label and date. Makes 600 ml (20 fl oz).

note: To prepare a sterilized storage jar, preheat the oven to 120°C (250°F/Gas ½). Wash the jar and lid in hot soapy water and rinse with hot water. Put the jar in the oven for 20 minutes, or until fully dry. Do not dry with a tea towel.

za'atar

This spice mixture is popular in Turkey, North Africa and Lebanon. Za'atar is also the name for a Mediterranean variety of wild thyme, which would have traditionally been used. Proportions vary, but the ingredients themselves remain fairly consistent, and include dried thyme, dried and crushed sumac berries, sesame seeds and salt. Za'atar is used as a seasoning for meats and vegetables, is mixed with oil to form a dip for bread, and is added as a flavouring to fried eggs and marinated yoghurt balls. A popular street snack involves brushing flatbread such as Lebanese or pitta bread with olive oil, sprinkling over the spice mix and then lightly toasting the bread. Za'atar can be bought from specialist food stores, or made at home.

4 tablespoons dried thyme
1 tablespoon sesame seeds, toasted
1 1/2 tablespoons sumac

mix the ingredients with a pinch of salt, to taste. Store in an airtight container in a dark cupboard. The flavour will last for up to 1 year. Makes 6 1/2 tablespoons.

sumac

Due to its souring qualities, this ground-up berry is most popular in countries where lemons have historically been rare, such as Syria, Lebanon and Turkey. (Tart pomegranates are another traditional souring agent.) The reddish-purple berry has a fruity but mildly astringent, lemony flavour. The seeds are dried, then crushed or powdered and are also used to add colour and a pleasant tangy flavour to meat, kebabs, fish, vegetables and the bread salad *fattoush*. Sumac will keep well in an airtight container in a cool, dark cupboard.

sumac-crusted lamb fillets with baba ghannouj

2 tablespoons olive oil
750 g (1 lb 10 oz) small new potatoes
2–3 garlic cloves, crushed
60 ml (¼ cup) lemon juice
1 red pepper (capsicum), seeded and quartered lengthways

4 x 200 g (7 oz) lamb backstraps or fillets
1 tablespoon sumac
3 tablespoons finely chopped flat-leaf (Italian) parsley
250 g (9 oz) good-quality baba ghannouj

heat the oil in a saucepan big enough to hold the potatoes in one layer. Add the potatoes and garlic, and cook, turning frequently, for 3–5 minutes, or until brown all over. When golden, add the lemon juice and reduce the heat. Gently simmer, covered, for 15–20 minutes, or until tender; stir occasionally to prevent sticking. Remove from the heat. Season well.

meanwhile, lightly oil a chargrill pan (griddle) or barbecue plate and heat to very hot. Cook the pepper pieces skin-side-down for about 2 minutes, or until the skin starts to blister and turn black. Cook the other side for 1–2 minutes. Remove from the heat, then place in a plastic bag or bowl covered with plastic wrap. Set aside.

coat the lamb with sumac. Cook on the chargrill pan or barbecue plate for 4–5 minutes on each side, or until cooked to your liking. Remove from the heat, cover with foil and leave to rest for a few minutes. Remove the skin from the peppers and slice the quarters into thin strips.

stir the parsley through the potatoes. Divide the baba ghannouj among 4 plates. Cut the lamb into 1 cm (½ inch) slices on the diagonal and arrange on top of the baba ghannouj with the pepper strips. Serve with the potatoes and a green salad. Serves 4.

vanilla

biscotti

True vanilla comes from the pod of a climbing orchid vine native to Central America. The pods are picked when green, at which stage they have no flavour, then left to sweat and dry in the sun, causing them to shrivel, turn deep brown and acquire a coating of small, white vanillin crystals. Good-quality vanilla beans have a warm, almost caramel aroma and flavour, and are soft, not hard and dry. Vanilla is sold as beans or distilled into natural vanilla extract (essence). A synthetic vanilla flavouring is also available but it is cheaper and of an inferior flavour.

250 g (2 cups) plain
  (all-purpose) flour
1 teaspoon baking powder
250 g (1 cup) caster
  (superfine) sugar
3 eggs

1 egg yolk
1 teaspoon natural vanilla
  extract (essence)
1 teaspoon grated orange zest
110 g (³/4 cup) pistachio nuts

preheat the oven to 180°C (350°F/Gas 4). Line 2 baking trays with baking paper and lightly dust with flour.

sift the flour and baking powder into a large bowl. Add the sugar and mix well. Make a well in the centre and add 2 whole eggs, the egg yolk, vanilla extract and orange zest. Using a large metal spoon, stir until just combined. Mix in the pistachios. Knead for 2–3 minutes on a lightly floured surface. The dough will be stiff at first. Sprinkle a little water onto the dough. Divide the mixture into 2 portions and roll each into a log about 25 cm (10 inches) long and 8 cm (3 inches) wide. Slightly flatten the tops.

put the logs on the trays, allowing room for spreading. Beat the remaining egg and brush over the logs to glaze. Bake for 35 minutes, then remove from the oven.

reduce the oven to 150°C (300°F/Gas 2). Allow the logs to cool slightly and cut each into 5 mm (¼ inch) slices. Put flat-side-down on the trays and bake for 8 minutes. Turn the biscuits over and cook for another 8 minutes, or until slightly coloured and crisp and dry. Transfer to a wire rack to cool completely. Store in an airtight container. Makes 45.

PANINI
~A~
PIACERE

delicatessen

amaretti biscuits

Amaretti are light, macaroon biscuits made with both sweet and bitter almonds. The bitter almonds give amaretti their characteristic flavour—and their name, which means 'little bitter things'. There are many varieties of amaretti, often seen wrapped in pairs and served with coffee. Amaretti can also be eaten with a dessert wine, crumbled as a topping for trifles, or used in desserts such as creamy almond semifreddo. This Italian dessert is a parfait-style ice cream made without churning. Amaretti also give a special flavour to savoury dishes such as *tortelli di zucca*, a pumpkin ravioli that is a speciality of northern Italy.

almond semifreddo

310 ml (1¼ cups) cream
4 eggs, at room temperature, separated
85 g (²⁄₃ cup) icing (confectioners') sugar
60 ml (¼ cup) amaretto
80 g (½ cup) toasted almonds, chopped
8 amaretti biscuits, crushed
fresh fruit, for serving

whip the cream until firm peaks form, then cover and refrigerate. Line a 10 x 21 cm (4 x 8½ inch) loaf tin with enough plastic wrap so that it overhangs the 2 long sides.

beat the egg yolks and icing sugar in a large bowl until pale and creamy. Whisk the egg whites in a separate bowl until firm peaks form. Stir the amaretto, almonds and amaretti biscuits into the egg yolk mixture, then carefully fold in the chilled cream and the egg whites until well combined. Pour or spoon into the lined loaf tin and cover with the overhanging plastic. Freeze for 4 hours, or until frozen but not rock hard. Serve in slices, topped with fresh fruit. Serves 8–10.

note: If you leave the semifreddo in the freezer overnight, put it in the refrigerator for 30 minutes before serving.

1 Whip the cream until it is thick and firm but not overbeaten.

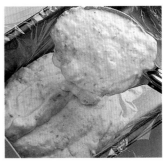

2 Spoon the mixture into a lined tin, ensuring an even surface.

capers

These are the small unopened flower buds of a Mediterranean shrub. Once picked, they need to be pickled in brine or cured in salt before they are edible, as is the case with olives. Capers are tart, piquant, and a wonderful companion to fish such as swordfish and tuna. Capers are also added to tomato sauces for pasta, such as puttanesca; sprinkled on pizzas; or used raw or fried in salads such as Sicilian *caponata*. They should be rinsed, drained and patted dry before use. The caperberry is the fruit of the same shrub, but appears after the flower. They are usually preserved in brine and can be used on antipasto plates, in salads or eaten like olives.

Caperberries.

caponata with tuna

caponata

500 g (1 lb 2 oz) ripe tomatoes
750 g (1 lb 10 oz) eggplant (aubergine), cut into 1 cm (½ inch) cubes
125 ml (½ cup) olive oil
1 onion, chopped
3 celery stalks, chopped

2 tablespoons capers
125 g (4½ oz) green olives, pitted
1 tablespoon sugar
125 ml (½ cup) red wine vinegar

6 x 200 g (7 oz) tuna steaks
olive oil, for brushing

score a cross in the base of each tomato. Put the tomatoes into a bowl of boiling water for 20 seconds, then plunge into cold water. Drain and peel the skin away from the cross. Cut the tomato into small cubes.

sprinkle the eggplant with salt and leave in a colander for 1 hour. Rinse under cold water and pat dry. Heat 2 tablespoons oil in a frying pan over medium heat and cook half the eggplant for 4–5 minutes, or until golden and soft. Remove from the pan and drain on crumpled paper towels. Repeat the process with 2 tablespoons oil and the remaining eggplant.

heat the remaining olive oil in the same pan, add the onion and celery and cook for 5–6 minutes, or until softened. Reduce the heat to low, add the tomato and simmer for 15 minutes, stirring occasionally. Stir in the capers, olives, sugar and vinegar, season and continue to simmer, stirring occasionally, for 10 minutes, or until slightly reduced. Add the eggplant and gently stir through. Remove from the heat and cool to room temperature.

heat a chargrill pan (griddle) and brush lightly with olive oil. Cook the tuna for 2–3 minutes each side, or to your liking. Serve with the caponata piled on top. Serves 6.

cheese

Cheese-making has long been a part of Mediterranean life—the ancient Egyptians knew how to make cheese, as did the Greeks and Romans. In Islamic countries, where the consumption of fresh milk is forbidden, cheese, butter, yoghurt and clotted cream are all common. Although all cheeses are made following the same basic method, they can vary dramatically, often due to long-established regional traditions.

making cheese

Cheese is made by coagulating or curdling milk with rennet so that it separates into curds (solids) and whey (liquid). The majority of cheeses are made by separating the curds from the whey, then processing and maturing the curds to make cheese. However, whey cheeses such as ricotta are made from the whey itself and fresh, unripened cheeses do not go through a maturing process.

The type of animal yielding the milk, or the milk itself, can make a great difference to the taste and texture of the cheese. The milk may be from a cow, sheep or goat. It may be from a morning or an evening milking, or a combination of both. It may be skimmed or have cream added to it, or it may have come from a particular breed of cow, or from a cow fed on a particular diet. Finally, the milk may be raw or pasteurized. Great variation also occurs through the addition of rennet and lactic starters; in the way in which the curds are cut; and the final pressing, salting and forming of the cheese. As well, crusts are formed in various ways and the cheese may be immersed in brine, alcohol or various spices. All this results in a great variety of cheeses. Many are intended for the cheeseboard only; the following pages look at those cheeses suitable for use in cooking.

storing and serving cheese

Cheese is a living substance and should be stored carefully until eaten or used in cooking. It needs humidity, but it must not get wet. Never freeze or store cheese in plastic wrap. Put it in a box in the vegetable crisper, wrapped in waxed paper, aluminium foil or in a cloth cheese bag. Cheese destined for the cheeseboard should be served at room temperature, so remove it from the refrigerator a few hours before serving. Serve cheese with slices of pear, some muscatels, candied citron, and some good bread.

Making Parmigiano Reggiano: milk containing rennet is heated in huge copper cauldrons to form curds. These are then cut in two and left to drain in linen cloth.

feta

This cheese is traditionally made using goat or ewe's milk, though milk from cows is also used nowadays. Feta cheese is made in large blocks and cured and stored in brine. It develops a rich salty flavour and quite a crumbly texture. Greece is famous for its feta but Turkey and other countries of the Eastern Mediterranean make similar cheeses, which vary according to region but are generally creamier and sometimes also saltier. Feta and similar cheeses are eaten almost daily, as part of a mezze spread or in cooking, such as in the Turkish cheese-filled filo pastries, *borek*. The Greeks also combine feta with filo pastry, in pies and triangles, and also use feta in salads and baked with prawns.

greek salad

cut the cucumber in half lengthways and discard the seeds. Cut it into bite-sized pieces.

cut each pepper in half lengthways, remove the membrane and seeds and cut the flesh into 1 cm (½ inch) wide strips. Gently mix the cucumber, green pepper, tomato, onion, olives, feta, parsley and mint leaves in a large salad bowl and gently toss to mix.

put the oil, lemon juice and garlic in a screw-top jar, season and shake well. Pour over the salad and serve. Serves 4.

1 Lebanese (short) cucumber, peeled
2 green peppers (capsicums)
4 vine-ripened tomatoes, cut into wedges
1 red onion, finely sliced
16 Kalamata olives
250 g (9 oz) Greek feta cheese, cubed
24 flat-leaf (Italian) parsley leaves
12 whole mint leaves
125 ml (½ cup) virgin olive oil
2 tablespoons lemon juice
1 garlic clove, crushed

goat's cheese

Known in France as *fromages de chèvre*, these goat cheeses are uncooked, unpressed cheeses, with a slightly wrinkled rind and fresh, tart taste when young. Older goat's cheeses are more wrinkly, often with a blue mould (sometimes encouraged by lightly dusting with ash) and a more intense, nutty flavour. They are produced all over France, with some of the more famous examples hailing from Provence, the Loire Valley and Corsica. Traditionally, they were made in the spring, taking advantage of the new season's rich milk.

goat's cheese and ricotta galette

pastry
125 g (1 cup) plain (all-purpose) flour
60 ml (¼ cup) olive oil
3–4 tablespoons chilled water

filling
1 tablespoon olive oil

2 onions, thinly sliced
1 teaspoon thyme leaves
125 g (4½ oz) ricotta
100 g (3½ oz) goat's cheese
2 tablespoons pitted Niçoise olives
1 egg, lightly beaten
60 ml (¼ cup) cream

to make the pastry, sift the flour and a pinch of salt into a large bowl and make a well. Add the olive oil and mix with a flat-bladed knife until crumbly. Gradually add the water until the mixture comes together. Remove and pat together to form a disc. Refrigerate for 30 minutes.

to make the filling, heat the olive oil in a frying pan. Add the onion, cover and cook over low heat for 30 minutes. Season and stir in half the thyme. Allow to cool slightly.

preheat the oven to 180°C (350°F/Gas 4). Lightly flour the work bench and roll out the pastry to a 30 cm (12 inch) circle. Evenly spread the onion over the pastry leaving a 2 cm (¾ inch) border. Sprinkle the ricotta and the goat's cheese evenly over the onion. Scatter the olives over the cheeses, then sprinkle with the remaining thyme. Fold the pastry border in to the edge of the filling, gently pleating as you go.

combine the egg and cream in a small jug, then carefully pour over the filling. Bake the galette on a heated baking tray on the lower half of the oven for 45 minutes, or until the pastry is golden. Serves 6.

other french cheeses

roquefort cheese This strong, creamy blue cheese must ripen in the caves of Cambalou in the southwest of France to legally carry the name. Legend has it that it was discovered by a goatherd who returned for some food he had left in the caves a few days before. It is served as either a table cheese or used in soufflés or in savoury pastries.

fattoush with fried haloumi

1 small cucumber
2 pitta breads
1 garlic clove, crushed
1 tablespoon lemon juice
3 tablespoons olive oil
2 spring onions (scallions), sliced
2 tomatoes, diced
1 green pepper (capsicum), diced
1 large bunch flat-leaf (Italian) parsley, chopped
1 tablespoon mint, chopped
1 tablespoon oregano, chopped
500 g (1 lb 2 oz) haloumi cheese, cut into 4 slices
sumac (optional)

preheat the grill (broiler). Peel the cucumber, cut it into quarters lengthways, then cut each piece into thick slices. Put them in a sieve and sprinkle with a little salt to help drain off any excess liquid, which would make the salad soggy.

split each pitta bread in half and toast them on both sides. When the bread is crisp, break it into small pieces.

mix together the garlic, lemon juice and 2 tablespoons of the oil to make a dressing. Rinse and drain the cucumber. Put the cucumber, spring onion, tomato, green pepper and the chopped parsley, mint and oregano in a large bowl. Add the dressing and toss everything together well.

heat the last tablespoon of oil in a non-stick frying pan and fry the haloumi cheese on both sides until it is browned. Scatter the bread over the salad and fold it through. Serve the fattoush with the slices of haloumi on top. Sprinkle with a little sumac, if you are using it. Serves 2.

haloumi

This salty, semi-hard sheep's milk cheese is a popular cheese in countries such as Lebanon, Syria and Cyprus, which is where much of this cheese comes from. It has a distinctive, almost rubbery texture when fresh, and is squeaky when cooked. Haloumi is often thickly sliced and grilled (broiled) or fried, then served with a squeeze of lemon juice or a sprinkling of mint. Taken with a glass of ouzo, this is a classic Greek mezze dish. It also makes an ideal accompaniment to *fattoush*, a Middle Eastern salad that features crispy pieces of flatbread tossed with vegetables.

At left, Valdeon queso tradicionales, a cow's milk blue cheese, matured in limestone caves in Valdeon, from the León region of Spain. It is wrapped in sycamore leaves. At back, Murcia al vino, a smooth goat's milk cheese doused with Murcia's local red wine. At right, 6 month old manchego cheese from La Mancha.

manchego

This Spanish sheep's milk cheese is from La Mancha in Spain's interior and is made exclusively from the milk of the manchego sheep. The sheep graze on wild herbs, which contribute to the distinctive salty, slightly nutty taste. It is a firm, ivory-coloured cheese that is traditionally pressed in moulds made of esparto, a native grass, giving a zigzag pattern on the rind. Manchego is served with bread and *membrillo*, a quince paste, for a light breakfast meal or for afternoon tea.

other spanish cheeses

cabrales Considered by many to be Spain's premier cheese, this blue cheese is made in only four villages, including the village of Cabrales, from the Asturia region in the country's northwest. Following a jealously guarded process, the cheese is made in the spring and summer, mainly from cow's milk but also sheep and goat's milk, and is left to mature in the local caves for up to six months. It has a thick, creamy texture, is streaked blue, and has a strong aftertaste. It is a table cheese only. Valdeon queso, from the León region of northern Spain, is another blue cheese, matured in the area's limestone caves for three to six months.

murcia al vino This goat's cheese is from Murcia, in the southeast of Spain. It is distinctive for being bathed in red wine during the ripening process, which gives it a burgundy tinge and pleasing aroma. The region's prized goats graze on wild herbs and grasses.

mozzarella

At one time, all mozzarella in Italy was made from the prized milk of water buffaloes, which produced a creamy, fragrant fresh cheese known as mozzarella *di bufala*. These days, cow's milk is increasingly used and such mozzarella is called *fior di latte*. It is cheaper to make but the resulting texture and taste are slightly different. To make mozzarella, the curds are stretched and shaped into balls by hand (though some balls are now factory made). Mozzarella should be white, fresh-smelling and have tiny holes that weep whey when it is very fresh. It is available in a variety of sizes that are sold in their own whey and also as plaits. Bocconcini literally means 'small mouthful' and is the name given to the smooth, mild-tasting, bite-size balls of mozzarella. Mozzarella balls will last for three weeks if stored in the refrigerator and covered in the whey in which they are sold.

insalata caprese

8 ripe Roma (plum) tomatoes
3–4 mozzarella balls, preferably buffalo mozzarella
2 tablespoons extra virgin olive oil
15 small basil leaves

slice the tomatoes, pouring off any excess juice, and cut the mozzarella into slices of a similar thickness.

arrange alternating rows of tomato and mozzarella on a serving plate. Sprinkle with salt and freshly ground black pepper and drizzle the olive oil over the top. Scatter with basil leaves, tearing any large ones. Serve immediately. Serves 4.

parmesan

This world-famous hard, crumbly cheese is made from skimmed or partially skimmed cow's milk. The best is Parmigiano Reggiano, produced in the Parma and Reggio provinces of northern Italy using techniques that are seven centuries old. It is aged for up to four years and is unrivalled in flavour and texture. It is grated and used in countless dishes; younger ones are eaten as a table cheese. Grana Padano tastes like and is made in a similar way to Parmigiano Reggiano, but it can be produced in other areas. It, too, is suitable for grating or eating. Always buy Parmesan cheese in a chunk and grate it as needed. To store, wrap in greaseproof paper, then in aluminium foil.

eggplant parmigiana

1.5 kg (3 lb 5 oz) eggplants
   (aubergines)
plain (all-purpose) flour,
   seasoned with salt
   and pepper
350 ml (12 fl oz) olive oil
500 ml (2 cups) tomato
   passata
2 tablespoons roughly torn
   basil leaves
250 g (9 oz) mozzarella,
   chopped
90 g (3¼ oz) Parmesan
   cheese, grated

thinly slice the eggplant lengthways. Layer the slices in a large colander, sprinkling salt between each layer. Leave for 1 hour to extract the bitter juices. Rinse and pat the slices dry on both sides with paper towels, then coat lightly with the flour.

preheat the oven to 180°C (350°F/Gas 4) and grease a shallow 2.5 litre (10 cup) baking dish. Heat 125 ml (½ cup) of the olive oil in a large frying pan. Quickly fry the eggplant slices in batches over high heat until crisp and golden on both sides. Add more olive oil as needed and drain on paper towels as you remove each batch from the pan.

make a slightly overlapping layer of eggplant slices over the base of the dish. Season with pepper and a little salt. Spoon 4 tablespoons of passata over the eggplant and scatter some of the basil over the top. Sprinkle with some mozzarella, followed by some Parmesan. Continue with this layering until you have used up all the ingredients, then finish with a layer of the cheeses. Bake for 30 minutes. Remove from the oven and allow to cool for 30 minutes before serving. Serves 8.

ricotta

In Italian cooking, ricotta is often combined with pasta. It is used as both a topping and a filling, such as in *culingiones*, the Sardinian moon-shaped ravioli. Desserts such as rich Sicilian *cannoli* are widely eaten, as is a ricotta cake flavoured with citrus, almonds and candied peel. In Eastern Mediterranean countries, a cheese similar to ricotta is widely available and is often served as a breakfast food, eaten with honey, or is made into syrupy desserts featuring kataifi pastry. Similarly, the Spanish and South Americans serve requesón, a ricotta-style cheese, with honey and pine nuts as a simple dessert. When buying, choose firm ricotta, store in the refrigerator and use within a few days as it quickly turns rancid.

Made from the whey that remains after the making of other cheeses, ricotta in Italian literally translates as 'recooked'. It can be made from cow, ewe and goat's milk and is not strictly a cheese, as cheeses are made from milk curd, not whey. Ricotta is a fresh, low-fat, slightly sweet cheese created by boiling the whey from cooked milk, then scooping off the solid particles that float to the top and draining off the solid remnants. Like other fresh cheeses, ricotta is most often used in cooking, where the delicate flavour and creamy texture are complemented by other stronger savoury flavours such as spinach or sweet flavours such as citrus and dried fruit.

other italian cheeses

caciocavallo This southern cheese is moulded into a pear shape, then dried. Eaten as a table or melting cheese when young, it can be grated over dishes like a Parmesan cheese when aged.

pecorino This is one of Italy's most popular cheeses. Versions of it are produced in many areas but the one from Sardinia is particularly famous. Pecorino is made from sheep's milk and always by the same method, although it may be aged in different ways. Pecorino sardo is a highly flavoured salty cheese, softer than the hard pecorino romano. Both are good for grating and using in cooking.

Pecorino cheese is one of Italy's most popular cheeses, and virtually every region produces a version. It is made from sheep's milk and always by the same method, although the result varies according to the milk and ageing process used.

sardinian ravioli

filling

**4 tablespoons mixed fresh herbs such as flat-leaf (Italian)
parsley, basil, mint, marjoram, oregano and thyme, chopped**
250 g (9 oz) ricotta cheese (preferably sheep's milk)
250 g (9 oz) pecorino cheese (preferably Sardinian), grated
1 egg
pinch freshly grated nutmeg

1 quantity fresh pasta dough (see page 36)
1 egg
2 teaspoons milk

to make the filling, mix the herbs with the ricotta, pecorino, egg and nutmeg. Season to taste.

to make the ravioli, roll out the pasta dough to the thinnest setting of the machine or with a rolling pin. Don't roll out more than you can handle at a time.

cut circles out of the dough with a 9 cm (3½ inch) round cutter or an upturned wine glass. Mix together the egg and milk and brush over each circle just before filling.

put 2 teaspoons of the filling in the centre of each circle. Fold over the top of the circle to make a half-moon shape. Use your finger to press down around the filling to remove any air pockets. Run your finger firmly around the edge to seal well.

put the ravioli, well spaced out, on a tray dusted with semolina and leave to dry for a few minutes before cooking. The ravioli can be cooked immediately or left for up to 1 hour.

cook the ravioli in batches in a large saucepan of boiling salted water until *al dente*. Remove with a slotted spoon and briefly rest the spoon on a tea towel to drain away any remaining water. Serve with melted unsalted butter or a tomato sauce and grated pecorino. Serves 4.

Put enough filling in the middle to fill the ravioli when folded over.

ricotta cake with almonds and candied peel

150 g (5½ oz) flaked or whole almonds
50 g (1¾ oz) Italian pandoro sweet cake
6 eggs
100 g (3½ oz) caster (superfine) sugar
grated zest of 1 orange
grated zest of 1 lemon
500 g (1 lb 2 oz) ricotta cheese
200 g (7 oz) candied peel, chopped

A by-product of cheesemaking, ricotta is a fresh, sweet-flavoured cheese. It can be eaten on its own or used to fill pastas or in desserts.

preheat the oven to 180°C (350°F/Gas 4). Toast the almonds on a baking tray in the oven for 8–10 minutes until golden brown.

put the almonds and pandoro in a food processor and process until the mixture resembles coarse breadcrumbs. Alternatively, finely chop the nuts and pandoro and mix them together. Grease a 20 cm (8 inch) springform tin with a little butter. Tip some of the mixture into the tin and shake it around so that it forms a coating on the bottom and side of the tin. Reserves the remaining nut mixture.

whisk the eggs and sugar for several minutes until pale and a little frothy. Add the orange and lemon zest, ricotta, candied peel and the remaining nut mixture and mix together very briefly.

pour into the tin and bake for 40–50 minutes, or until the cake feels just firm to the touch. Cool in the tin. Dust with icing (confectioners') sugar before serving at room temperature. Serves 6.

note: To save having to clean fiddly citrus zest out of your grater, hold a piece of greaseproof paper against the grater before you use it. When you pull off the paper all the zest will come with it.

clarified butter

Along with olive and vegetable oils, clarified butter or *samna*, as it is called locally, has generally replaced rendered lamb fat as a cooking medium in kitchens across the Middle East. It was traditionally made from buffalo milk butter that was slowly melted over boiling water and strained through squares of damp muslin. This process separates the milk solids, eliminating impurities as well as the water. Clarified butter is a favoured frying medium due to its distinct flavour and high smoking point. While an Indian form of clarified butter called ghee is now sold in many supermarkets, it is fairly simple to make your own at home. Melt unsalted butter very slowly over low heat, skimming off any foam that forms on top. The remaining clear butter is then strained through a cloth into a sterilized jar. Store in the refrigerator.

coffee

Transforming the raw coffee bean into an aromatic, rich brew involves washing, fermenting, husking, drying, roasting and blending, then grinding and finally adding the grains to water and heating. These many stages may account for the ritualistic fervour many coffee fans bring to the bean and the drink, and nowhere is this more true than in the Mediterranean. Coffee, as a drink, originated in Yemen, and spread throughout Europe in the sixteenth century with Arab traders. Today, it is hard to imagine Mediterranean breakfast without coffee, and Italy, in particular, also features coffee in cooking: in desserts, granitas and gelatos. Naples is particularly well known for its coffee granitas, traditionally served topped with whipped cream.

coffee granita

200 g (7 oz) caster (superfine) sugar
1.25 litres (5 cups) very strong espresso coffee

heat the caster sugar with 25 ml (³/₄ fl oz) hot water in a saucepan until the sugar dissolves. Simmer for 3 minutes to make a sugar syrup. Add the coffee and stir well.

pour into a plastic or metal freezer box. The mixture should be no deeper than 3 cm (1¼ inches) so that it freezes quickly and breaks up easily. Stir every 2 hours with a fork to break up the ice crystals as they form. Repeat this 2 or 3 times. The granita is ready when almost set but still grainy. Stir a fork through it just before serving. Serves 6.

cured meats and sausages

cured and cooked hams

At its most basic, ham is the salt-cured hind leg of a pig. But the flavour of the ham is due to numerous factors—the breed and age of the pig, its diet and the method of curing. Curing methods may vary, but the process is always based on salt, using either a dry-cure or brine, sometimes with added herbs, spices and treacle or molasses. Most hams are then either smoked or air-dried and possibly aged for months or even years to give each its unique flavour. Though pork is the most common choice, beef, wild boar and venison have also been used in the Mediterranean to make cured meats; one example is bresaola, a salt-cured or air-dried beef from Italy.

types of ham

air-dried hams These have been salt-cured, usually dry-salted, then hung in cool air to dry. They are traditionally made in mountain areas that have steady breezes and little pollution and in climates that are low in humidity. The most famous dry-cured ham is prosciutto di Parma from the area around Parma in Italy, though San Daniele from the northeast of Italy, is also excellent. So, too, are Spanish jamon Iberico and jamon serrano; this latter ham is left to dry for as long as 18 months. Parma ham is a favourite antipasto dish, often served with fresh figs or slices of melon, eaten with bread, or used in cooking. Serrano ham is eaten across Spain as a tapas dish, simply served in thick slices and topped with pimiento (cooked Spanish red peppers).

cooked hams Known as *prosciutto cotto* in Italy, the cut of ham is the same as for air-dried hams but is made by being pressed into a mould and steamed. Prosciutto cotto is eaten as an antipasto or in cooking.

smoked hams These are hams that have been salt-cured either in dry salt or brine, then smoked. The smoking further cures the hams as well as adds flavour. Well-known smoked hams for eating raw include the French jambon de Bayonne and jambon d'Ardennes.

non-leg hams These are not true hams as they are not from the whole leg but are cuts of the leg or other cuts such as the shoulder or loin, cured like hams. Italian coppa is made from the collar of pork, salt-cured in brine, then air-dried. It is a mixture of meat and fat, with the best ones having equal amounts of each. It is sliced thinly for antipasto. Italian culatello is made from the rump in the same way as prosciutto is. It has a sweet taste and can be eaten on its own.

The salting and drying of meat are techniques known since Classical times. During the Middle Ages, the practice really hit its stride, driven by the continuing need of poorer people to ensure food for themselves over winter but given extra impetus by the need to feed armies and sailors embarking on ever-longer voyages. However, like so many ingredients in the Mediterranean, what began out of necessity has developed, over the centuries, into the many wonderful and sophisticated regional specialities that we enjoy today.

meat antipasto

a meat antipasto plate is probably the quickest to put together. It is, however, very important that you choose a really good selection of meats. Buy the best quality you can afford: the fresher the meat is, the better it will taste. If you are planning on serving this dish often, you may want to buy a few whole salami and slice them yourself at home as you need them.

serve the meat with strong accompaniments such as caperberries, cipollini and olives, as these cut through any fattiness, or with sweet fruit like figs and melon that enhance its flavours.

to put together an attractive platter, cut the meat in different ways. The lardo needs to be sliced very thinly, almost shaved. The salami can be sliced according to your personal taste—generally the smaller salami such as cacciatore are cut into thicker slices than the large ones. Mortadella is often cut into cubes instead of slicing.

lay out the meats on a platter, folding some and rolling others. Arrange a choice of the accompaniments on the platter with them so your guests can help themselves, and serve with plenty of bread. The bresaola should be sprinkled with a little olive oil and lemon juice just before serving. Always serve a meat antipasto platter at room temperature—meat taken straight from the refrigerator will not have as much flavour. Serves 6.

6 slices lardo
6 slices felino salami or
    1 or 2 cacciatore salami
6 slices coppa di Parma
6 slices bresaola
6 slices prosciutto di Parma or
    San Daniele
selection of plain olive oil
    bruschetta or crostini,
    topped with flavourings
    such as chicken liver
6 slices mortadella
black olives, in brine and
    unpitted
pickled baby onions (cipollini)
caperberries
sun-dried tomatoes
3 figs, halved
6 slices rockmelon
    (cantaloupe)
country-style bread, to serve
extra virgin olive oil and
    lemon juice, to serve

sausages

Generally, sausages consist of chopped meat and flavourings stuffed into tube-shaped casings. However, a much wider range of products can be grouped under the term 'sausage'. Sausages can be made from meat, fish or vegetables; can be fresh, cooked or cured and fermented; can range in size and shape; and don't necessarily have to be stuffed into casings. Fresh sausages tend to be made into links, as are some cured and cooked sausages; some, however, are sold as spirals or lengths. Cured and cooked sausages can also be bought sliced.

cooked and cured sausages

cooked sausages Sausages may be cooked or partially cooked. The most famous of the Mediterranean's cooked sausages is Italy's largest sausage, mortadella. This large, finely textured pork sausage has lengths of lard running through it, and some versions also contain pistachio nuts. It should be eaten very fresh, either thinly sliced or in cubes. Traditionally made in Bologna, mortadella is also known as bologna or boloney in the USA.

cured or dried sausages These are made with raw meat, salt and saltpetre and are usually flavoured with spices such as black pepper, chilli or paprika. The meat mixture is stuffed into casings and then hung to dry, either in cool or hot air, until they have reduced their weight by about half. Some cured sausages are also smoked, further enhancing their preservation properties. There are countless local examples of cured or dried sausages, from all parts of the Mediterranean, and Spanish chorizo is one of the best known. Of note among the Italian *salame* is the strongly flavoured *salame di napoli*, a long dried sausage made from pork, beef and pork fat, with garlic, pepper, wine, chilli and paprika. In France, Lyon is a celebrated centre for *saucissons secs*, producing rosettes, made from seasoned pork and back fat in a natural case, and Jésus, so named because of a supposed resemblance to the swaddled baby Jesus. Both types should be eaten sliced thinly.

Above, left to right: mortadella, fresh sausages and Italian *salame di Napoli*. Opposite, top right, Spanish chorizo.

chorizo This cured sausage is very popular in Spain and most regions have their own variety. In Catalan alone, there are seventeen officially recognized varieties. Chorizo is a pork sausage with a coarse texture, highly seasoned with paprika and garlic, and is either mild or made spicy with the addition of chillies. The sausages are generally sold cured or smoked, and are indispensable in many traditional Spanish recipes, as well as constituting one of the all-time favourite tapas dishes.

spanish chorizo in cider

3 teaspoons olive oil
1 small onion, finely chopped
1½ teaspoons paprika
125 ml (½ cup) dry alcoholic apple cider
60 ml (¼ cup) chicken stock
1 bay leaf
280 g (10 oz) chorizo, sliced diagonally
2 teaspoons sherry vinegar, to taste
2 teaspoons chopped flat-leaf (Italian) parsley

heat the oil in a saucepan over low heat, add the onion and cook for 3 minutes, stirring occasionally, or until soft. Add the paprika and cook for 1 minute.

increase the heat to medium, add the apple cider, stock and bay leaf to the pan and bring to the boil. Reduce the heat and gently simmer for 5 minutes. Add the sliced chorizo and simmer for 5 minutes, or until the sauce has reduced slightly. Stir in the sherry vinegar and parsley. Serve hot, with plenty of crusty bread. Serves 4.

fresh sausages

Sausages tend to be eaten fresh in those parts of the Mediterranean that have colder climates or where the air is too moist for successful drying and curing, such as northern Italy and parts of France and Spain. Pork remains the most popular ingredient, though some feature beef, and bread and cereal may also be added as a filler. The sausages are usually flavoured with salt, pepper and mace along with herbs and spices according to their variety. One well known example is Toulouse sausage, a coarse pork sausage flavoured with wine, garlic and seasonings added. It is usually braised, fried or grilled (broiled).

merguez Originally from Tunisia but now adopted by the French, this fresh sausage is increasingly popular around the world. It is flavoured with harissa and is usually grilled (broiled) and served with couscous but its spiciness makes it a great companion for a variety of ingredients including pasta, bread, and summery vegetables.

merguez with harissa and couscous

1 tablespoon butter
150 g (5½ oz) instant couscous
1 teaspoon harissa
2 tablespoons olive oil
1 tablespoon lemon juice
1 tablespoon grated lemon zest
1 tablespoon chopped parsley
70 g (2½ oz) grilled (broiled) red pepper (capsicum), sliced
2 tablespoons raisins
6 merguez sausages
Greek-style natural yoghurt

put the butter in a saucepan with 250 ml (1 cup) water and bring to the boil. Add the couscous, mix it into the water, then take it off the stove. Cover and leave it to sit for 5 minutes. Turn on the grill (broiler).

put the harissa, olive oil, lemon juice and zest in a bowl and stir together until well mixed. Add the parsley, red pepper and raisins and leave everything to marinate briefly.

grill (broil) the sausages for 8 minutes, turning them so they brown on all sides. Meanwhile, take the lid off the couscous, stir it for 2 minutes to separate the grains, then stir in the harissa mixture. Serve the couscous with the merguez sliced over it and topped with a large dollop of yoghurt. Serves 2.

salsicce In Italy, fresh sausages come under the general name *salsicce*, and one of the more commonly available varieties is cotechino, a speciality of northern Italy. These are made from pork and pork rind and have a gelatinous texture. They are often flavoured with cloves and cinnamon.

salsicce with white beans and gremolata

3 tablespoons olive oil
6 salsicce, cut into chunks
4 garlic cloves, smashed
125 g (4½ oz) grilled (broiled) red or yellow pepper (capsicum)
400 g (14 oz) tinned cannellini beans, drained and rinsed

1 tablespoon grated lemon zest
3 tablespoons parsley, chopped
1 tablespoon lemon juice
virgin olive oil, for drizzling

heat the olive oil in a frying pan and cook the salsicce until they are browned all over and cooked through. Lift them out of the frying pan with a slotted spoon and put them to one side.

put 2 garlic cloves in the frying pan and cook them over low heat until they are very soft. Cut the pepper into strips and add to the pan, along with the beans and salsicce. Stir everything together and cook over low heat for 2 minutes to heat the salsicce through. Season well with salt and pepper.

to make the gremolata, put the remaining 2 garlic cloves and some salt into a mortar and smash to a paste with the pestle. Mix in the lemon zest and the chopped parsley and season with salt and pepper. Just before serving, stir the gremolata through the beans and then finish with a sprinkling of lemon juice and a drizzle of olive oil. Serves 2.

other pork cuts and ingredients

guanciale The cured cheek of a pig, guanciale tastes and resembles pancetta. It is the traditional ingredient in spaghetti carbonara and spaghetti all'Amatriciana.

lardo This is the cured lard from pork. It is often flavoured with herbs, pepper and salt. It is used as a flavouring in cooking, or is sometimes finely shaved and eaten on its own or as part of an antipasto platter.

pancetta Coming from the Italian word *pancia*, which means belly, pancetta is exactly the same cut of meat as bacon but it is not normally smoked. There are two main types of pancetta: pancetta stesa, a flat type that is cured for about three weeks and then hung to dry for up to four months, and pancetta arrotolata, which is rolled into a salami-like shape. Pancetta stesa is used to flavour sauces, stews and pastas, and the rolled pancetta is mainly used as an antipasto meat.

spaghetti carbonara

1 tablespoon olive oil
250 g (9 oz) guanciale or
  pancetta, cut into cubes
4 tablespoons thick
  (double/heavy) cream

6 egg yolks
500 g (1 lb 2 oz) spaghetti
50 g (1/2 cup) grated
  Parmesan cheese, plus
  extra, to serve

put the olive oil in a saucepan and cook the pancetta over medium heat, stirring frequently, until it is light brown and crisp. Tip the pancetta into a metal colander to strain off the fat. Mix together the cream and egg yolks. Add the pancetta to the mixture when it has cooled.

cook the pasta in a large saucepan of boiling salted water until *al dente*. Drain, reserving a little of the cooking water.

return the pasta to the pan to retain as much heat as possible, add the egg mixture and Parmesan, season and mix together. Add a little of the reserved water if the sauce is too thick and the pasta is stuck together. Serve in warmed bowls with extra Parmesan on top. Serves 6.

honey

The world's first sweetener, honey has been used for a lot longer than sugar. It was regarded in ancient times as a food of the gods and a symbol of wealth. In the Middle East, Syrian bees were said to produce the best honey, and soaking food such as pastries and cakes in honey was a traditional method of perfuming and extending the life of dishes. Honey was also used as a means of refreshing cakes if stale.

types and uses of honey

The fragrance and flavour of honey depends on the flowers that the bees have fed on, not the bees themselves, as honey is really processed flower nectar. Regional honeys include thyme honey and French lavender honey. The general rule is that the darker the colour, the stronger the flavour. For all-purpose cooking and eating, it is best to use a pale, mild honey such as clover. In cooking, honey is mainly used in desserts, fruit salads, biscuits and cakes, but it is also an essential part of North African sweet-and-spicy savoury dishes, such as marinated aromatic eggplant (aubergine), and sweet chicken dishes.

ricotta with honey and pine nuts

300 g (10½ oz) ricotta cheese or requesón
2 tablespoons honey
pine nuts, toasted, for serving

divide the ricotta between 2 bowls, drizzle with honey and sprinkle with the pine nuts. Serves 2.

pastry

The epoch when female slaves would spend their days working in the kitchens of the extremely wealthy producing dishes of exquisite beauty and skill are over, but the many small and large pies and pastries that date back to that age still remain, nowadays made in specialist pastry shops.

In the Eastern Mediterranean, where households pride themselves on being able to offer delicious little morsels of food whenever a guest may arrive, these pies and pastries are the perfect offering.

types of pastry

filo pastry Also known as phyllo, this is a paper-thin pastry made from flour and water. This simple description does not do justice to the skill, or the arms, needed to stretch the dough to tissue-like thinness, and today most cooks in the Mediterranean gratefully buy fresh or frozen commercially made filo. Filo is used widely in Eastern Mediterranean countries in numerous sweet and savoury dishes. Savoury dishes include the more-ish Lebanese and Turkish fried filo cigars, Tunisian *briks*, and Greek *spanakopita* pies, while sweet dishes include Moroccan almond filo snake and the famous baklava. The invention of baklava is claimed by more than one country, but it is probably rather like the pastry itself: the result of layers of involvement by different cultures, starting with the Assyrians in the eighth century BCE, who first placed chopped nuts between layers of pastry and soaked it in sugar. The Greeks, Armenians and Arabs later refined it and the famed pastry chefs of the Ottoman Empire put the finishing touches on its presentation and form. Needless to say, baklava is a favourite right across the Eastern Mediterranean.

kataifi This shredded pastry is used throughout Greece, Turkey and the Middle East, where it is also known as *konafa* or *kadaif*. A flour and water batter is poured through a sieve onto a rotating hot plate. As it hits it sets to become soft, white vermicelli-like strands of pastry, which are immediately lifted off for use. Most cooks these days buy rather than make their own; outside of the Mediterranean, kataifi is available from Greek delicatessens and other speciality food stores. It is used to make syrupy pastries with cheese or nuts.

baklava

put the sugar, lemon zest and 375 ml (1½ cups) water in a saucepan and stir over high heat until the sugar has dissolved, then boil for 5 minutes. Reduce the heat to low and simmer for 5 minutes, or until the syrup has thickened slightly and just coats the back of a spoon. Add the honey, lemon juice and orange flower water and cook for 2 minutes. Remove from the heat and leave to cool completely.

preheat the oven to 170°C (325°F/Gas 3). Combine the nuts, extra sugar and cinnamon in a bowl. Brush the base and sides of a 30 x 27 cm (12 x 10¾ inch) baking dish or tin with the melted butter. Cover the base with a single layer of filo pastry, brush lightly with the butter, and fold in any overhanging edges. Continue layering the filo, brushing each new layer with butter and folding in the edges until 10 sheets have been used. Keep the unused filo under a damp tea towel.

sprinkle half the nut mixture over the pastry and pat down evenly. Repeat the layering and buttering of 5 more filo sheets, sprinkle with the remaining nuts, then continue to layer and butter the remaining sheets, including the top layer. Press down with your hands so the pastry and nuts stick to each other. Using a sharp knife, cut into diamond shapes, cutting through to the bottom layer. Pour any remaining butter over the top and smooth with your hands. Bake for 30 minutes, then lower the temperature to 150°C (300°F/Gas 2) and cook for 30 minutes more.

while still piping hot, cut through the original diamond markings, then strain the cold syrup evenly over the top. Cool completely before lifting the diamonds out onto a serving platter. Makes 18 pieces.

- 515 g (2¼ cups) caster (superfine) sugar
- 1½ teaspoons grated lemon zest
- 90 g (¼ cup) honey
- 60 ml (¼ cup) lemon juice
- 2 tablespoons orange flower water
- 200 g (7 oz) walnuts, finely chopped
- 200 g (7 oz) shelled pistachios, finely chopped
- 200 g (7 oz) almonds, finely chopped
- 2 tablespoons caster (superfine) sugar, extra
- 2 teaspoons ground cinnamon
- 200 g (7 oz) unsalted butter, melted
- 375 g (13 oz) ready-made filo pastry

Baklava is not for those on a diet. It is made from layers of buttered filo pastry, which are filled with chopped nuts, sugar and spices, cut into triangles and doused in a rich sugar syrup.

preserved lemons

Preserved lemons are a speciality of Morocco, made by tightly packing lemon quarters in jars with salt and lemon juice. They are traditionally served with dishes such as grilled (broiled) meats or used to flavour couscous, tagines, stuffings and casseroles. They can lend an intense citrus tang to a surprising variety of savoury dishes, such as prawn (shrimp) skewers, risotto, pasta and vinaigrettes. Only the rind is used in cooking. Discard the flesh and bitter pith, rinse and finely slice or chop the rind before adding it to the dish. Preserved lemons can be stored for up to six months in a cool, dark place.

note: To prepare a sterilized jar, preheat the oven to 120°C (250°F/Gas ½). Wash the jar and lid in hot soapy water and rinse in hot water. Put the jar in the oven for 20 minutes, or until dry. Do not dry with a tea towel.

preserved lemons

10 lemons
1 tablespoon rock salt
250 ml (1 cup) lemon juice

1 teaspoon black peppercorns
1 bay leaf
2 tablespoons rock salt, extra

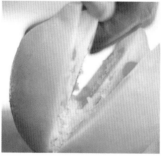

1 Rub the salt into the lemon.

2 Pack the lemons in the jar.

scrub 10 lemons under warm running water with a soft bristle brush to remove the wax coating. Cut into quarters, leaving the base attached at the stem end. Open each lemon, remove any visible pips and pack 1 tablespoon rock salt against the cut edges of each lemon. Push the lemons back into shape and pack into a 2 litre (8 cup) sterilized jar with a clip or screw-top lid. (Depending on the size of the lemons, you may not need them all—they should be firmly packed and fill the jar.)

add the black peppercorns, bay leaf and extra rock salt to the jar. Fill the jar to the top with lemon juice. Seal and shake to combine all the ingredients. Leave in a cool, dark place for 6 weeks, inverting each week. (In warm weather, store in the refrigerator.) The liquid will be cloudy initially, but will clear by the fourth week.

to test if the lemons are preserved, cut through the centre of one of the lemon quarters. If the pith is still white, the lemons are not ready. Re-seal and leave for a week before testing again. The lemons should be soft-skinned and the pith should be the same colour as the skin.

once the lemons are preserved, cover the brine with a layer of olive oil. Replace the oil each time you remove some of the lemon pieces. Makes a 2 litre (8 cup) jar.

roe

These are the eggs or spawn of a female fish, also called hard roe. Soft roe is the sperm of a male fish. In the Mediterranean, fish roe is mostly obtained from grey mullet and is often salted, pressed and dried. Its main uses in cooking are in the form of bottarga or tarama.

bottarga with scrambled eggs

8 eggs
25 g (1 oz) bottarga
1 tablespoon olive oil
4 slices country-style bread

lightly beat the eggs together, and season with pepper only (the bottarga is very salty). Warm 4 serving bowls by filling them with boiling water. Leave to stand for a few minutes before drying. Slice the bottarga with a sharp knife or mandolin.

heat the oil in a saucepan and add the eggs. Turn the heat down to low and gently scramble the eggs until they are creamy but not completely set. Tip the eggs into the serving bowls and put the bottarga on top where it will soften. Serve with the bread. Serves 4.

bottarga

This is made from either the roe of grey mullet or tuna, which is cured and then pressed into a solid block and dried. Bottarga is thought to be an Arabic invention, and is consequently most popular in countries with an Arabic influence: Andalusia in Spain's south, Sardinia and Sicily off Italy's coast, southern France and North Africa. It is eaten thinly sliced and seasoned with lemon juice and olive oil or grated or sliced onto scrambled eggs or pasta. Tuna bottarga is sold as a large piece, without the skin, and mullet bottarga is a neat block with its silvery skin still on. Refrigerate or freeze, wrapped tightly as it has a strong smell.

tarama

This is salted, dried and pressed grey mullet roe, and has been considered a great delicacy for centuries. Traditionally, intact roes were salted, dried in the sun until very firm, coated with beeswax, then eaten thinly sliced with bread, or skinned and used to make taramosalata, a creamy dip popular in Greek and Turkish mezze. Tarama is sold as whole roes from fishmongers or is available in tins.

taramosalata

5 slices white bread, crusts removed
80 ml (⅓ cup) milk
100 g (3½ oz) tin tarama
1 egg yolk
½ small onion, grated
1 garlic clove, crushed
2 tablespoons lemon juice
80 ml (⅓ cup) olive oil
pinch ground white pepper

soak the bread in the milk for 10 minutes. Press in a strainer to extract excess milk, then mix in a food processor with the tarama, egg yolk, onion and garlic for 30 seconds, or until smooth. Add 1 tablespoon of the lemon juice and mix in.

with the motor running, slowly pour in the olive oil until you have a smooth mixture. Add the remaining lemon juice and white pepper. If the dip tastes too salty, add another piece of bread. Makes approximately 375 ml (1½ cups).

salt cod

salt cod fritters

500 g (1 lb 2 oz) salt cod
1 large potato (about 200 g/
7 oz), unpeeled
2 tablespoons milk
3 tablespoons olive oil
1 small onion, finely chopped

2 garlic cloves, crushed
30 g (¼ cup) self-raising flour
2 eggs, separated
1 tablespoon chopped flat-leaf
(Italian) parsley
olive oil, extra, for deep-frying

soak the cod in cold water for 24 hours, changing the water regularly to remove as much salt as possible. Cook the potato in a pan of boiling water for 20 minutes, or until soft. When cool, peel and mash with the milk and 2 tablespoons of the olive oil.

drain the cod, cut into large pieces and put in a saucepan. Cover with water, bring to the boil over high heat, then reduce the heat to medium and cook for 10 minutes, or until soft and there is a froth on the surface. Drain. When cool enough to handle, remove the skin and any bones, then mash well with a fork until flaky.

heat the remaining oil in a small frying pan and cook the onion over medium heat for 5 minutes, or until softened and starting to brown. Add the garlic and cook for 1 minute. Remove from the heat.

combine the potato, cod, onion, flour, egg yolks and parsley in a bowl and season. Whisk the egg whites until stiff, then fold into the mixture. Fill a large heavy-based saucepan one-third full of olive oil and heat to 190°C (375°F), or until a cube of bread dropped into the oil browns in 10 seconds. Drop heaped tablespoons of the mixture into the oil and cook for 2 minutes, or until puffed and golden. Drain and serve. Makes 35.

Salting was one of the earliest forms of preservation and meant that the cod, which was plentiful in the North Atlantic Sea, could be readily and inexpensively transported to the more southerly countries of the Mediterranean. Salting is a simple process in which the fish are gutted and packed flat in salt, later washed and then dried. The fish are rehydrated in several changes of water to be used in cooking. Salt cod is an important ingredient in the cuisines of Provence and Spanish Catalonia, in particular, but also throughout much of the Mediterranean. It is known by its Spanish name *bacalao*.

tomato products

Originally grown as an ornamental garden plant only, the tomato is now a mainstay of Mediterranean cooking. Not just in the Western countries either; from Morocco to the Middle East, the tomato is found in a great many dishes. It is not surprising, therefore, that techniques have evolved to make the juicy, ripe summer tomatoes last all year. This includes preserving by sun-drying, bottling as sauces and storing in tins.

sun-dried tomatoes

These are widely available either dry and loosely packed, or in jars in oil. The dry variety needs to be rehydrated before use. To do this, cover the tomato with boiling water and leave for about 10 minutes. If buying sun-dried tomatoes in oil, choose those that are in olive oil as you can use the oil for cooking.

notes: The marinated feta will keep for 1–2 months if stored in the refrigerator. The oil in the bottle will partly solidify when refrigerated, but will liquefy when returned to room temperature. Use the oil to flavour pasta or to make salad dressings.

To prepare a sterilized jar, preheat the oven to 120°C (250°F/Gas ½). Wash the jar and lid in hot soapy water and rinse with hot water. Put the jar in the oven for 20 minutes, or until dry. Do not dry with a tea towel.

marinated feta and sun-dried tomatoes

350 g (12 oz) feta cheese
1 tablespoon dried oregano
1 teaspoon coriander seeds
1 tablespoon cracked black
  pepper

125 g (4½ oz) sun-dried
  tomatoes in oil
4 small fresh red chillies
3–4 rosemary sprigs
olive oil

pat the feta dry with paper towels and cut into 2 cm (¾ inch) cubes. Transfer to a bowl and sprinkle the oregano, coriander seeds and black pepper all over the feta cheese.

drain the sun-dried tomatoes over a bowl so that you retain all of the oil. Arrange the feta, chillies, rosemary and sun-dried tomatoes in a sterilized 750 ml (3 cup) wide-necked storage jar with a clip-top lid. Cover with the reserved sun-dried tomato oil (there should be about 3 tablespoons) and top up with olive oil. Seal and refrigerate for 1 week before using. Serve at room temperature. Serves 6–8.

tomato passata and tinned tomatoes

Tomato passata is a bottled tomato sauce commonly used in Italian cooking. The sauce is made with fresh, ripe tomatoes that are peeled, seeded and slowly cooked down with fresh basil, onion and garlic. The thickened sauce is then passed through a sieve before being bottled. Tinned peeled tomatoes have been used in Italy since the end of the eighteenth century, and Italian, as well as Spanish, tinned tomatoes are now sold throughout the world. Chopped, peeled whole, crushed and pulped tomatoes are all available. It is perfectly acceptable to use tinned tomatoes for recipes such as sauces; add a pinch of sugar if necessary.

spanish albondigas en picant salsa de tomate

combine the pork, veal, garlic, breadcrumbs, spices, egg and some salt and pepper in a bowl. Mix by hand until smooth and leaving the side of the bowl. Refrigerate, covered, for 30 minutes.

roll tablespoons of the mixture into balls. Heat 1 tablespoon of the oil in a frying pan and toss half the meatballs over medium-high heat for 2–3 minutes, until browned. Drain on paper towels. Add the remaining oil, if necessary, and brown the rest of the balls. Drain on paper towels.

to make the sauce, heat the oil in a frying pan over medium heat and cook the onion, stirring occasionally, for 3 minutes, or until translucent. Add the garlic and cook for 1 minute. Increase the heat to high, add the wine and boil for 1 minute. Add the tomato, tomato paste and stock and simmer for 10 minutes. Add the cayenne, peas and meatballs. Simmer for 5–10 minutes, or until the sauce is thick. Serve hot. Serves 6.

175 g (6 oz) minced (ground) pork
175 g (6 oz) minced (ground) veal
3 garlic cloves, crushed
35 g (1/3 cup) dry breadcrumbs
1 teaspoon ground coriander
1 teaspoon ground nutmeg
1 teaspoon ground cumin
pinch ground cinnamon
1 egg
2 tablespoons olive oil

spicy tomato sauce
1 tablespoon olive oil
1 onion, chopped
2 garlic cloves, crushed
125 ml (1/2 cup) dry white wine
400 g (14 oz) tin crushed tomatoes
1 tablespoon tomato paste (purée)
125 ml (1/2 cup) chicken stock
1/2 teaspoon cayenne pepper
80 g (1/2 cup) frozen peas

truffles

These are the fruiting body of a family of fungi that grow underground in a symbiotic relationship with the roots of certain trees. Although truffles grow all around the world, the prized and expensive black Périgord truffles of western France and the white truffles of Alba in northern Italy are considered to be among the best. Truffles have a heady, intense, earthy aroma and flavour and consequently are treated simply in Mediterranean cooking. Shavings are added to salads or spread on toasted sourdough bread sprinkled with olive oil, or the truffle is stored with eggs for a few days to produce an earthy-scented omelette. The same is done with rice before making risotto. Preserved truffles and truffle-flavoured oil can also be bought.

truffle and rocket salad

bruschetta
- **6 slices sourdough bread**
- **1 garlic clove**
- **2 tablespoons extra virgin olive oil**

- **175 g (6 oz) rocket (arugula) (about 2 bunches)**
- **1 tablespoon lemon juice**
- **3–4 tablespoons extra virgin olive oil, plus extra for drizzling**
- **1 small truffle**
- **shaved Parmesan cheese, to serve**

to make the bruschetta, grill (broil) or toast the bread until it is crisp. Cut the garlic clove in half and rub the cut edge over both sides of the bread, then drizzle a little olive oil over each slice.

put the rocket in a small bowl and dress with the lemon juice, olive oil, salt and freshly ground black pepper. Mix together and divide the salad among 6 plates.

thinly slice the truffle, ideally using a truffle slicer or sharp mandolin. Slice the truffle over each plate—the pieces should be as thin as possible and will break up easily if touched by hand. Add some Parmesan shavings, arranging them around the truffle (you won't need much Parmesan or it will overwhelm the truffle) and drizzle with a little olive oil. Serve with the pieces of bruschetta. Serves 6.

vine leaves

These large green leaves of the grape vine are used in Middle Eastern and Greek cookery as handy food wrappers, imparting a fresh, lemony tang to dishes. They are most famously used to make Greek dolmades (*dolmas* in Turkey), a meat or rice mixture wrapped in vine leaves, then cooked in stock. They are also used to wrap small game birds or fish before braising or baking, or as a decoration for cheese plates and salads. For those lucky enough to have grape vines within reach, use them straight off the vine, otherwise, buy them fresh or tinned, preserved in brine. Fresh leaves need blanching in hot water until soft enough to be pliable. Tinned vine leaves should be rinsed in plenty of cold water to remove the salty brine.

dolmades

soak the vine leaves in cold water for 15 minutes, then remove and pat dry. Cut off any stems. Reserve some leaves to line the saucepan and discard any that have holes or look poor. Meanwhile, soak the rice in boiling water for 10 minutes to soften, then drain.

put the rice, onion, olive oil, pine nuts, currants, herbs and salt and pepper, to taste, in a large bowl and mix well.

lay some leaves vein-side-down on a flat surface. Put 1 tablespoon of filling in the centre of each, fold the stalk end over the filling, then the left and right sides into the centre, and finally roll firmly towards the tip. The dolmades should resemble a small cigar. Repeat with the remaining filling and leaves.

use the reserved vine leaves to line the base of a large, heavy-based saucepan. Drizzle with 1 tablespoon olive oil. Add the dolmades, packing them tightly in one layer, then pour the remaining oil and the lemon juice over them.

pour the stock over the dolmades and cover with an inverted plate to stop the dolmades moving around while cooking. Bring to the boil, then reduce the heat and simmer, covered, for 45 minutes. Remove with a slotted spoon. Serve warm or cold. Dolmades can be served with lemon wedges. Makes 24.

200 g (7 oz) packet vine leaves in brine
220 g (1 cup) medium-grain white rice
1 small onion, finely chopped
1 tablespoon olive oil
60 g (2¼ oz) pine nuts, toasted
2 tablespoons currants
2 tablespoons chopped dill
1 tablespoon finely chopped mint
1 tablespoon finely chopped flat-leaf (Italian) parsley
80 ml (⅓ cup) olive oil, extra
2 tablespoons lemon juice
500 ml (2 cups) chicken stock

vinegar

Vinegar has been made for thousands of years as a flavouring, pickling and preserving agent. Originally the by-product of the fermentation process of wine or other alcohols, today many vinegars are purpose made. In the Mediterranean, they are, not surprisingly, used primarily in non-Muslim countries. The French are known for their wine vinegars, the Italians for balsamic and the Spanish for their *jerez* (sherry) vinegars. Also available are cider, herb and fruit-flavoured ones. Store vinegar in a cool, dark place.

balsamic-roasted tomatoes

6 Roma (plum) tomatoes	**5 garlic cloves, unpeeled**
60 ml (¼ cup) olive oil	**1½ teaspoons sugar**
2 tablespoons balsamic vinegar	**12 small basil leaves**

preheat the oven to 170°C (325°F/Gas 3). Cut the tomatoes in half lengthways and put on a lightly greased baking tray, skin-side-down. Mix the olive oil with the balsamic vinegar and drizzle over the tomato halves. Bruise the garlic cloves with the back of a knife and scatter over the baking tray among the tomatoes. Sprinkle the sugar over the tomatoes, then cook in the oven for 35–40 minutes, or until quite soft. Arrange the tomatoes on a serving plate, scatter with the roasted garlic and top each tomato half with a small basil leaf. Drizzle with any remaining pan juices and season. Serves 4–6.

balsamic vinegar

This centuries-old speciality is produced in the province of Modena, just north of Bologna in Italy. It is made from boiled-down must, which is the concentrated sweet juice of white grapes. True balsamic vinegar is aged for up to 50 years in successive barrels, each made from a different wood to produce a syrupy sweet-and-sour liquid. This *aceto balsamico tradizionale di Modena* is often far superior to commercially made balsamic vinegar, which is sold without the traditional label. Use good-quality balsamic sparingly and in cooking add at the very end so that the aromas are present in the final dish.

pickled vegetables

The ancient art of pickling is very important in the Mediterranean region, where seasonal fluctuations and high temperatures make preserved foods an essential part of the diet. Though born of necessity, pickles are also highly prized for their crisp texture and wide range of strong flavours, as most Mediterranean vegetables can easily be pickled. They are served as part of a selection of starters or as an accompaniment to main meals.

garden pickles

**280 g (10 oz) carrots, cut into
    short lengths**
280 g (10 oz) pearl onions
225 g (8 oz) small gherkins
**875 ml (3½ cups) white
    wine vinegar**
1 tablespoon sea salt

2 tablespoons honey
**225 g (8 oz) stringless green
    beans, cut into short lengths**
10 black peppercorns
6 cloves
5 juniper berries
2 bay leaves

preheat the oven to 120°C (250°F/Gas 1–2). Put the carrot, onions, gherkins, vinegar, salt and honey in a saucepan with 600 ml (20½ fl oz) water and bring to the boil. Reduce the heat and simmer for 20 minutes. Add the beans and simmer for 5 minutes, or until the vegetables are tender but still slightly crisp.

drain the vegetables, reserving the liquid. Put the vegetables in a sterilized 1.25 litre (5 cup) jar and add the peppercorns, cloves, juniper berries and bay leaves. Cover with the liquid. Refrigerate for 24 hours before use. Keep for up to 2 months. Makes 1.25 litre (5 cups).

note: To prepare a sterilized jar, preheat the oven to 120°C (250°F/Gas ½). Wash the jar and lid in hot soapy water and rinse with hot water. Put the jar in the oven for 20 minutes until dry. Do not dry with a tea towel.

wine vinegars

Made from red and white wine and champagne, the best and most expensive wine vinegars are made by the traditional French Orleans method, where the vinegar is allowed to mature slowly in oak barrels. Commercial varieties use faster processes that don't give as good a flavour. Some wine vinegars are sold by grape variety, such as Cabernet Sauvignon, Rioja or Zinfandel. Wine vinegar is used in sauces, vinaigrettes and to preserve fish and vegetables.

wines and liqueurs

A glass of wine with simple food and plenty of crusty bread is the image many people have of classic Mediterranean dining. And historical records suggest they wouldn't be too far wrong. Though forbidden in Muslim countries, wine and liqueurs exist in great variety in other parts of the Mediterranean, and are an integral part of the cuisines, not just as an accompaniment to a meal, but as an ingredient in their own right.

wines and liqueurs used in cooking

amaretto This Italian liqueur is flavoured with almonds and apricots and *amaretto di Saronno* is the original Italian brand. Amaretto is drunk as an after-dinner liqueur or used in cooking in cakes and sauces.

marsala This fortified wine is Sicily's most famous drink. It is made from local grapes and can range from the very dry to the very sweet. While the dry Marsala is used more frequently in the kitchen and also drunk as an aperitif, sweet Marsala is used for sweet dishes such as zabaglione and is also drunk as a dessert wine. There are also special blends with added ingredients such as cream, eggs and almonds.

sherry This fortified wine was first made in, and named after, the Jerez de la Frontera region of southern Spain. Sherries (jerez) differ in colour and flavour and a number of types exist: manzanilla (dry and delicate); fino (dry and light); amontillado (darker and sweeter with a nutty flavour); and oloroso (used as a base for sweet sherries). Dry sherries are used in many savoury sauces and chicken dishes, and sweet sherries in cold desserts such as trifles.

wine Cooks from Greece to Spain use wine in cooking, mostly using their local wines. Wine is used in risottos, desserts such as syllabub and zabaglione, sauces and marinades. Some good choices are: Italian Valpolicella; Minervois and Corbières, both from the Languedoc region in southwest France; and Rioja from Spain. Remember to only use wine in cooking that you would be happy drinking. On the other hand, don't use wine that is too good, as much of the character of expensive wine will be destroyed in the cooking process.

zabaglione

whisk the egg yolks and sugar in the top of a double boiler or in a heatproof bowl set over a saucepan of simmering water. Make sure that the water does not touch the base of the bowl or the egg may overcook and stick. It is important that you whisk constantly to move the cooked mixture from the outside of the bowl to the centre. At this stage the mixture will be dark yellow and thin.

when the mixture is tepid, add the Marsala and whisk for 5 minutes more, or until it has thickened enough to hold its shape when drizzled off the whisk into the bowl.

whip the cream until soft peaks form. Gently fold in the egg yolk and Marsala mixture. Divide among 4 glasses or bowls. Cover and refrigerate for 3–4 hours before serving. Serves 4.

6 egg yolks
3 tablespoons caster (superfine) sugar
125 ml (½ cup) sweet Marsala
250 ml (1 cup) thick (double/heavy) cream

Zabaglione *(zabaione)* is one of those rare lucky accidents of the culinary world. It first came into being in the seventeenth century when a chef in the French court of Savoy mistakenly poured sweet wine into an egg custard. Today it is eaten on its own or served as a sauce over fruit, cake or pastries.

1 Add the Marsala to the egg and sugar and whisk vigorously.

2 Whip the cream until soft peaks form and it holds its shape.

yoghurt

Thousands of years ago, nomadic Bedouin tribesmen discovered the secret of preserving milk, probably through accident when fermenting milk came into contact with bacteria. Yoghurt continues to be a staple ingredient of Turkey and the Middle East, where it is commonly drained and made into a type of cheese called *labna*. The Turks are great consumers of yoghurt, eating it with honey at breakfast, serving it as an accompaniment to meals, using it for marinating and cooking meat (it also acts as a tenderizer) and adding it to sauces for meat and vegetable dishes. Today yoghurt is made by introducing non-harmful bacteria to milk, which causes it to ferment and coagulate, resulting in a creamy-textured yoghurt with a slightly sharp flavour.

marinated yoghurt cheese balls

1.5 kg (3 lb 5 oz) Greek-style natural yoghurt
2 clean muslin squares, about 50 cm (20 inch) square
2 fresh bay leaves
3 thyme sprigs
2 oregano sprigs
500 ml (2 cups) olive oil

put the yoghurt in a bowl with 2 teaspoons salt and mix well. Put the muslin squares one on top of the other and put the yoghurt mixture in the centre. Gather up the corners of the muslin and tie with string, suspended over a bowl. Refrigerate and leave to drain for 3 days.

once drained, the yoghurt will have the texture and consistency of ricotta cheese. Remove from the cloth, and put in a bowl. Roll tablespoons of the mixture into balls and put on a large tray. Cover and refrigerate for 3 hours, or until firm.

put the balls in a sterilized 1 litre (4 cup) glass jar. Add the bay leaves, thyme and oregano sprigs. Fill the jar with the olive oil then seal and refrigerate for up to 1 week. Return to room temperature for serving at breakfast or as an appetizer. Makes 18 balls.

yoghurt cake with syrup

preheat the oven to 180°C (350°F/Gas 4) and lightly grease a 20 x 10 cm (8 x 4 inch) loaf tin.

cream the butter and sugar in a bowl with electric beaters until light and fluffy. Add the egg yolks gradually, beating well after each addition. Stir in the yoghurt, lemon zest and vanilla essence. Fold in the sifted flour, bicarbonate of soda and baking powder with a metal spoon. Mix well.

whisk the egg whites in a clean, dry bowl until stiff, then gently fold into the mixture. Spoon into the tin and bake for 50 minutes, or until a skewer comes out clean when inserted into the centre of the cake. Cool in the tin for 10 minutes, then turn out onto a wire rack.

meanwhile, for the syrup, put the sugar and cinnamon stick in a small saucepan with 185 ml (3/4 cup) cold water. Stir over medium heat until the sugar has dissolved. Bring to the boil, add the lemon zest and juice, then reduce the heat and simmer for 5–6 minutes. Strain, then pour the syrup all over the hot cake and wait for most of it to be absorbed before you serve the cake. Cut into slices and serve warm with whipped cream. Serves 8–10.

175 g (6 oz) unsalted butter, softened
250 g (heaped 1 cup) caster (superfine) sugar
5 eggs, separated
250 g (1 cup) Greek-style natural yoghurt
2 teaspoons grated lemon zest
1/2 teaspoon natural vanilla extract (essence)
280 g (21/4 cups) plain (all-purpose) flour
1/2 teaspoon bicarbonate of soda
2 teaspoons baking powder
whipped cream, to serve

syrup
250 g (heaped 1 cup) caster (superfine) sugar
1 cinnamon stick
4 cm (11/2 inch) strip lemon zest
1 tablespoon lemon juice

index

Published by Murdoch Books®, a division of Murdoch Magazines Pty Ltd.

Murdoch Books® Australia
Pier 8/9
23 Hickson Road
Millers Point NSW 2000
Phone: + 61 (0) 2 4352 7000
Fax: + 61 (0) 2 4352 7026

Murdoch Books UK Limited
Erico House
6th Floor North
93/99 Upper Richmond Road,
Putney, London SW15 2TG
Phone: + 44 (0) 20 8785 5995
Fax: + 44 (0) 20 8785 5985

Design Concept and Design: Vivien Valk
Editorial Director: Diana Hill
Senior Editor: Margaret Malone
Photo Library Manager: Anne Ferrier
Production: Monika Vidovic

Chief Executive: Juliet Rogers
Publisher: Kay Scarlett

National Library of Australia
Cataloguing-in-Publication Data
Mediterranean Kitchen. Includes index.
ISBN 1 74045 222 4.
1. Cookery, Mediterranean
641.591822

PRINTED IN SINGAPORE by Imago.
Published 2004.

©Text, design, and photography Murdoch Books® 2004.
All rights reserved. No part of this publication may be reproduced, stored in a retrieval system or
transmitted in any form or by any means, electronic, mechanical, photocopying, recording or otherwise
without the prior written permission of the publisher.
Murdoch Books® is a trademark of Murdoch Magazines Pty Limited.

IMPORTANT: Those who might be at risk from the effects of salmonella food poisoning
(the elderly, pregnant women, young children and those suffering from immune deficiency
diseases) should consult their GP with any concerns about eating raw eggs.

acknowledgements

Photographers: Craig Cranko, Ben Dearnley, Joe Filshie, Jared Fowler, Ian Hofstetter, Chris L. Jones, Rob Reichenfeld,
Howard Shooter, Brett Stevens.

Stylists: Marie-Hélène Clauzon, Georgina Dolling, Mary Harris, Katy Holder, Cherise Koch, Michaela Le Compte, Ben
Masters, Sarah de Nardi, Michelle Noerianto, Bridget Palmer, Justine Poole.

Food Preparation: Ross Dobson, Rodney Dunn, Jo Glynn, Saskia Hay, Justine Johnson, Michelle Lawton, Valli Little,
Ben Masters, Kerrie Mullins, Kate Murdoch, Kim Passenger, Justine Poole, Wendy Quisumbing, Michelle Thrift,
Angela Tregonning.

Recipe Development: Ruth Armstrong, Sophie Braimbridge, Michelle Earl, Belinda Frost, Jo Glynn, Fiona Hammond,
Katy Holder, Deh-Ta Hsiung, Eva Katz, Jane Lawson, Barbara Lowery, Kerrie Mullins, Kate Murdoch, Maria
Papadopoulos, Wendy Quisumbing, Sarah Randell, Nina Simonds, Dimitra Stais, Jody Vassallo, Maria Villegas,
Richard Young, Sophia Young and the Murdoch Books Test Kitchen.

bibliography

Alexander, Stephanie. *The Cook's Companion.* Viking Australia, 1998.
Başan, Ghillie. *The Middle Eastern Kitchen.* Kyle Cathie Limited, 2001.
David, Elizabeth. *A Book of Mediterranean Food.* Penguin Books, 1991.
Davidson, Alan. *The Oxford Companion to Food.* Oxford University Press, 1999.
Grigson, Sophie and Black, William. *Fish.* Headline, 2000.
Malouf, Greg and Lucy. *Arabesque – Modern Middle Eastern Food.* Hardie Grant Books, 2002.
Roden, Claudia. *Mediterranean Cookery.* Penguin Books BBC Books, 1998.
Wright, Clifford A. *A Mediterranean Feast.* William Morrow and Company, Inc., 1999.